THE FACTORY THAT
BECAME A VILLAGE

First published in 2019 by Redshank Books

Redshank Books is an imprint of Libri Publishing.

Copyright © Jim Lewis

The right of Jim Lewis to be identified as the author of this work has been asserted in accordance with the Copyright, Designs and Patents Act, 1988.

ISBN 978-0-9954834-4-6

A CIP catalogue record for this book is available from The British Library

Cover and Design by Helen Taylor

Printed in the UK by Short Run Press

Libri Publishing
Brunel House
Volunteer Way
Faringdon
Oxfordshire
SN7 7YR

Tel: +44 (0)845 873 3837

www.libripublishing.co.uk

THE FACTORY THAT BECAME A VILLAGE

The History of The Royal Small Arms Factory at Enfield Lock

Jim Lewis

REDSHANK
BOOKS

Foreword by Terry Farrell

Jim Lewis is an extraordinary man. He is a traveller in that long tradition of indefatigable British explorers, journeying intellectually into unknown yet fascinating territory. Out of the glorious and chaotic metropolis which is London, Jim has discovered in his travels and revealed through his writing one of the great wonders of London – the extraordinary history of the Lea Valley.

The Lea Valley is the place where Jim spent his working life. The places he worked, and the characters he encountered there, drew him into the fascinating history of the place and inspired him to reveal the full story. I first encountered Jim through my own research into the Lea Valley, as part of my work in place making and characterisation of the Thames Gateway. Little did I know I could spend a lifetime struggling to learn only a fraction of what Jim has discovered.

Jim is a relentless advocate for this extraordinary place. For many years, he has been campaigning to seek recognition for the significance of the Lea Valley, as part of the rich history of London. For this small part of London changed the world – a crucible of scientific discovery and industrial firsts. His earlier books tell the unique story of the region, its scientists, engineers and entrepreneurs. But most significantly, Jim has revealed how the Lea Valley was the birthplace of the post-industrial revolution – the electronic technological revolution – which arguably began in the Lea Valley with the invention of the diode valve by Professor Ambrose Fleming. This small but inspired device allowed, for the first time, the control of a stream of electrons by electronic means, paving the way for modern electronic communication around the world and across the vast expanse of space.

Given the focus on the Lea Valley with the creation of the Queen Elizabeth Olympic Park, Jim is unique in the way he has recognised the significance of the place. In his last book, *From Ice Age to Wetlands, the Lea Valley's Return to Nature*, Jim discussed how the Lea Valley was formed and he skilfully uses the region as an example to warn us of the damage that our consumer driven lifestyles have created for our planet. In this new book Jim traces the story of the Royal Small Arms Factory at Enfield Lock and takes us on a fascinating two-hundred year trek through the challenges and politics of weapon development that ends in a good news story for a redundant historical building.

Therefore, I urge you to journey with him through a past which is shaping the future. It is people like Dr Jim Lewis who keep alive the magic of the place for present and future generations.

Sir Terry Farrell

ABOUT THE AUTHOR

Dr Jim Lewis has spent most of his career in the consumer electronics industry, apart from a three-year spell in the Royal Air Force servicing airborne and ground wireless communications equipment. When working in the Lea Valley for Thorn EMI Ferguson, he represented the company abroad on several occasions, and was involved in the exchange of manufacturing technology. Currently he is a Consultant to Terry Farrell & Partners on the historical development of London's Lea Valley. He is at present a volunteer with Social Services teaching students who have learning difficulties. A freelance writer (with thirteen published books), researcher and broadcaster for his specialist subject – London's Lea Valley – he also has a genuine passion for encouraging partnership projects within the local community, which, in the long term, are planned to help stimulate social and economic regeneration.

In 2012 Dr Lewis was appointed Contributory International Professor by the Clark H. Byrum School of Business, Marian University, Indianapolis, for his work with students on The Modern British Service Economy.

Dr Lewis is married with four grown-up children and lives in Lincolnshire.

The author filming a piece about the Great War for
ITV News outside large machine room. Ray Tuthill,
President of RSAF Apprentice Association waiting
behind camera for his turn

ACKNOWLEDGEMENTS

The author wishes to thank the following organisations, companies, societies and individuals for their encouragement, support and advice and for supplying many of the illustrations within this book:

Enfield Enterprise Agency, Hertford Road, Enfield

Enfield Local Studies Library and Archive, London Road, Enfield

Fairview New Homes, Lancaster Road, Enfield, Middlesex

RSA Trust, Enfield Island Village, Enfield Lock

Royal Armouries, Leeds, Yorkshire

House of Lords Record Office, Westminster

BAE Systems, Farnborough, Hampshire

Imperial War Museum, Duxford, Cambridgeshire

National Army Museum, Chelsea, London

The Institution of Engineering and Technology, Savoy Place, London

The National Archive, Kew, Richmond, Surrey

The British Library, London

The Waltham Abbey Royal Gunpowder Mills Company Ltd, Waltham Abbey, Essex

The Science Museum, Kensington, London

The Royal Air Force Museum, Hendon, London

Gary Walker, Chairman of RSA Trust

Michael Polledri MBE, Chairman of Lee Valley Estates Limited

Martin Jewell, Chairman of RSA Enfield Island Village Limited

Mike Wehrmann, former Banking Executive with Barclays Bank

Patrick Gray, Heritage Manager RSA Trust, Enfield Island Village

Ray Tuthill, President RSAF Apprentices Association

Dan Bone, Chairman CIVIX

Gladys Anoqah, Natgab Services Limited, Enfield Island Village

Andy Bell, Enfield Business Centre, Hertford Road, Enfield

Peter Taylor, Senior Partner, Taylor Associates

Dr Nicholas Falk, Urban and Economic Development Ltd

Dr Kostakis Evangelou, Edmonton Eagles Boxing Club

Joan Kearns, Nightingale Cancer Support Centre, Enfield

Mike Taylor, responsible for overseeing the RSA Enfield Island Village site's early development

James Musgrave, Enfield Island Youth and Community Trust

Melvyn Lee, Thwaites

Ralph Ward, former officer with Government Office for London

Eric Fletcher, RSA Trust site caretaker

Annette Mitchell, North London Chamber of Commerce

Ian Campbell, RSA Trust manager of the Enfield Island Village site

Denys Dowling, Financial Director, Lee Valley Estates Trustees

Doug Taylor, Enfield Councillor

Michelle Kypranou, Administrative Assistant, Lee Valley Estates Trustees

David Morris, former manager at the Royal Small Arms Factory, Enfield Lock

While many individuals have freely given their knowledge, some unknowingly, which has contributed greatly to the production of this book, some have been given credit elsewhere in the overall text.

I could not let the occasion pass without recording my sincere thanks to my wife Jenny for her superb editorial skills and outstanding patience. The author freely admits that this voluntary sacrifice on Jenny's part has comprehensively tested the cement that holds our wonderful marriage together.

CONTENTS

INTRODUCTION

When I originally met the directors of the RSA Trust, the charity responsible for the concept and the running of Enfield Island Village, in January 2015, it was to discuss the commissioning of a book that would tell the story of the former government-controlled Royal Small Arms Factory (RSAF) after privatisation and closure in 1987. However, during discussions it soon became clear, with the impending two-hundredth anniversary of the birth of the Enfield Lock armoury, that a unique opportunity existed to link the story of the RSAF site with the founding of the RSA Trust. And as one Trust director put it, this is the classic story of "from swords into ploughshares". Surprising as it may seem, the story of the birth of the Enfield Lock armoury in 1816 and the methods of manufacture that then existed within the British small arms industry has never been completely told.

In telling this story it will be essential to carry out some in-depth research and also to use and expand some of the narrative within the popular Lea Valley series of books to ensure that the continuity of history from armoury to Trust status is fully maintained and understood. To do this it will be necessary for me to revisit my unpublished research, carried out in the 1990s, to give the reader a unique understanding of the influence of government and its officers on what was, in the early nineteenth century, the disorganised and antiquated British gun trade. This eventually led to the establishment of the armoury at Enfield Lock. It will also be necessary, where appropriate, to set the various developments at Enfield Lock against a background of an evolving and at times an aggressive world to show how external influences had a significant effect on what happened on site.

At the time of writing this book I wanted, in the two-hundredth anniversary year of the founding of the RSAF, to commemorate the contribution made to our armed forces by the former workforce which, by their skills and dedication, helped keep Britain safe during times of world instability. Also, I wanted to acknowledge the contribution made to our community by the four founding fathers of the RSA Trust that has benefited so many worthwhile good causes.

Unfortunately, this publication became delayed due to my having to write From Ice Age to Wetlands the Lea Valley's Return to Nature to coincide with the official opening of the Walthamstow Wetlands, Europe's largest urban wetland nature reserve, in November 2017.

However, I have now managed to put computer to printer to complete the RSAF story. In a world full of increasingly depressing news it is uplifting to have the opportunity to write about a group of four local businessmen who had the vision, courage and tenacity to take on the mammoth task of rescuing a Grade II listed building that no sane entrepreneur would have contemplated taking on and turn it into a vibrant sustainable business for the benefit of the local community. The model created pays a service charge into a limited liability company, RSA IV, which in turn transfers the surplus to the not-for-profit RSA Trust which is then able to fund many community good causes.

Jim Lewis

Further reading:

From Gunpowder to Guns, the story of two Lea Valley armouries, Jim Lewis, Middlesex University Press (2009)

Weapons, Wireless and World Wars, the vital role of the Lea Valley, Jim Lewis, Libri Publishing (2010)

PART ONE

1. THE ROYAL SMALL ARMS FACTORY ENFIELD LOCK THE EARLY YEARS – AN OVERVIEW

Due to considerable local interest the author has been persuaded to deviate from the original intention for the format of this book, that of keeping chapters deliberately short, to include a fuller treatment of the beginnings of the Royal Small Arms Factory at Enfield Lock. It is therefore hoped that the reader will be given a greater insight into the site's development during the first half of the nineteenth century. In setting the scene, it will also be necessary to highlight the various issues which slowed the rate of progress and innovation within the British small arms manufacturing industry in comparison to the speed of technological achievement attained by its American counterpart particularly in the field of machine tool development. Unfortunately, due to limitations of space, it will not be possible to cover the whole range of influences which affected the British small arms industry in detail. However, it is hoped to show that the path of the British small arms industry towards interchangeability and standardised mass-produced weapons was anything but straightforward.

Establishing the armoury

The construction of the small arms factory beside the River Lea at Enfield Lock on the Essex and Middlesex borders came about through a British Government initiative. The decision to proceed with construction had been provoked by what the Board of Ordnance regarded as the failure of the private gun trade to provide sufficient quantities of weapons for the British Army and Navy during the Napoleonic Wars.

By 1816 the factory and houses for the workmen and their families had been completed. Also, during this year, the barrel branch from the Royal Manufactory at Lewisham was incorporated into the site as water power for the south London armoury began to fail. The lock and finishing sections from Lewisham were integrated later, adding to the site's gradual expansion. However, it was not until after some forty years of further building and equipping that the Royal Small Arms Factory (as it was to become known) became capable of producing large quantities of weapons by standardised methods of machine manufacture. Up until the middle of the century the factory acted largely as a research and development establishment, an assembly and small weapon modification shop, and a repair facility. Because of the expert knowledge of arms production and assembly contained within the factory, the establishment was also used to monitor the price and quality of finished parts and complete weapons produced by private contractors for the Board of Ordnance.

Despite the early initiative taken by the British Government to control and secure regular supplies of military small arms by building the factory at Enfield Lock, it took over four decades before regular supplies to the armed forces could be guaranteed from this plant. It is the circumstances which were responsible for this somewhat ironic situation that provide an interesting study in which it can be shown that it was the private sector and not, as commonly believed, the public sector which was still producing the bulk of military small arms up until c1857.

An early engraving of the Royal Small Arms Factory, Enfield Lock

The influence of George Lovell

George Lovell was appointed Storekeeper, a position similar to today's General Manager, at Enfield Lock on 1st April 1816, the date coinciding with the barrel branch being moved from Lewisham. Most students of the history of the RSAF agree that it was Lovell more than any other individual, who, with his expertise and dedication laid the foundations and set the bench-marks for quality and reliability which were to become synonymous with the RSAF in later years.

Lovell was determined to improve the tolerance standards of weapons and piece parts delivered to the Board of Ordnance (a powerful department of government similar to today's Ministry of Defence (MoD)) by the various private contractors. In 1833, armed with a new micrometer, he was able to ascertain that the instruments used for measuring the bores of barrels of small arms varied between 0.752 and 0.760 of an inch. He therefore set the standard at 0.754 of an inch, a measurement which would be strictly adhered to in the future. By necessity, increased levels of accuracy call for greater standards of skill and improved manufacturing techniques if high rejection rates are to be avoided. Improvements of this scale in the short term can lead to a decrease in manufacturing output, accounting for a reduction in profit margins. As might be imagined, Lovell's demands for tolerances to a thousandth of an inch brought considerable criticism from the private contractors. One anonymous observer unhappy with the new standards called Lovell "a cabinet or bedstead maker by trade". Going on, this nameless person criticised the strictness imposed by the Ordnance viewers (quality control and inspection personnel) upon the private gun trade which led "to a litigious vexatious nicety of gauging, and finished appearance unknown in the highest finished fowling pieces". He described as absurd "the principle of exact jigging, gauging, moulding and other fantastic accuracies".

Lovell's problems did not subside after his appointment as Inspector of Small Arms in 1840, the most influential position in all aspects of British military weapon design, manufacture, and procurement below that of the Master General of Ordnance. If anything, the personal attacks increased and considerable controversy was to surround his later years. These issues and the consequences of Ordnance imposing strict quality standards form part of the complex story of the British small arms industry, illustrating the somewhat delicate character of the military gun trade, during the first half of the nineteenth century.

Ordnance dilemma

It is clear from the many written accounts of the British gun trade in the period to the middle of the nineteenth century that production was essentially uncoordinated and fragmented, being split mainly between the London and Birmingham private gun makers. As the demand for arms changed during times of military conflict the private sector gun manufacturing industry suffered not only from the indecisiveness of government policies, but also from the general lack of understanding of their needs and requirements by the Ordnance procurement agencies. Skilled men were lost to the industry, sometimes never to return, as many gun makers were unable to find work for their craftsmen or were denied the stability of long-term Ordnance contracts. The apparent reluctance of government to initiate a policy of major intervention into the arms industry was primarily due to the private gun trade's successful lobby of Parliament, which effectively stopped Ordnance encroaching into their area of business, but was in part due to the

An early picture of Ordnance Road, Enfield Lock

strong influence of the Duke of Wellington, who, as Commander in Chief of the Army, believed that arms themselves needed no improvement, the only improvement required being the degree and extent of the troops' instruction in their use.

In addition, the contract system operated by the Board of Ordnance moved from one of favoured manufacturers to one of open tender at the lowest price. This helped create supply and price difficulties for military weapons, as rejection rates increased and contractors tried to recover lost Ordnance business by increasing costs. This helped to deepen the impression that the private sector was incapable of meeting the reasonable demands of Ordnance. As the middle of the century approached, these were just some of the issues facing both Ordnance and the private gun trade.

In October 1853, Mr (later Sir) John Anderson, the chief engineer of the Royal Arsenal at Woolwich, was sent to Enfield and instructed to find out whether the factory was capable of manufacturing bayonets by machinery. Following his visit Anderson issued a report to which the official response of Ordnance was to appoint a committee to consider the whole question of small arms provision for Her Majesty's Service. Lieutenant Colonel Alexander Tulloh, Royal Artillery, Inspector of the Royal Carriage Factory at Woolwich, and Colonel James Archibald Chalmer, R.A., Inspector of Artillery, reported to the Committee making the following observations:

> It appears that the system hitherto adopted to procure small arms is so heterogeneous in its character that it could not fail to produce considerable difficulties. The Government establishment at Enfield Lock is comparatively small and of a mixed nature, some parts of the work being performed by the establishment, some by contractors; many of the lathes and tools are the property of the workmen; others belonging to the establishment. The men possessing lathes hire them out to other men.

> The establishment at Enfield Lock being small, and forming part of the heterogeneous system, is unable to hold that check or control over the contractors to prevent exorbitant demands and serious delays. The principal part of the gun trade upon which the Government mainly depends for supply in case of emergency, is carried on in Birmingham and London, by men working by hand in wretched cellars and garrets, and great evil arises from the slowness of manufacture.

It can be seen from these findings that the Committee was reinforcing the image, already held by Ordnance, that the small arms industry in Britain was in rather a perilous state. This would appear especially true if one considers the imperial role of Britain in the nineteenth century with a need to police her far flung Empire. Furthermore, for a nation which had been at the heart of the industrial revolution, it must have been extremely embarrassing for government to witness senior Ordnance officers being forced to purchase quantities of arms from continental manufacturers in times of conflict. Having to go abroad to find ways of bridging the gaps brought about by recurring delays and non-fulfilment of military contracts by local industry was clearly an unsatisfactory political outcome.

Further scorn was heaped upon the private gun trade when Sir Thomas Hastings, the Ordnance Principal Storekeeper, in evidence to the Committee, read some of the written excuses given by contractors for delays. These were strikes amongst the workmen, difficulty in procuring coal, illness of a skilled

Napoleon pictured at Waterloo, his last battle in 1815

artisan, and accident to machinery. It would seem there was little sympathy with the contractors' reasons for delay as Lord Raglan, the Master General of Ordnance, and Sir Thomas Hastings had already formed the view that Ordnance should take control of small arms manufacture. They stated:

... they had been guided in their opinion partly by the report of the Commissioners who, during the last year, visited the manufactories of the United States, and partly from communications with Mr Anderson and other persons conversant with machinery.

Reading the report, and considering the evidence from the Committee's point of view, it would be difficult to see how they could have reached any other conclusion than for the Board of Ordnance to assume overall responsibility for military small arms manufacture. The previous three years had seen a worsening of arms deliveries to Ordnance and the commencement of war in the Crimea had heightened pressure for a radical review of procurement. Given that the British armed forces were again placed in the position of being without sufficient quantities of reliable small arms in time of war, as they had been during the Napoleonic conflict, it might be considered strange that by the middle of the century, Ordnance still relied heavily upon the independent gun trade for its weapon supplies. The private sector had not modernised its methods of manufacture and did not do so until well into the second half of the century, instead relying heavily on traditional manual skills. Only after their hand had been forced through competition from the new government factory at Enfield Lock did the private contractors set up the Birmingham Small Arms Company (BSA) in 1861. Further pressure for radical change was heaped on the private sector when Ordnance began placing contracts for weapons manufactured only with interchangeable parts.

Delaying change

By 1854 the Board of Ordnance had received reports from the Commission led by Lieutenant Colonel Burn, and the previous year from Joseph Whitworth (later Sir), detailing the fact that the government armouries in America were employing large amounts of machinery in the manufacture of rifles. The level of mechanisation was reported as being particularly advanced in the operations of forming, shaping, and fitting out gun stocks, formerly considered a highly labour-intensive part of the gun manufacturing process. It was not as if the American Government was keeping the technology a secret, for machinery capable of making 130 to 160 gun stocks per day was offered to the Board of Ordnance by an American agent Samuel Cox as early as 1841. In fact, the technology for manufacturing large scale irregular and complex shapes in wood had existed in Britain since the early part of the century. Less than one hundred miles from Enfield, in the Portsmouth dockyards, the relatively complicated ship's pulley block had been manufactured for the Navy on a sequence of machines invented by Marc Isambard Brunel (father of Isambard Kingdom Brunel) and built by Henry Maudslay the eminent London engineer. Maudslay's workshops were located within one hour's travel from Enfield, so it is hard to imagine that senior Ordnance personnel were ignorant of the available manufacturing technology, especially as it was

*Picture of Portsmouth block
making factory c1900*

*Ship's pulley blocks similar to those
manufactured on Marc Brunel's machines*

the Admiralty, another branch of government, which had been responsible for financing the Portsmouth block-making factory. However, the process seems not to have been adopted in Britain for the purpose of manufacturing gun stocks although there is evidence which suggests that the principles were probably "borrowed" by American machine tool inventors and the ideas incorporated into their own designs. These eventually found their way back to Britain via Enfield through the machine tool contract with the Ames Manufacturing Company, Chicopee, Massachusetts, later in the century.

*Marc Isambard
Brunel inventor of
the early Portsmouth
block making
machinery*

*An Ames Manufacturing
Company, USA, lock
bedding machine*

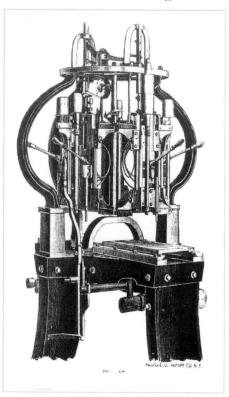

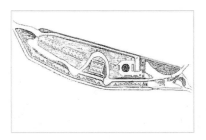

Early map of RSAF, Enfield Lock, clearly showing the site as an island

Further examples of differences between British and American manufacturing techniques were observed by Ordnance personnel, prominent engineers, and private small arms contractors at the time of the Great Exhibition of 1851 in London's Hyde Park. Here the American company Robbins and Lawrence had sent six US Army rifles for display and demonstration, all manufactured with parts that interchanged. Samuel Colt exhibited his revolvers which he claimed were made almost entirely by machinery and having parts that were interchangeable for everyone to see. From the evidence it can be seen that both the Board of Ordnance and the private gun makers were aware of the advances made in machine tool technology on the other side of the Atlantic, yet there was still an apparent reluctance to embrace the processes of mechanisation and mass production. For this reluctance to have existed for so long, it would seem fair to conclude that strong and compelling forces were at play.

Grasping the nettle

When the second Commission, led by Lieutenant Colonel Burn R.A., was sent to America in 1854 it had been given quite specific instructions to inspect the different gun factories and to purchase such machinery and equipment as found necessary for the proposed new factory at Enfield. This was quite a different approach to that of the Commission of 1853 which included Joseph Whitworth the distinguished engineer. Whitworth did not go expressly to America to view the gun manufacturers as might be implied by reading some accounts of the visit. Initially he went to attend the New York Industrial Exhibition. This would seem to indicate that in less than a year, the procurement of small arms for the British army and navy had reached an extremely critical state. Accompanied by George Wallis, Headmaster of the Birmingham School of Art, Whitworth appears to have taken it upon himself to alter his itinerary, as it is suggested "and while there they extended their enquiries by visiting several establishments, among others the Government Arms Factory at Springfield". This observation is further substantiated in Whitworth's evidence to the 1854 Select Committee when he stated "that he had not been specially directed to inspect the manufactories of fire-arms, and had not therefore given the close attention to the subject which he would have done if he had foreseen the present inquiry".

The introduction to the 1854 Committee on Machinery's 87 page report sets out their terms of reference and provides an insight into some of the circumstances which helped bring about a marked change of direction by Ordnance. From the following extract of the report, the reasons can be seen which were eventually to cause Ordnance to take on the responsibility of becoming a major manufacturer of military small arms.

> Owing to the delays constantly recurring in the fulfilment of contracts for arms, the high price demanded by contractors, and the inconvenience occasioned to the Service by these causes, the Honourable Board of Ordnance, towards the end of the year 1853, considered it advisable, in order to secure a regular supply of them, to take this branch of manufacture into their own hands, and erect a Government establishment capable of producing muskets in large numbers, and at a moderate price by the introduction of machinery into every part of the manufacturing where it was applicable... Having caused a plan of the building they proposed to erect to be drawn out,... set to work as speedily as possible; and hearing from Mr Whitworth and others that machinery was extensively applied to this branch of manufacture in the United States of America,

where, on account of the high price of labour, the whole energy of people is directed to improving and inventing labour-saving machinery, the Honourable Board consider it advisable to send over to that country some of their officers, with a view to obtaining every information in their power connected with the manufacture of arms as there conducted, and with the power of buying such machinery as they might consider would be more productive than that used in England for similar purposes.

The second Commission to America placed contracts for machine tools with Robbins & Lawrence of Windsor, Vermont, and the Ames Manufacturing Company, Chicopee, Massachusetts. This latter company produced machinery for fashioning gun stocks, bedding the barrel, and letting in the lock. The machinery proved to be so efficient and reliable that when writing the history of the Royal Small Arms Factory in c1930, G. H. Roberts, the then Superintendent proudly wrote:

> It is interesting to note that several of the woodworking machines supplied by the Ames Co. are still in use today and giving good service, in fact one well known Firm of English machinists recently declared that even today they could not improve upon the American machines in the matter of output etc.

Sir Joseph Whitworth (1803-1877) gave evidence before the Select Committee of 1854

Roberts commented further:

> As regards Messrs. Robbins & Lawrence machines, a small Horizontal Milling Machine of their make, probably one of the last of the plant supplied by them, has been scrapped within the last year or two, although it has not been worked for some time.

From the report of the Commission when visiting the US Armoury at Springfield, it would appear that their decision to purchase what must be considered a substantial quantity of machinery, was influenced by at least two important factors; that of the sequenced operation of the gun stock forming machinery and the ability of a workman to randomly assemble arms from parts taken from weapons manufactured over a ten-year period. To oversee the installation and the commissioning of the machinery at Enfield Lock, James H. Burton, former Master Armourer of Harpers Ferry Armoury, was brought to England on a five-year contract.

James Henry Burton came to Enfield from the USA on a five-year contract to oversee installation of American machine tools

Enfield comes of age

The years 1855 to 1859 saw the rapid expansion of building at Enfield Lock. Construction work was carried out by the Royal Engineers under the supervision of Captain Thomas Bernard Collison, R.E. During this period the large machine room was completed specifically to house the new machinery, much of which was purchased in America by the 1854 Commission. The plant was designed for an estimated annual production of 130,000 muskets and bayonets. In the early years, although expenditure on land, buildings, machinery, and gas works amounted to £315,000, the success of the plant was such that, according to Roberts, by 1862 this sum together with depreciation of £48,000 was said to have been entirely repaid by the reduced cost of production.

The large machine room, completed in 1856 to house the American machine tools

Before 1861 the energy source for the Enfield manufactory had been water taken from the River Lea to drive two 18 foot diameter cast iron water wheels, each having an estimated output of 46 horse power. The design of the drive, which did not incorporate governors, was reported to have made the outputs very irregular. Primarily the main function of the water wheels was to run the barrel grinding shop which, according to reports, continued with this source of power until 1887. Amazingly it has been recorded that the use of the traditional grit grindstone was not finally discontinued until c1926.

In 1852 a new Barrel Rolling Plant was installed and by 1853 Roberts reported that the factory capacity was 50,000 muskets and 3,000 swords per annum. Prior to this, and using only an average of 25 horse power before steam was introduced, it was claimed that the production rate of the Enfield factory had been in the order of 7,000 small arms and 1,500 swords annually. However, Professor Tim Putnum, an historian of industrial technology, when referring to George Lovell suggests that "the number of complete weapons in his period never approached that figure". This, he concludes, is based upon the assumption that Enfield was using a number of individual components purchased from the private contractors rather than manufacturing the complete arm in-house.

Once the American machine tools had been installed at Enfield, not only was there a dramatic increase in arms production, but also their introduction made the RSAF the first British plant to be able to claim that their machined parts were so accurate that they could be interchanged between weapons. This is the first true example of a British factory using mass production techniques, as defined by the manufacture of standardised machine-made parts that interchanged completely, rather than those which are made to fit on an individual basis, usually by hand finishing. The new system of manufacture was so successful that by year ending 30th June 1860 the output of rifles alone had increased to 90,707, an average of 1,744 per week, later to go up to 1,900. By the year 1861 1,700 men were employed at the plant and it is recorded that the large machine room (currently the Grade II listed building with the clock tower) was driven by two 40 horse power steam engines with Fairbairn expansion gear, while in the barrel mill a 70 horse power steam engine was employed along with the existing water wheels.

It would therefore seem that one could proclaim with confidence that the "American system of manufactures" (as it has popularly become known) had truly arrived at Enfield and was seen to be working. The private gun trade had yet to respond to the challenge of producing military weapons with standardised and interchangeable parts by the extensive use of machine tools.

In this chapter a number of issues have been highlighted which have arisen out of the installation of the "American system" at Enfield Lock. Should the reader wish to gain a deeper knowledge of the complexities surrounding the British small arms industry in the nineteenth century, an analysis, together with the effects, problems, and advantages for both the Board of Ordnance and the independent gun trade, can be derived from the recommended reading in the References at the end of this chapter.

The Royal Small Arms Factory at Enfield Lock lasted for over one hundred and seventy years, providing arms for the Allied forces in two World Wars. Many of the famous Lee Enfield magazine rifles can still be seen in use around the world today. This is a lasting tribute to the quality of the product produced

The ferry, Enfield Lock

by the RSAF workforce. It was a sad day for manufacturing in the Lea Valley when the factory closed in August 1987. During its life the factory created work for generations of local people, in many cases whole families. It has often been said that once you had served an apprenticeship or had been employed at the RSAF then your skills would in great demand from other employers.

Early picture of RSAF, Enfield, showing school building and main gate

REFERENCES

Bailey De Witt, "George Lovell and The Growth of the RSAF Enfield", paper presented at MA Day School, Middlesex University (4th July 1992)

Blackmore Howard L., "Military Gun Manufacturing in London and the Adoption of Interchangeability", *Arms Collecting Vol.29, No.4* (November 1991)

Cottesloe, Colonel, Lord, C.B., "Notes on the History of the Royal Small Arms Factory, Enfield Lock", *Historical Research Vol. 12* (undated, probably c1932)

Gilbert K. R., "The Ames Recessing Machine: A Survivor Of The Original Enfield Rifle Machinery", *Technology and Culture, Vol.4, Part 2* (1963)

Putnam Tim & Weinbren Dan, *A Short History of the Royal Small Arms Factory Enfield*, Middlesex University (1992)

Whitworth J. & Wallis G., *The Industry of the United States in Machinery, Manufacturers and Useful and Ornamental Arts* (1854)

Royal Ordnance, Nottingham. "Notes on the History of the Royal Small Arms Factory, Enfield Lock", Unsigned typed manuscript c1930, accompanied by a memorandum, dated 24th December 1930, signed, G. H. Roberts, (Superintendent RSAF 1922-1931), clearly showing that he is the author of the RSAF history.

C. H. Gregory, "Address of the President", *Institute of Civil Engineers – Minutes of Proceedings, Vol. 27* (London 1867-68)

House of Lords Record Office, London. "Report of the Committee on the Machinery of the United States of America, Presented to the House of Commons, in Pursuance of their Address of 10th July, 1855"

"Report from the Select Committee on Small Arms, House of Commons", May 1854

Farming near the Royal Small Arms Factory

Note.1.

There does appear to be some confusion with regard to the actual date when the RSAF was first established. R.H. Roberts in his notes suggests the establishment was, "about the year 1804". Colonel Lord Cottesloe, C.B. confirms this date in his article, "Notes on the History of the Royal Small Arms Factory, Enfield Lock", Volume 12 of *Army Historical Research*. This is not particularly surprising as Cottesloe bases most of his article on the notes of Roberts. In A. Robinson's and J. Burnby's "Occasional Paper No. 50" for the Edmonton Hundred Historical Society, *Guns and Gun Powder in Enfield*, it suggests that negotiations were started for the land to build the new manufactory on 14th July 1811. George Lovell (appointed as Storekeeper at Enfield Lock, 1st April 1816), in his report on the background and present state of the Enfield factory (W.O.44/682) to Sir Henry Hardinge (Board of Ordnance) lists the following under "Lands":

Government Row built for the workers at the RSAF

> 4 Acres, 2 Rods, 5 Poles of Sedgy and Swampy Ground adjoining the River, purchased therewith from William Sotherby, Esq. in 1808.

Note.2.

There has been some confusion as to who actually led the 1854 Commission on Machinery during their American tour. For example, David A. Hounshell, in his book, *From the American System to Mass Production 1800-1932: The Development of Manufacturing Technology in the United States*, The John Hopkins University Press,

(Baltimore, 1984), (p.4) suggests that John Anderson was the leader. However, it is clear from the "Report of the Committee on the Machinery of the United States of America, Presented to the House of Commons, in Pursuance of their Address of the 10th July, 1855", p.2 (548), (House of Lords Record Office, London) that Anderson was not the leader. Here it is clearly documented that Lieutenant Colonel Burn, Royal Artillery, who held the position of Assistant Inspector of Artillery at Woolwich, had been appointed to lead the Commission. A communication dated 13th February 1854, from the Office of Ordnance shows that the Secretary to the Board of Ordnance, J. Wood, had passed on the Board's instruction to Burn stating "I am to add that Lieutenant Warlow, Royal Artillery, and Mr Anderson, have been instructed to proceed thither on the 4th March next, and to place themselves under your direction; and I am to request you will give them such instructions previous to your departure as you may consider necessary".

Interestingly, in the unpublished history of the RSAF written by G. H. Roberts he mistakenly lists a Major Turborville accompanying Lieutenant Colonel Burn, Lieutenant Warlow and Mr Anderson as part of the Commission sent to America in 1854. All the documentary evidence which includes the Report of the Committee on the Machinery of the United States of America, lists only the latter three members. In fact, this report which describes their findings during the tour of American manufacturing establishments in 1854 and was presented to the House of Commons, "in Pursuance of their Address of the 10th July, 1855", is signed only by Burn, Warlow and Anderson.

Roberts' mistake is curious as he clearly had access to material which may not have been freely available to other historians at the time. In the preface to his *Notes on the History of the Royal Small Arms Factory, Enfield Lock*, he states "The writer wishes to place on record his indebtedness to Sir Herbert J. Creedy, Secretary of the War Office, for permission to consult a number of War Office records".

Apart from this one transgression, Roberts is to be congratulated for having the interest and enthusiasm to begin assembling the facts which have assisted later historians with their researches into the history of the RSAF.

Note.3.

The possible explanation for Lovell being called a "bedstead maker", is that in the late 1820s, to keep the Enfield factory going, Lovell took on all kinds of work, including making bedsteads.

It is worth noting that George Lovell, the first Storekeeper at the RSAF, should not be confused with Frederick Lovell, his brother, Clerk 1824, or Francis George Lovell, his son, Assistant Inspector of Arms 1843. Robert Lovell, another son, also worked in the industry.

2. THE ORDNANCE CONTRACT SYSTEM AND THE "VIEW"

In this chapter the opportunity will be taken to examine the relationship between the Board of Ordnance and the private gun trade. To help understand the interplay between the private and the public sectors, it will be necessary to explore the workings of the Ordnance contract system and to discover how "the view" (inspection) was performed by Ordnance personnel. By studying these two areas and their effect upon the private gun trade, particularly in the period from 1840 to 1854, we can resolve a number of complex issues. While research has shown that there were several reasons governing the slow progress of British industry in the nineteenth century towards a fully mechanised system of small arms manufacture, in many ways it was the Ordnance viewing and contracting systems which had the strongest influence upon the industry's shape and structure.

In the complicated and multifaceted nature of Ordnance practice, the pivotal role played by the Inspector of Small Arms, George Lovell, will be treated in greater detail in a later chapter. There, a reassessment of the available evidence will allow a fresh look at the influence of this complex and talented man upon the operation of the Ordnance small arms inspection and procurement which was firmly linked to the functioning of the weapons contract system.

To assist this study and to gain a better understanding of how Ordnance viewed the performance of the independent gun trade during the first half of the century, it will be necessary to look at the prevailing situation from an Ordnance perspective. Fortunately, a detailed and quite vivid account of the Ordnance viewpoint survives, recorded in a memorandum written on the 18th February 1854 by Joseph Wood, Secretary, War Office, which encapsulates the unsatisfactory history of weapon supply as he saw it. From the text of the memorandum it is possible to detect the increasing tension between Ordnance and the private sector.

Wood's memorandum

Highlighting the relevant sections of Wood's memorandum allows the backdrop of events to unfold, giving a clear image of the circumstances which were to dramatically change the methods of weapon supply and procurement for the British armed forces:

> In 1803, when the war with France was renewed, the scarcity of arms was so great, and the want of them so urgent, that the Government had recourse to foreign markets, and bought up all they could obtain. These were bad in quality, cumbersome and heavy in pattern, and comparatively few in number. ... At the peace in 1815, the manufacture of arms for Government ceased, and the workmen were dispersed. Little was afterwards done with regard to the provision of arms, until the adoption of the percussion principle, when a re-equipment of the army became necessary. The trade had fallen into a very disjointed state, and there was a difficulty in collecting together men capable of making the new arm in a satisfactory manner. In 1840 the inspector of small arms represented the very unsatisfactory state of affairs; the masters complaining of the workmen, the workmen of the masters; the lock-filers and the stockers striking for wages; the masters exposed to serious combination of

workmen, and the latter having a fair ground of complaint against the masters; the result being higher prices to the department, or injury to the service by delay. Again, in 1842, the inspector of small arms represented the injury to the service, ... and in 1848 he further represented the disadvantages of the system then pursued for obtaining arms, ... The opinions of the inspector of small arms expressed coincided with those which the Board had previously entertained. ... In March 1850 they decided upon putting up to competition the supply of arms then required, for calling for tenders of the several parts of the musket except the stocks, of which there was a store, and then for setting them up. The result showed a great reduction in the cost of the arms; ... Many of the tenders were at one price, showing that the parties had acted in concert, ... Great difficulties arose in the execution of the contracts; the setting up was delayed for want of materials, the lock-filers having struck for wages; and it was also impeded by the very unsettled state of the workmen in the military-gun trade generally. In February 1851 the Board were desirous of obtaining a further number of muskets, before the end of the financial year, 31st March 1851, but were informed by the contractors that there were not enough workmen in the trade to enable them to increase the number they were under engagement to supply.

In May 1851 a new pattern rifle musket was adopted by the British Army, and tenders, by competition, were obtained for the supply of the materials requisite, in addition to those in store which were applicable, for setting up 28,000 rifle muskets. Great delays occurred in the supply of the materials and sufficient were not collected to enable the Board to make contracts for setting up the muskets, until the month of December 1851; and the muskets were not completed until November 1853. ... In January 1853 a new pattern rifle carbine was adopted for the artillery, and the contracts were made for the materials for setting them up; but so great has been the difficulty and the delay in obtaining them, notwithstanding all the efforts of the Board, that not more than 500 carbines were completed by the end of January 1854. The rifle musket of 1851 having been superseded in 1853 by another of smaller bore, and somewhat different construction, the Board, in July last, called for tenders for materials for 20,000 muskets of the latter description. The offers received were so unsatisfactory as to price, and evinced so perfect a combination amongst the parties, that they were, after some correspondence, declined; ... The consequence is, that, up to the present time, the Board have not been able to commence the setting up of the muskets; and though they have made a contract for that purpose, it is uncertain, even if the materials should now come in with regularity, when it will be carried out, from the difficulties which the contractors may again encounter from the workmen.[1]

From Wood's memorandum, it can readily be established that after almost half a century the Board of Ordnance had hardly improved its position as a weapons procurer. As the second half of the century began, the Board was still unable efficiently to equip the British Army with small arms. This was the sorry state in which Ordnance found itself after initially planning to avert such future disasters by constructing the factory at Enfield Lock in 1816. The predicament poses two questions. How had such an unsatisfactory set of circumstances arisen after active measures had been taken to rectify the problem of arms supply, and was the position as one-sided as Wood had described?

Procurement problems

Prior to 1850 the contract system of arms procurement relied on Ordnance working with an established list of approved contractors. These contractors in turn used their own discretionary authority to employ sub-contractors and to engage the workers they required. There was considerable distrust between Ordnance and the private sector almost from the start.

In May 1816 the Birmingham and district gun manufacturers held a meeting which passed a resolution opposing the Board of Ordnance on the erection of the Enfield factory. Subsequently a petition was drawn up, but not presented to Parliament. Ordnance subsequently made an offer to the private sector only to use the facilities at Enfield for repair and not the manufacture of small arms. This promise was accepted by the trade.[2]

The short-term nature of the contract system and the strictness of the view had resulted in complaints to Parliament by the independent gun trade through their political representatives.

This had helped create difficulties and delays for Ordnance in their weapon procurement programme. Tensions did not improve between the two sides when George Lovell was promoted to Inspector of Small Arms in 1840. Lovell effectively took responsibility for every aspect of military weapon procurement. Under him, the Ordnance inspection system of gauging and measuring to pattern was tightened, no doubt spurred on by the drive towards improvements in standardisation he had begun at Enfield. Tolerances were becoming so stringent that contractors were having great difficulty in getting their work accepted byOrdnance. The private gun trade suffered considerably from the high rate of rejection and were in constant fear that Enfield would eventually undertake all military business in-house. This was the unsatisfactory state of the military gun trade as the second half of the century commenced. With war looming in the Crimea, the British Government found itself placed in the same embarrassing position it had been nearly half a century before at the start of the Napoleonic conflict, that of not having the ability to supply good quality arms in quantity to the front line troops.

Examining correspondence between the Board of Ordnance, the new Inspector of Small Arms, R.W. Gunner (promoted after Lovell's death in 1854), and some of the private contractors in the period September 1854 to March 1855, suggests that the demands and requirements of the Ordnance arms procurement programme had unfairly placed great strain upon the private contractors. In a letter to Joseph Wood, dated 12th September 1854, the Birmingham contractor Hollis & Sheath stated "we believe that we can complete the 20,000 musket pattern 1853 in March next, providing we have the materials (less sights) issued to us at the rate of 200 each per week from this date. We have received up to the 9th instant 10,000 sets". The letter goes on to explain:

> We beg again to assure the Honourable Board that every effort is being made to supply the sights so as to keep the pace with the setting up and we have already made from 9 to 10,000 sights, the greater part of which have not passed the view but we shall be able (as soon as the proper tools are prepared for viewing the sights) to deliver them in such quantities as to fetch up the lost time.[3]

Hollis & Sheath factory, Birmingham

At first glance the reference in the letter to the tools not yet having been prepared for viewing the sights might imply self criticism on the part of the contractor for failing to produce these items on time. However, reading a later letter from the contractor dated 16th November 1854 to Wood does place a somewhat different interpretation on who should be supplying the tools. In the correspondence Hollis & Sheath state that between 27th May and 28th October 1854, they had delivered 14,636 sights for viewing. Out of these, 8,613 had been "marked" (passed inspection) and 5,823 rejected. The following section of the letter is most revealing when the contractor complains "We believe that the immense number of rejections would not have taken place had the viewers been supplied with proper tools to test their accuracy – to which we refer in our letter of September 12th and with which tools the viewers have not yet been supplied".[4] While it cannot be categorically deduced from the correspondence that Ordnance should have actually made the tools, there is certainly a strong implication that they were responsible for their supply on time in support of the contract.

The reference in the correspondence to "the viewers" not being supplied with tools seems to imply the Ordnance viewers rather than those employed by Hollis & Sheath. However, even if this was not the case Ordnance would still be at fault for being the root cause of the delay.

A further revealing piece of evidence comes to light when examining a letter from R. W. Gunner to the Board of Ordnance, dated 22nd November 1854, in response to complaints of delays in the delivery of the pattern 1853 musket. Gunner reported that between April and November 15th, 16,880 sets of material had been issued, but he had only received 8,080 completed sights. Interestingly, there is no mention of tools not being supplied to the viewers. However, he does go on to say "sights have been obtained from other sources and issued for their service making up the numbers as stated by the contractors to about 10,000 Rifled and Sighted, whereas only 5,000 finished arms had been delivered up to the 6th instant".[5]

Cartridges for Enfield 0.577 (pattern 1853) used at time of Indian Mutiny, 1857

On 2nd March 1855 the Board of Ordnance wrote to Gunner regarding the contract for the 20,000 pattern 1853 muskets entered into on 21st February 1854, reminding him that "the whole should be delivered by the 5th March". Gunner responded on 10th March, reporting that the "four old contractors" had delivered 18,406 Pattern 1853 [muskets] which had all passed the view, and that he had another 385 muskets in hand, leaving an outstanding balance of 1,209. On 31st March 1855, Gunner wrote to Wood "I beg to report to the Honourable Boards information that the four old contractors have delivered 20,000 Musquets Rifle Pattern 1853 (first pattern) in completion of their contract of the 21st February 1854". He then went on to give the following totals as "set up and finished complete":

```
Set up Birmingham    20,000
Set up Enfield        1,000

Set up London         1,500  = Total. 22,500 [6]
```

Studying the evidence surrounding this particular contract has revealed what might be construed as a "cover-up" on behalf of certain individuals working for the Board of Ordnance who appear to have either withheld or not supplied important gauges or patterns to the contractors. This may have been an individual deliberate act, and not necessarily a piece of Ordnance collusion. However, in the future the incident along with other similar examples could easily strengthen the Board's hand when arguing the case for expanding the Enfield Lock small arms manufacturing facility, on the grounds of the gun trade's inefficiency. This would be a trump card to play against the private sector's opposing Parliamentary lobby. Although the Board was eventually to take a major controlling interest in the manufacture of military weapons by the introduction of American manufacturing technology at Enfield, this was not before a complex series of events had unfolded.

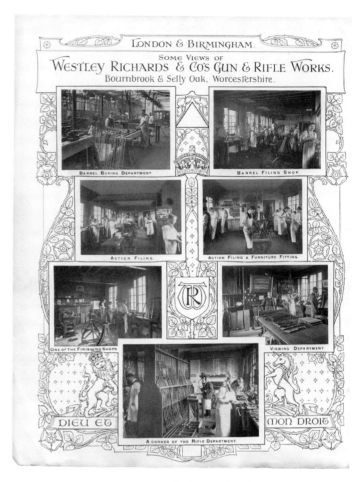

Wesley Richards, Birmingham 1912 catalogue images

Unfair criticism?

Although the private gun trade had been much maligned over its poor manufacturing and delivery performance by Ordnance, perhaps in some instances rightly, nevertheless, with regard to the contract for 20,000 weapons, it has been shown that in spite of being denied specialist setting-up tools, a substantial order had been completed within a few weeks of the agreed date. This was achieved in the face of strict viewing procedures, a reliance on hand production methods and, as Wood had pointed out in his memorandum dated 18th of February 1854, "there was a difficulty in collecting together men capable of making the new arm in a 'satisfactory manner'".[7] While the information above suggests that the fault was not always with the private sector, there is, in addition, further strong evidence which is at variance with the Ordnance criticisms of the gun trade. This information also conflicts with the generally accepted view of arms experts and historians like De Witt Bailey who have suggested that at the time, there was within the gun trade many "slovenly workmen".[8]

Giving evidence to the Select Committee on Small Arms in March 1854, Colonel John George Bonner, the Inspector of Stores to the East India Company for the past 21 years, when asked, "How do you provide your supply of fire-arms?" replied:

> As regards the musket, the materials are provided from various bona fide manufacturers at Birmingham and its neighbourhood, such as locks, bayonets, barrels, ramrods, and brass work; the smaller articles, such as screws, nails, swivels, and the minor parts of the gun, are entrusted entirely to the setters-up, viz., the gunmakers of London, and they provide the stock also, the Company not deeming it advisable to accumulate a store of stocks; no difficulty has been found in getting them at all times from the

East India House, Leadenhall Street, London

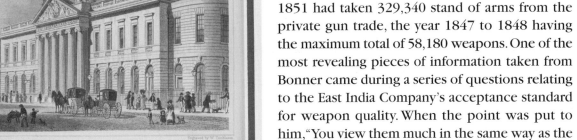

East India Company coat of arms

gunmakers in London; that forms part of their charge of course for setting up.[9]

From Bonner's evidence it can be seen that the East India Company between the years 1840 to 1851 had taken 329,340 stand of arms from the private gun trade, the year 1847 to 1848 having the maximum total of 58,180 weapons. One of the most revealing pieces of information taken from Bonner came during a series of questions relating to the East India Company's acceptance standard for weapon quality. When the point was put to him, "You view them much in the same way as the Government view their muskets, do you not?" Bonner replied, "Just the same".[10]

It can readily be deduced from following the probing cross examination that Bonner and his highly experienced long serving assistants were the final arbitrators in any controversial issues over standards of acceptable quality. One gets the distinct impression that should a dispute arise over the dimensions or finish of a particular weapon or part, then a practical common sense settlement would be found and mutually agreed. In the continuing cross examination Bonner was asked "When you have required so large a supply as 58,000 for one year, and 48,000 for the next year, have you found the contractors raise their prices?" To this Bonner replied "Never, except it was called for by those circumstances which enhance all prices".[11]

Interestingly, and in contrast, Wood in his memorandum of 18th February, had complained of "... high prices, which resulted from the organised combinations both of the masters and men in the gun trade..."[12]

When probed deeper on the subject of charges, "You met with nothing unfair on the part of the contractors?" Bonner made the following telling statement

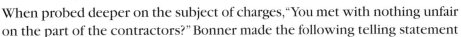

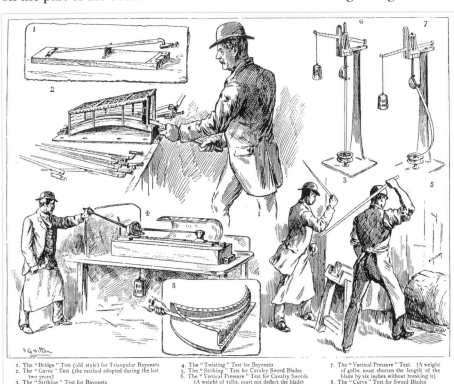

1. The "Bridge" Test (old style) for Triangular Bayonets
2. The "Curve" Test (the method adopted during the last two years)
3. The "Striking" Test for Bayonets
4. The "Twisting" Test for Bayonets
5. The "Striking" Test for Cavalry Sword Blades
6. The "Vertical Pressure" Test for Cavalry Swords (A weight of 32lbs. must not deflect the blade)
7. The "Vertical Pressure" Test. (A weight of 40lbs. must shorten the length of the blade by six inches without breaking it)
8. The "Curve" Test for Sword Blades

TESTING BAYONETS AND CAVALRY SWORDS AT THE ROYAL SMALL ARMS FACTORY, ENFIELD

Bayonet and sword testing at Enfield Lock c1850

which implied a good working relationship between customer and supplier. He explained, "I must do them the justice to say that they were always particularly anxious to do what was right and proper between the Company and themselves, which is my duty to watch."[13]

This display of mutual trust appears genuine and probably accounted for the East India Company getting the weapons they required at the right price. In fact there is evidence of the good relationship between the private sector and the East India Company, and the somewhat strained alliance between the Board of Ordnance and the gun contractors, dating back to the eighteenth century. At the time a dispute arose between Ordnance and the private sector over the design, price and conditions of a contract for the manufacture of the pattern 1777 flint lock. On this occasion the East India Company were having a simpler form of the lock manufactured for which they paid the contractors one shilling more than Ordnance were offering. Not unnaturally, their work was given preference over Ordnance.[14]

Further evidence of fairness and a good working relationship can be seen when inspecting the price of some popular nineteenth century weapons. Although not exactly the same as the then current British service pattern, by 1850 the cost of a weapon to the East India Company from the private sector was £2-7s-7d, which at the time was not excessive.[15]. This figure compared more than favourably with a Baker rifle costing £4-8s-3d in 1810, or the Minié rifle manufactured at the RSAF Enfield in 1853 costing £3-4s.[16]

With regard to pricing, it should be remembered that Ordnance had a distinct advantage over the private sector, as Enfield had the ability to estimate the various manufacturing costs. However, the gun trade, being denied long-term contracts, were reluctant to invest in capital equipment which over a reasonable period of time would have helped reduce the labour cost content of a weapon. Allegations by Ordnance of the private sector overcharging may have been the result of contractors trying to maintain sensible profit margins to compensate for high reject rates and the short-term nature of the contract system, rather than a deliberate policy of making excessive profits from the government. This observation would appear to be validated if the quantities of weapons delivered (shown later in this chapter) to the East India Company and Ordnance are compared. Over a nine-year period (1841-1850), the private sector sent on average almost three guns to the former, against only one to the latter, suggesting that the best prospects for the future of the independent trade lay with customers like the East India Company rather than Ordnance.

Ordnance on the other hand was supported by, and were part of, government. Before the end of the 1850s Enfield, a public sector factory, would receive substantial internal orders for weapons allowing them to sustain high annual volumes of production. While it is beyond the scope of this book to examine the methods of Ordnance financial accounting to see if all overhead costs had been properly administered and apportioned to the weapon, it is however recognised that government departments have historically been clever at concealing the true cost of products and services through the vastness of the budgetary machine. Therefore, without an in-depth study, it would not be possible to guarantee that the Ordnance price for a weapon supplied to the military reflected all the attributable overheads, like warehousing, material deterioration, wastage, packing and transport.

The importance of good relationships

The working relationship between customer and supplier is one that should not be overlooked, as often it can provide vital clues and broaden our understanding of why a particular set of circumstances arose, or why certain situations prevailed. From Wood's memorandum of 18th February 1854, it can be seen that relationships had remained strained between Ordnance, the contractors and their workers for a number of years, as he speaks of "... organised combinations both of the masters and men..."[17] This, he implies, caused contractual delays and higher prices for Ordnance. However, as with all forms of accusations and counter accusations, there is seldom one side which is completely innocent or correct in its assessment of the situation. Reasons governing the difficulties are often complex and not always what they appear on the surface. Under such circumstances, there is a need for mutual trust and understanding if issues are to be resolved.

Although there were some calm and conciliatory voices from within the ranks of the gun contractors, there was a growing general belief that Ordnance was planning to take away their livelihoods by increasing the number of manufacturing functions carried out in-house. As it will be seen later, the fears of the gun trade were not without foundation.

It is quite usual today to discover examples of strained relationships between customer and supplier, resulting in lack of mutual trust. Often the customer will take advantage of the contractor or supplier, when the market demand for the product is weak, by offering a lower price. This is on the grounds of the product being more difficult to sell, which on occasions can be quite genuine. Nevertheless, when the market becomes buoyant, then it can be the turn of the contractor or supplier to take advantage of the customer by putting up the price, often on the grounds that material costs have risen, prompted by increased demand. Both forms of commercial blackmail are the basis for distrust, each party awaiting the earliest opportunity to regain the upper hand. When such breakdowns in relationships occur, it is normal for the customer to seek to place business with other contractors or suppliers, while the supplier strives to gain contracts with other customers. Such behaviour is not conducive to the maintenance of good quality products, as both customer and supplier have to go, once more, through a fresh learning cycle with their new partners. Inevitably this can lead to higher product reject rates as new procedures are adopted, with the added risk of failure to meet delivery schedules. While these may not have been the exact circumstances experienced by the Board of Ordnance and the private gun trade, research has revealed that a number of the elements outlined certainly existed, particularly when Ordnance moved from a list of established contractors to an open tendering system in 1850.

These complex issues of relationships, the short-term intermittent nature of contracts, the strictness of view, and what might be seen as the delaying or withholding of essential measuring equipment by Ordnance made up a cocktail of events which in turn eventually influenced Parliament into voting large sums of money to re-equip the Royal Small Arms Factory at Enfield Lock with the latest American machine tool technology. This action thereby enabled Ordnance to take virtual control of all military small arms manufacture. However, in the ensuing period until the improved manufacturing facility was firmly established, the private gun trade was to be called upon once more to supply the British Army in time of war.

A different relationship

It would be difficult for the researcher sifting through the considerable documentation of the period not to escape the clear impression that there was a general feeling of mutual respect and trust between the East India Company and the private gun contractors. This understanding had developed over a number of years, resulting in a good long-term working relationship. Much of this had come about through the stewardship of Colonel John George Bonner with his more practical approach to the viewing of arms which was more about serviceability and functionally, rather than standards of high finish. The same could not be said of the relationship which existed between the private contractors and the Board of Ordnance. Much of the ill feeling came about after George Lovell was promoted to Inspector of Small Arms in 1840, when he had insisted on stricter standards of viewing for weapons and parts. Lovell's endeavours to improve the quality of British military firearms and, to his credit, the contractual relationship with the independent gun trade, were generally not understood by government officials, lacking the whole-hearted support of Ordnance. The years from 1840 to the middle of the century saw a rapid deterioration in the relationship between the private gun trade and the Board of Ordnance, with increasing acrimony, much of the venom being directed at Lovell.

By the time Joseph Wood had written his critical memorandum on the performance of the private gun trade in February 1854, and Bonner had given an opposing view in his evidence before the Select Committee on Small Arms in the following month of March (this being given some prominence in the Committee's summing up in the May), the situation had been overtaken by events. On the 28th March 1854, Britain declared war on Russia. This loosened the private gun maker's lobbying grip on Parliament. In the national interest, Bonner's contrasting testimony would have to be ignored as Ordnance pushed home the initiative to expand the Enfield Lock manufacturing facility.

A misunderstood private sector

Several contemporary writers have given the impression that the private gun trade in Britain was woefully inadequate and generally slovenly in its performance, producing sub-standard weapons and parts. While one can understand how such an impression had grown and remained with some commentators, by examining the available evidence in detail a somewhat different and more balanced picture emerges.

The British private gun trade can be looked upon as being extremely flexible and adaptable in its methods of manufacture, coping with a range of weapon types. These essentially fell into three main categories. At the bottom of the scale there were the cheap flint-locks with beech-wood stocks made for the African market, at a unit price of around ten shillings. Then there were the different types of contract military patterns for supply to overseas markets and to the British Government, typically selling at £3-0 to £3-10s. At the top were the sporting guns or fowling pieces. These could command prices in the order of £18 or more.[18] Some of these sporting guns can be considered as lovingly hand-crafted masterpieces, even desirable works of art, many having engraved lock plates and barrels, with highly figured and polished walnut stocks, the wood in the most expensive models coming from selected areas of the tree root. Much of the criticism of the private gun trade had come from Ordnance sources such as Joseph Wood (alluded to earlier). No doubt from his particular point of view the situation of arms quality and delivery was as bad as it could be. When he wrote his memorandum in February 1854, giving his analysis regarding the state of the gun trade, it is doubtful if he was fully aware, or, for that matter, understood, the intricacies surrounding arms procurement, particularly the constraints placed upon manufacturers by the contract system. Due to the private gun trade being loosely organised around a flexible system of out-working, employing small jobbing artisans using mainly manual skills, it was able on the whole to cope extremely well with the three main categories of weapon manufacture. This was particularly true of the African and sporting gun trade, and that of the East India Company. Problems arose when the trade tried to fulfil contracts for the Board of Ordnance because it did not appear to understand the nature of the private sector's business, and had therefore unilaterally set standards of high quality and finish. This level of perfection was not compatible with the more practical requirements set by other major customers, such as the East India Company. Naturally these differing standards for military weapons caused confusion and even resentment among the private contractors, as large numbers of their arms were rejected by the Ordnance viewers, when their work was generally accepted elsewhere. If Ordnance had really understood the workings of the private gun trade, they would have realised what they had before them was what might be described collectively as a large and versatile factory system. Admittedly the production processes were widely spread throughout Birmingham and London, but the overhead costs were relatively low and not borne by Ordnance. This "factory" had certain advantages over the machine-intensive plant which would eventually be installed at Enfield. Firstly, its manufacturing processes were not locked into producing mainly one type of weapon in volume, as Enfield would effectively be. Due to its heterogeneous nature the private trade had the ability to satisfy different markets with different grades of weapons, sub-assemblies, and parts, all at the same time. Because of this flexible approach, and despite the level of complaint from Ordnance, the private sector remained the most reliable and effective supplier of small arms to the Board until 1859, only reducing deliveries of military weapons when the Enfield factory came fully on-stream in 1857.[19]

Reading the well documented evidence of the many witnesses called before the 1854 Select Committee on Small Arms, and taking into account the previous accusations of Ordnance that the private gun trade had acted in combination against them, it would be difficult to accept, if the evidence is viewed objectively, that the problems of poor quality and supply was wholly a one-sided affair. There is sufficient information provided from a good cross-section of witnesses, who were interrogated in depth, for the researcher to form the opinion that the private gun trade had been treated rather shabbily by the Board of Ordnance. However, if one reads only the critical reports from Ordnance members, and accepts, in isolation, the failure of contractors to meet completion dates, then it will not be too difficult to understand why the private gun trade has been held in such low esteem by some for so long.

In recent times the poor image has been perpetuated by Nathan Rosenberg, perhaps inadvertently, when he quoted from a section of Joseph Wood's memorandum (February 1854) relating to arms "… of an inferior description". The arms to which Wood refers, inter alia, is the India pattern musket supplied to the British Army during the Peninsula Wars. Although Rosenberg acknowledges that at the time when this weapon was supplied there was a "rapid growth in the output of military firearms", he suggests that this was "achieved in part by a relaxation of standards of quality".[20] Whether the "rapid growth" alluded to by Rosenberg had been achieved by the deliberate "relaxation of standards" is not clear. The information contained within Wood's memorandum covers a period of over half a century and the point relating to quality and acquisition of arms is quite general and refers also to weapons purchased from abroad. However, what is clear is that the Birmingham gun trade alone was able to average a grand total of 158,484 muskets, rifles, carbines and pistols per annum for the Board of Ordnance throughout an eleven-year period between 1804 to 1815. During this time Birmingham also manufactured some 3,037,644 barrels and 2,879,203 locks for setting up into arms by the London gun trade for Board of Ordnance contracts. Also, there was an estimated 1,000,000 sets of material produced for the London trade to set up into arms for the East India Company and in excess of 500,000 fowling pieces manufactured, all during the same period.[21]

Considering the reliance upon mainly manual methods of production, and all the other problems alluded to above, the private sector's achievements can be viewed as outstanding. The "factory" concept of out-working within the private sector, which can be viewed as a "collective industry" was not quite as archaic as it might first appear. While certainly there were difficulties for the private sector in the way Ordnance organised the system of view, nevertheless by the 1840s the London and Birmingham trades had easy access to each other through the rapidly expanding railway network. This effectively brought together and improved communication between the more distant assortment of typically small, yet diverse component manufacturers. John Dent Goodman, the respected Birmingham manufacturer and writer, lists the chief branches of these as "Stock, barrel, lock, furniture, and odd-work making; and for military guns there are in addition, bayonet, sight, and rammer".[22] While it is generally accepted that the private sector relied mainly on manual methods for the manufacture of the lock and stock, from early in the century the barrel making branch of the industry had invested in machinery. Goodman reports, "Barrel making is quite a distinct trade. For the manufacture of military barrels, a somewhat large plant of rolling, boring, and grinding machinery is required."[23]

Birmingham Gun Barrel Proof House

Birmingham gun trade quarter map of 1815

Taking the earlier quoted figures for the private gun trade in Birmingham alone between the years 1802 and 1814, Goodman makes the somewhat chauvinistic point that "upwards of 200,000" more arms for the British Government were produced when comparisons were made with the combined output of the ten national manufactories of France. He further suggests that during this period, Birmingham turned out "500,000 to 600,000" more barrels and locks than the same French manufacturers.[24] Without this quite outstanding manufacturing commitment by the British private sector in the face of growing Ordnance criticism, achieved under the gathering cloud of a poor supplier contractor relationship, it is doubtful if Wellington would have been victorious over Napoleon.

Throughout the period of the Napoleonic Wars Ordnance made only a minute contribution to weapon manufacture. The barrel and lock factory at Lewisham, which began production in 1807, fell woefully short of its expected target of 50,000 barrels per annum. Beset by failing water power, production was eventually transferred to the newly constructed, although rather modest, government manufactory at Enfield Lock. The factory and its workers cottages were not completed until 1816. This meant the artisans took no part in providing military small arms for the war with France.[25]

Understanding the supply background

The build up of friction between the Board of Ordnance and the private sector over allegations of poor quality products, and the failure of gunsmiths to meet contractual obligations, had reached critical proportions by the 1850s. However, the private gun trade countered and complained bitterly about the strictness of the view imposed by Ordnance, which in the eyes of many contractors was "vexatious" and quite unnecessary. Ordnance were seen to be uncompromising, constantly imposing financial penalties upon the gun makers for late delivery; and non-payment for parts which failed the view was a common occurrence. There were criticisms by Ordnance over the quality of finished parts, the allegation being that the gun trade placed too much reliance on individual sub-contractors who employed low standard workmen who would toil for the lowest wage. There were further complaints aimed at the trade's slowness and apparent reluctance to invest in modern machinery. While some complaints against the gun trade were probably justified, research has shown that the overall picture as painted by Ordnance seems to have come from the brush of an impressionist artist.

The nature of the contract system as operated by Ordnance had changed by the early 1850s from a list of approved suppliers to one of open tender. Suppliers who tendered had to put up with a system which was price competitive, with contracts that were short-term. Implementation of the new contract system did not help the gun trade maintain a stable work-force as masters laid off skilled workers when business was lost or slack. This, as we have learned from Select Committee reports, helped exacerbate insecurity within the private sector. Further problems for the private sector occurred during the inter-war years due to the lack of Ordnance orders. This was partly due to the high levels of arms in store long after the cessation of hostilities between Britain and France. Putting all the above factors together, it is not difficult to understand why it was the private sector rather than the public which took the brunt of the industrial down-turn, with skill losses as craftsmen were forced to find work elsewhere, in some cases never to return to the trade again. To a large extent, this was the situation in which the industry found itself when George Lovell took up the post of Inspector of Small Arms in 1840. From this period to the mid 1850s there were gathering complaints by Ordnance over the seeming inability of the private gun trade to meet order schedules. There was also a growing mistrust of the trade's willingness to produce reasonably priced military small arms and parts, with accusations of firms operating cartels. Certainly this was the view of a number of Ordnance officials who, in fairness, probably lacked the overall experience and vision to know what was required when it came to administering contracts at grass root level. This observation is supported by the fact that it took an independent Select Committee to identify the problems of contractors not being supplied with specialist equipment to check their work prior to submission to the Ordnance viewing houses. While it is not denied that the private contractors had joined trade associations and discussed matters of mutual interest, the Ordnance policy of not issuing long-term contracts or guaranteeing follow-up work, would of necessity have forced prices upward as the independent trade had little other opportunity of recovering the costs of setting-up and material losses incurred through the high rate of product and component rejection. However, in contrast, it is interesting to note that Colonel Bonner of the East India Company had not complained that he had experienced a cartel operating against him.

On balance, who was to blame for supply failures?

From the continuing allegations of Ordnance over the failure of the private gun trade to meet delivery schedules and pass the view, it would be a simple matter to assume that the fault was always with the contractor. However, the evidence would suggest that these allegations should not be taken as a wholly one-sided affair. Reading the correspondence between the private gun makers and the Board of Ordnance (much of which is engrossed and included within the appendix to the report of the Select Committee on Small Arms 1854) and studying the evidence given before the Committee has allowed an insight into the difficulties experienced by both Ordnance and the private sector. Here we have clear indicators which show that the private gun makers were not always to blame for the poor quality and late delivery of which they were accused by Ordnance. To illustrate the point, it is worth examining extracts from the evidence of masters, workmen and experts who came before the Select Committee of 1854. The Committee had been appointed with a prime objective to "consider the Cheapest, most Expeditious, and most Efficient Mode of providing Small Arms for Her Majesty's Service".[26]

Although the Committee were finally to recommend to Parliament "... that a manufactory of Small Arms under the Board of Ordnance should be tried to a limited extent. This manufactory would serve as an experiment of the advantages to be derived from the more extensive application of machinery, as a check upon the price of contractors and as a resource in time of emergency...". The Committee made it clear that "... the system for the contracting for the supply of Small Arms should not be discontinued...". They further recommended that the Enfield factory should be expanded to accommodate their plan for the increased use of machinery.[27]

In achieving their objective, the Committee had to investigate very thoroughly the complaints of the Board of Ordnance over the difficulty of procuring sufficient numbers of small arms on time and made to a particular quality and standard. On the other hand, to be objective, the Committee had to address seriously the many criticisms made by the private contractors over the Board's strictness of view. This, the trade alleged, had prompted delays in delivery and, in some cases, non-fulfilment of contracts. The witnesses called to give evidence before the Committee were subjected to very close scrutiny. The procedures adopted were not too dissimilar from a cross-examination in a court of law. Making a careful study of the questions and replies allows a greater awareness of the problems surrounding the gun trade. This helps to bring about a more balanced view which enhances our understanding of the difficulties which the Ordnance contractors experienced.

Joseph Brazier, a prominent Wolverhampton lock manufacturer, who had been making locks for the Board of Ordnance since 1836 had not continued to be a contractor after 1850. In evidence he explained that the "Tower at Birmingham" had rejected a new musket lock of his and he was unable to discover the reason why. Brazier even produced the lock before the

*The Great Exhibition, 1851,
where Joseph Brazier exhibited
his prize-winning gun locks*

*Showing tightened spring cramp
that was used to remove or
replace the main spring of a mid
nineteenth century rifle lock*

Committee and challenged any member to pass an opinion. During questioning it was learned that Brazier had exhibited this very lock at the Great Exhibition of 1851, for which he had received a prize. Brazier stated "The lock was looked at by the commissioners appointed by government from Belgium and France, and Mr Lovell was there also." The question was then put, "Mr Lovell was one of the commissioners, was he not?" To this Brazier replied, "Yes".[28] This must have given Brazier great satisfaction as his evidence shows he attributed the strictness of view solely to George Lovell. In reply to the question "Has there been any improvement in the view during the last month?" Brazier answered, "They are not so strict; they were aware of this investigation, and that has put a check upon them, I suppose." In reply to the next question, "Since when have they ceased to be so strict?" "Since Mr Lovell's indisposition" came the response.[29]

Brazier was asked further questions about why complaints were not generally made about the viewer. This was said to be because the viewers would "punish them for it". It was explained to the Committee that the method of view was by jig and gauge. Brazier produced a gauge for them to see, suggesting it was identical to those used by the viewers. When a part was rejected by the viewer it was customary to identify the problem area with a chalk mark.

Even after these measures, it was suggested on many occasions the contractor was still unable to discover the reason for rejection. If an explanation was sought from Ordnance often no new information was forthcoming. From the evidence it can be discovered that many parts were rejected on the basis of what the viewer perceived to be questionable finish and not because the piece failed the gauge test, these judgements being purely subjective and having no bearing on the mechanical working of a particular mechanism or part.

When questioned further, Brazier revealed there were different qualities of lock which were price dependent. His locks tended to cost in the order of thirty shillings each, while the current contract lock was eight shillings and three pence. The point was therefore put to Brazier, "Does not the price at which it is possible to produce the Government lock depend on the view?" To which Brazier replied, "Yes, it depends upon the view as a matter of course". The questioner then concluded, "If the view is too strict, it would not be possible to produce it at the price?" "It cannot be", Brazier replied. Staying with the point, the questioner confirmed, "In short, the possible production at the price depends upon the view?" "Yes"; came the response from Brazier.[30] From this very crucial piece of evidence it would appear that Ordnance would have had extreme difficulty in getting any locks past the viewer if they insisted upon a high level of finish for the lowest price. It would seem the only sensible way for the Board of Ordnance to break out of this "endless loop" would be by accepting mechanically functional and correctly dimensioned locks, with a lower standard of finish than they had hitherto set. Presumably this was the way in which the East India Company was able to obtain satisfactory quantities of serviceable weapons.

In answering the question "What do you think has been the cause of the delay in producing arms, which is complained of by the Board of Ordnance?" William Scott, a Birmingham gun maker who had been in the trade some thirty years, and had previously worked as an Ordnance viewer, gave the opinion that it was because manufactories were having to close due to lack of orders from the Board. As an example, he explained that "since 1851, I, amongst others, have had nothing at all to do for my men; the vices, the benches, the machinery, and the rifling machines are lying idle". He then went on to say "I have seen men often about the London Docks and wharves, scores of them, almost shoeless and stocking-less, and in a state of destitution and starving, and seeking labour and occupation elsewhere".[31]

While Scott's experiences are not directly related to the strictness of view, it will be obvious that if skilled men are lost to the trade, or at best return after a period of lay-off, then the standard of workmanship will generally not be the same as that where craftsmen have been continually employed. Until such times as the artisan can once more regain confidence in his ability to work accurately and fast the standard of workmanship will in general be below his best. So it can be seen that if a government lacks a well thought out strategy for the arms industry, on which it relies for its supply of military weapons, taking into consideration such aspects as continuity of orders, fairness of inspection and good communication, then indirectly the standards of quality and delivery will be influenced by default. Scott had identified the problems of a weapon procurement system which was not designed to place regular long-term orders on its suppliers. The reasons for this were probably due to a combination of ignorance on behalf of some members of the Board in not having a clear understanding of manufacturing requirements, and political pressure created by the private sector to limit Ordnance encroachment into their area of livelihood.

Of course it could be argued that if Ordnance had an understanding of manufacturing needs and the will to work amicably with the private sector, the difficulties encountered by both sides would not have arisen. However, with the technical and structural problems identified by Brazier and Scott, it would have been almost impossible for military gun making in the private sector to develop efficiently and to prosper. That was unless government adopted a consensus strategy with the gun makers, similar to that operated by the East India Company. By 1854, with war for Britain looming in the Crimea, any idea of such a policy materialising from a government initiative would have passed into obscurity.

John Stephenson, a lock filer who at that time resided in Birmingham, had previously worked at the RSAF, Enfield. He explained to the Committee that he had a contract in November 1851 with the Board of Ordnance for hardening and freeing 10,000 sears and tumblers. Unfortunately he had been unable to get any of his work past the Ordnance viewers and he had now left this branch of the industry. Stephenson had contracted to do the work at seven shillings per 100, when he had previously been paid 25 shillings per 100. Even then he stated that he "could have got a living at it if they had been looked at as they were when they were 25s. a hundred". Stephenson informed the Committee that he had been a lock filer for 17 years. The work, he explained, which had recently been rejected, was similar to that undertaken during his time at Enfield which had passed inspection without any problems. When asked, "was anything said to you about the difference in the price?" Stephenson replied, "Yes, there was an item made in Mr Lovell's office, and he said it was a most awful price". Reading through Stephenson's evidence, a rather ironic story emerges. He had only completed 150 pieces of his contract, all of which he was unable to get past the viewer. In his words, "I let them lie for some time, and sold them to another contractor, and he sent them in, and I heard no more of them".[32]

From this evidence it is possible to offer two probable causes which might have accounted for the viewer's rejections, providing the assumption is made that Stephenson's work had not deteriorated in any way since he left Enfield.

(a) There was a difference in viewing standards operating between Birmingham and Enfield.

(b) The strictness of view had increased in the period between Stephenson getting 25s. per 100, to when he contracted to the Board for 7s. per 100.

Considering the evidence, it would appear on balance that the two proposed reasons for rejection probably carry similar weight.

For example, Brazier was of the firm belief that different standards of view were operating between Birmingham and Enfield. He cited an incident to the Committee concerning a particular consignment of gun locks which had been rejected. He explained, "... they sent them back at Birmingham when they did not do so at Enfield".[33]

Interestingly there was the distinct possibility that reason (b) was operating against Stephenson. Brazier in his evidence had alluded to the "view" being "much more strict" after the open tendering system "made its appearance" in 1849 (it will be recalled that Wood gave the date for the introduction as March 1850).[34] Under the circumstances, and given this latter fact, it would have been logical for Ordnance to impose a tighter level of inspection to ensure that standards of workmanship by any new contractor did not further compromise quality. This could have accounted for the difficulty experienced by Stephenson.

George Lovell, in a letter dated December 1848, had recommended to the Board, inter alia, that "The Board's List of Tradesmen" be scrapped and that "tenders should be called for by public advertisement, ... and that such selection will be governed solely by reference to the lowest price offered, and by consideration of the capabilities of the parties to fulfil their contracts."[35] This clear recommendation by Lovell, and Brazier's evidence to the Committee, would suggest that the system of open tendering had been implemented, further confirming Brazier's allegation of the view becoming "much more strict". With the contracting system being thrown open to all and sundry, and Lovell stating that acceptance would be "governed solely by reference to the lowest price offered", Ordnance would have had little option but to tighten its inspection procedures to make sure that lower prices did not equate to lower standards.

While the precise reasons behind the rejection of Brazier's and Stephenson's work, with its subsequent alleged acceptance when sent to Enfield or passed on through another contractor, may never be known, it is difficult to believe that these incidents were unique or would have passed unnoticed. In the atmosphere of distrust and suspicion which existed in the private sector, Brazier's and Stephenson's stories would have, no doubt, gained credence as they circulated within the gun trade, helping to convince the contractors that Ordnance was operating unequal inspecting standards in different viewing departments. With the bulk of British military weapons being manufactured in the Birmingham district and the procurement system having changed to open tender at the "lowest price", it is conceivable that the Birmingham viewers might have been more severe with their level of inspection than Enfield. There is also the fact that George Lovell took up residence in Birmingham in the autumn of 1852 to fulfil the duties of Assistant Inspector.

This may have increased pressure on the local viewers to apply a stricter standard of inspection.[36]

Functionality or finish?

The evidence given to the Committee by John Barnett, a prominent London gun maker whose family had been a contractor to the Board of Ordnance since 1794 was seriously to challenge the Ordnance notion that the fault of quality and late delivery lay mainly with the private sector. Barnett explained he had not had an order from the Board since 1849 and had to rely on orders from "merchants and foreign parts". He stated that in 1852 he had made "repeated applications", both personally and by letter, to the Board of Ordnance for part of a contract which he had heard was being issued to the Birmingham gun trade. In his words "I begged that the Board would give a portion to London, and I offered to take them at a price which I afterwards found was lower than they issued to Birmingham for".[37] Apart from obviously wanting the business, it does appear from the evidence that Barnett was desperately trying to secure work to keep his men employed. In an attempt to ensure the survival of his business, Barnett had secured orders over the years with North America, the East India Company and the Hudson Bay Company. It so happened that at the time of the Select Committee's investigations, Barnett had a legal action pending in Belgium over what was a blatant case of forgery. This was revealed in Barnett's answer to a question concerning the sale of Belgian arms to the Hudson Bay Company, "Do they buy any in Liège?" – "No; the Belgians only copy that gun, the English gun, and put my name on it; and the Belgians, to a very great extent, send them out to New York. That is one of the guns that I have an action pending now about; the gun sent to America". A further question followed, "They put your name on it to give the gun a better character?" – "Yes; not only the name, but the address, and they imitate every mark; they are exceedingly clever at that".[38]

From this last piece of evidence it would seem reasonable to conclude that John Barnett's company was capable of making arms to a sufficiently high standard that others wished to jump on the band-wagon of his success by making copies. If one was taking a sceptical view point, it might be argued that the Belgium gun makers were only putting Barnett's identification on their arms to command a higher price, which we know from the evidence Barnett was able to get. However, if this particular conclusion is drawn, then one should acknowledge that the quality and finish of Barnett's weapons must have been universally known and therefore perfectly acceptable to the Belgian gun maker's customers. The corollary to this would be to conclude illogically that a higher price would have been paid for an inferior weapon. This example of Barnett raises a further question regarding the private sector. How was it, if the standard of manufacture was so poor, that the Birmingham and London gun makers were able to successfully supply arms in quantity to customers other than the Board of Ordnance, seemingly without high levels of rejects? The facts are, as the evidence shows, that although the private gun trade did have rejects from the non Ordnance trade, the bulk of the problems seem to have been confined to barrels and locks. In the case of John Barnett's company, he suggested that, out of a total of 105,000 complete arms made for the East India Company he had experienced a reject rate of between 15 and 25 per cent before and after proof of barrels, which incidentally were made in Birmingham, and a figure of 10 to 15 per cent for the locks. Even given these relatively high rates of component rejects, the London gun trade alone was able to deliver the following quantities of arms between 1841 and 1850:

DATE.	EAST INDIA COMPANY.	GOVERNMENT.	TOTAL.
1841	20,150	7,660	27,810
1842	36,353	12,926	49,279
1843	34,880	12,270	47,150
1844	25,362	13,496	38,858
1845	49,623	2,539	62,162
1846	50,880	16,336	67,216
1847	57,214	18,376	75,590
1848	55,068	23,862	78,930
1849	71,381	26,366	97,747
1850	26,025	3,607	39,632
Total:	**426,936**	**157,440**	**584,376**

It will therefore be seen, that the London trade over a period of nine years was supplying almost three guns to the East India Company to every one supplied to Ordnance. Also it should be remembered that these figures are exclusive of supplies to foreign governments and the commercial trade generally. In fact, Barnett was confident that "Under proper management, the productive power of the London gun trade alone for Military Arms is 100,000 per annum; while the trade of Birmingham is capable of furnishing, with ease, a similar amount".[39]

An independent assessment

It has been shown that the private gun trade was capable of producing large quantities of arms mainly by manual methods, there being a general reluctance amongst the gun makers to invest in costly capital equipment. Without an Ordnance system that supported the principle of issuing long-term contracts, it is difficult to see how the trade's attitude could have changed. However, the strictness of view, which was felt to be so unreasonable by the private sector, the nature of contracts and the reluctance of the Board of Ordnance to issue patterns and gauges had not gone entirely unnoticed by the Select Committee on Small Arms. In their report to Parliament dated 12th May 1854 they were to state:

> With a view of expediting supplies, and giving confidence to the trade, Your Committee recommend that contracts should only be entered into with such men as have means and capital to fulfil engagements; that in future the contract should be understood to commence from the time of the delivery of the pattern; and that in all cases of doubt on the part of the viewer, or remonstrance on the part of the contractor, a ready appeal to a competent person should be afforded.[40]

The Committee also took the opportunity to point out that, in their view, while recognising the contractor's need for continuous orders to stop skilled workmen drifting away from the industry in slack times, they were in general against the principle. It was argued that if contracts had been placed for periods of three years or more, then "... in this age of rapid invention, such a course might be attended with very inconvenient consequences". As an example, they referred to the change of pattern from the 1851 rifle to that of the 1853, suggesting that had long-term contracts been in operation then

Ordnance would have been supplied with a large quantity of out of date arms.[41] This might suggest that financial penalty clauses were not in operation at the time for cancelled orders or perhaps Ordnance did not wish to enter into this kind of agreement. While it is not appropriate to deal with the arguments of "rapid invention" here, it is worth remembering that a factory is usually unable to cope efficiently with hasty product changes. These invariably lead to loss of production volume until experience of manufacturing the new article is gained. Initially this might result in poor quality products, as the workforce go through a learning phase before the required standards are reached. It would also seem reasonable to conclude that the uncertainty which would have been caused by a period of "rapid invention" was yet another factor which confronted the private gun trade, furthering their reluctance to invest in increased levels of new machinery. If the trade had opted for higher levels of mechanisation over the traditional methods of production, it could be argued that they would have lost the advantage of flexibility in the event of frequent model changes. Also, by adopting dedicated machine production methods it would have made it more difficult to manufacture their three main weapon categories, sporting, African and military. There is of course a further consideration for the private sector, which is that it is not always the first company to install the latest technology which benefits in the longer term. It has often proved better to leave a period of time to allow the technology to stabilise before the decision is taken to install the latest plant and equipment. This particular point was experienced by the author when working for Thorn EMI Ferguson, in relation to the competitors of the British television industry, when it was argued that a waiting strategy could often bring about economic and cost benefits.

What emerges from the research into the strictness of view is that the Board of Ordnance appeared to be demanding standards, particularly that of finish, which the gun trade could not consistently meet, until George Lovell was replaced by Gunner. It also seems remarkable from the evidence that, if one excludes Ordnance, the customer did not generally want arms manufactured to such a high standard of finish. This was particularly true in the case of the East India Company who were looking for functional replacement weapons, with the minimum amount of design change, at a reasonable price. To support this view it is worth examining a report dated 6th August 1839 written by Colonel Bonner. This document highlights an extremely important point concerning the private gun trade which hitherto seems to have gone unnoticed. That is, even if Ordnance had the capacity to manufacture large quantities of small arms, it could not be sufficiently flexible to meet efficiently the individual requirements of a section of the widespread military market (as Bonner would have wanted).

Bonner's report is addressed to the Honourable Political and Military Committee and sets out, inter alia, his objections to taking quantities of new arms fitted with percussion caps. From the evidence it is clear that Bonner had already studied reports of the superiority of the cap over the earlier flint lock and had accepted that it was infinitely more reliable. He went on to say "I hope I shall not be deemed presumptuous in offering an opinion somewhat at variance with that recognised with the Board". Bonner complained that the new pattern muskets had "a heart stock instead of the usual and less expensive description, both the interior and exterior of the barrel have a finish beyond what is given or is necessary to be given to military arms – it is provided with a double sight, flat bolts, box trigger, and Ram-rod and Bayonet springs and the cost is stated to be £3:12:1/2". What Bonner was really objecting to was changes to design and price, since he stated that the cost is "much beyond what has ever been paid for a musket". Going on, Bonner explained that as far as the Indian Army were concerned, he could provide modifications which in his opinion would cost far less than what was on offer from Ordnance. He further suggested that there were no problems with the current East India barrel regarding "strength and correctness of bore and requires no improvement". With regard to his suggested modifications he wrote:

> I have therefore in the musket No.4 applied the percussion principle of the Ordnance Pattern – substituting round bolts for the flat bolts of the Ordnance and for the wire pins heretofore in use: with these exceptions it is the existing pattern of the Company's musket. The lock is the same in principle, workmanship and value as that of the Ordnance – but I have made some alterations in the screws and tumbler pin, which I consider improvements.[42]

Bonner also stated that he had "not applied the double sight, box trigger, bayonet spring, or new ramrod spring, as I consider them unnecessary and I have retained the present pattern bayonet". In concluding his report Bonner remarked:

> With regard to the stock, I am clearly of the opinion, that although a heart stock may improve the appearance of the musket, its exclusive adoption is neither necessary or desirable – The difference of expense is considerable and great difficulty would be experienced, particularly in the event of war, in obtaining them in any quantity. I am the more satisfied of what is technically termed Sap Stocks (that is stocks cut indiscriminately from the Plank) from an examination of upwards of 100 muskets recently brought from India by invalids bearing dates from 1808 to 1816 – not one of these have heart stocks, yet after a period of service, of from 23 to 31 years they are perfectly sound and exhibit no tendency to decay.[43]

By Bonner's clear evaluation of the weapon from the perspective of the customer, it can be seen that the interests of the East India Company were not being served. Had Ordnance wished to take over the role of supplier of military weapons, then they had clearly got this customer's requirements wrong. Bonner had demonstrated that from the East India Company's standpoint, the product had been over engineered in both specification and finish. Therefore, it did not meet the criteria of the army in India who were clearly looking for a straightforward and reliable weapon. The report illustrates that, during the first half of the century, the requirements of the British armed forces, as perceived by Ordnance, were quite different from those of other large consumers like the East India Company. This would suggest that it was highly unlikely that Ordnance could or would fulfil, in the same way, the role of the private sector. This branch of the gun trade was capable of manufacturing military weapons to suit differing customer requirements. The key strength of the private sector was its heterogeneous structure which allowed them to manufacture weapons flexibly without being constrained by a rigid factory system. Until internationally, the military market accepted a standard type weapon, it could be argued that the labour-intensive nature of the private sector was a key factor in its own survival.

A different approach

The report of the 1854 Select Committee, probably for the first time, formally recorded a somewhat different and more amicable method of dealing with the private gun trade when it revealed how Colonel Bonner purchased arms on behalf of the East India Company for its regular army of over 200,000 men. While the Committee, in its final recommendations, pointed out that the East India Company as well as the Board of Ordnance "provide only one pattern of the articles for contract", they did however suggest that "... there seems no reason why a larger number should not be provided if by this means the operations of the contractors could be saved from needless delay". The Committee were clearly impressed by Bonner's method of procuring small arms which they summarised in the following detail:

Sikh officers of the British 15th Punjab Infantry Regiment

> Colonel Bonner described to Your Committee the system under which Small Arms were procured by the East India Company. They have a list of contractors for setting up and making the materials of muskets. The smaller articles, such as screws, nails, and swivels, together with the stocks, are provided by the setters up. Each of the other parts of the musket is got directly from the persons whose trade is to manufacture it. When a supply of muskets is required by the Company, Colonel Bonner ascertains the Ordnance prices, and calls together the setters-up and material makers. He shows them the pattern gun, and discusses with them the price. The price is then fixed by discussion and arrangement, and not by competition.[44]

It is perhaps the last sentence of the summary which gives the true meaning and allows us to understand more fully Bonner's method of dealing with the private sector. With references to "discussion and arrangement" and "not by competition", it can be seen how his methods of procurement differed radically from that of Ordnance.

To gain a greater understanding of a labour-intensive industry without incentive to change the respected Ordnance engineer John Anderson had been sent in March 1853 with Lieutenant Warlow, Royal Artillery, on a fact finding tour of British manufacturers associated with the forging of wrought iron. As the tour embraced Birmingham, Warlow, accompanied by Anderson, took the opportunity to call upon some of the gun makers he was acquainted with as a matter of courtesy.

On returning to Woolwich, Anderson produced a report covering the whole tour, within which he was able to provide a unique glimpse of mid century small arms industry in Birmingham from the perspective of a respected engineer. He describes the status of the trade thus: "We then visited a number of establishments engaged in military musket and bayonet work, all of which, however, are in a low mechanical state, and at least 50 years behind most of the other branches of manufacturing industry which we have been examining."[45] Anderson lists these other branches of manufacturing as "... cotton, flax, and woollen trades, engineering and machine making, the tool-makers of Leeds and Manchester, steel pen and wood screw making of Birmingham. Those we were very much pleased with."[46]

Two interesting observations emerge from Anderson's report in connection with the Birmingham gun trade. Firstly, he comments on the backwardness of the industry with regard to the lack of machinery employed in weapon production, but makes no comment on the skill of the workmen or the quality of the product, apart from mentioning the "great waste" of the out-work system with parts being carried from the profusion of workshops to the setter-up. This Anderson compared to the efficiency of the flow-line process he had proposed for Enfield, with self-acting machines where "... everything connected with it passing consecutively on from one stage to another, never passing over the same ground twice, so that the raw materials which go in at one side shall come out a finished musket at the other".[47]

Anderson's report, with his observations of the Birmingham gun trade, may simply have been a case of him publicising his strongly held views. He was a committed machine enthusiast with an exceptional record of inventing and modifying. It is known that he had been responsible for devising and introducing new mechanical manufacturing processes at Woolwich Arsenal.[48]

Nevertheless, the fact that he had not commented on the Birmingham workforce or the product might suggest that what he had witnessed of the manual system of manufacture did not strike him as being unduly odd or slovenly, perhaps no less than an engineer of his calibre would have expected, given the way the industry was structured. If Anderson had encountered poor standards of workmanship to the levels implied by Ordnance and some later commentators, then it would seem reasonable to assume that he would have mentioned the fact in his report. After all, he did see fit to comment that the gun trade was "50 years behind most of the other branches of manufacturing industry". Secondly, and even more interestingly, the industries which were mechanised and up to date, which he was "pleased with", do not appear to have any direct links with Ordnance and small arms contracts. Perhaps there is a subtle lesson to be learned here. The suggestion being, that if you are a company in the private sector wishing to do business with Ordnance, then it would seem wise to negotiate a contract with mutual terms and conditions of trading, in a similar way to Bonner for the East India Company.

The first signs of an atmosphere of normality descending upon the private sector can be detected from the evidence given before the 1854 Select Committee, when several of the old established contractors began to experience less severe viewing standards when R. W. Gunner accepted responsibility for the Ordnance office in Birmingham after Lovell's health began to fail in 1853. This was not a case of contractors now being able to

W. W. Greener, gunsmiths factory, Birmingham before demolition

turn in shoddy work, they still had to comply with Ordnance inspection standards, but it would appear that a mutually agreeable common sense approach was starting to develop. An example of this emerges from the evidence given by Brazier when he described what he considered to be a good functional gun lock. Under questioning, Brazier wholeheartedly agreed that if a lock sent to Ordnance "did not meet all the requirements of the gauge" it should be rejected. However, he did make the point that it should not "fit the gauge to a hair's breadth", as in his considered opinion "it cannot be better or worse for it".[49]

This would seem to be a perfectly reasonable position to adopt under the system of out-work which employed mainly manual methods of manufacture. After all, it would not have been possible under such an arrangement to supply large quantities of weapons made to close tolerance at prices attractive to Ordnance. The exactness, repeatability and interchangeability of machine-intensive manufacture could not be expected from men filing to gauge. Support for Brazier's position of unreasonable standards of tolerance eventually came from the late twentieth century. The author, using a set of the Pattern 1853 rifle gauges, belonging to the Ministry of Defence Pattern Room then situated in Nottingham, to measure the dimensions of a nineteenth-century Birmingham gun lock revealed a minutely raised surface on the lock's bridle. This area of raised metal had been caused by the viewer stamping his pass mark on the part, so that the bridle, which we know from the viewer's stamp had already passed inspection, was made to fail the gauge test retrospectively. This interesting and highly significant discovery adds further authenticity to the documentary evidence of witnesses like Brazier recorded in the Select Committee Reports and supports the private sector's claims that Ordnance were operating too tight an inspection criterion. The gun lock in question was still operating perfectly over 120 years after manufacture, the viewer's mark having been stamped in an area of the bridle which was in free air and had no detrimental effect whatsoever on the function of the mechanism.

Of course it could be argued that the viewer placing his mark on a surface which remained in free air was a deliberate act. However, the point being made is this: if the bridle dimension when originally gauged had measured to the minutely increased width caused by the viewer's stamp, then the Ordnance inspector would have had little option but to reject it as failing the test. Here we have a classic example of a standard being set and applied without taking account of the function or physical position of the part in question. Even if the bridle had been one or two thousandths of an inch thicker it could not in any way have affected the part's ability to function correctly and it would have made no difference whatsoever to its interchangeability with other like components. It is not often that one is fortunate to discover such a good example of physical evidence which supports the interpretation of data obtained from documentation, suggesting that Ordnance were in fact applying too strict a standard of inspection.

The discovery would also support the notion that Ordnance viewers were not allowed to exercise individual discretion; the part either fitted the gauge or it did not. While measurement by a gauge was precise and left little room for doubt, the viewer's judgement of finish, by its very nature, was subjective and open to challenge. However, it will be recalled from the evidence obtained from the Select Committee Reports that there was a slightly more relaxed approach to viewing when Gunner took over the responsibility of

Close up of the plaque on the former RSAF pattern room wall to Bert Woodend

inspection from Lovell. This might have meant the acceptance of a bridle which was marginally over gauge. Unfortunately one can only speculate on the possible outcome, as the opportunity to prove this point has probably been lost with the passing of time and the difficulty of obtaining authentic samples which could be identified as being manufactured after Gunner took over.

REFERENCES

1. House of Lords Record Office, London. "Memorandum from Secretary, War Office, J. Wood, 18th February 1854". Included under Appendix to *Report from the Select Committee on Small Arms. Reports Committee's Vol. XVIII-1854*, pp.451-2 (489-90)

2. Birmingham Proof House Library, Young, D. W., "History of the Birmingham Gun Trade up to Mid 1935", Unpublished document, No.19 (Birmingham, 1936)

3. National Archive, Kew. Letter to J. Wood, Office of Ordnance, from Hollis & Sheath, 12th September 1854. Reference WO 44/701

4. National Archive, Kew. Letter to J. Wood, Office of Ordnance, from Hollis & Sheath, 16th November 1854. Reference WO 44/701

5. National Archive, Kew. Letter from R. W. Gunner, to Board of Ordnance, 22nd November 1854. Reference WO 44/701

6. National Archive, Kew. Letter from R. W. Gunner, to J. Wood, Office of Ordnance, 31st March 1855. Reference WO 44/701.7. Op.cit., Wood, memorandum 18th February 1854

8. Bailey, De Witt, "George Lovell and the Growth of the RSAF Enfield", paper presented at MA Day School, Middlesex University (4th July 1992), p.6

9. House of Lords Record Office, London. "Examination of Colonel J. G. Bonner, 31st March 1854", *Select Committee on Small Arms. Reports Committee's Vol. XVIII-1854*, p.361

10. Ibid., pp.361-5

11. Ibid., pp.361-2

12. Op.cit., Wood, memorandum 18th February 1854

13. Op.cit., Bonner, p.361

14. Bailey, De Witt, "Development of the British Ordnance Musket Lock-part 2", *International Arms and Militaria, No.2 Quarterly*, p.13

15. Op.cit., Bonner, p.361

16. Goodman, John D., "The Birmingham Gun Trade", Samuel Timmins Ed. *Industrial History of Birmingham and the Midland Hardware District*, Robert Hardwick, (London, 1866) p.388

17. Op.cit., Wood, memorandum 18th February 1854

18. Op.cit., Goodman, pp.419-28

19. Ministry of Defence Pattern Room, Nottingham. Roberts, G. H., "History of the RSAF Enfield Lock", Unpublished manuscript, p.C10

20. Rosenberg, Nathan, *The American System of Manufacture* Edinburgh

University Press (Edinburgh, 1969) p.38

21. Op.cit., Goodman, pp.412-13

22. Ibid., pp.388-9

23. Ibid., pp.388-9

Also see Op.cit., Goodman, pp.388-9, and "Examination of Richard Prosser, 21st March 1854", *Select Committee on Small Arms. Reports Committee's Vol. XVIII-1854*, pp.172-4. According to Goodman, military barrels were made by a rolling process. The barrel started life as a piece of iron measuring 12 x 5.5 inches and 0.5 inches thick which was first turned in a pair of grooved rolls until the edges met. The piece was then brought to welding heat in a furnace and "closed in a third groove of the roll". Subsequently the piece was heated again then "passed through a succession of grooves on a mandril until the 12 inch tube is drawn out to the required length of about 40 inches". The invention of barrel rolling machinery has been credited to Osborne, a Birmingham manufacturer, in 1817. Because up to 25 per cent of barrels could be lost in the proof and barrels for a range of weapons could be accommodated relatively simply on one machine, it would seem that these were important factors in determining the early mechanisation of this branch of the gun trade in Britain. The lock mechanism comprising of typically 12 separate parts could not be accommodated on one machine, neither could the irregularly shaped gun stock with its various cut-outs and holes for the lock, barrel, rammer, heel plate and so on. From an industry point of view, it would have been logical to use the plentiful supply of cheap labour to manufacture these two latter items.

24. Ibid., p.414

25. Putnam, Tim & Weinbren, Dan, *A Short History of the RSAF Enfield*, Middlesex University (Enfield 1992), pp.5-8

See also: Blackmore, Howard L., "Military Gun Manufacturing in London and the Adoption of Interchangeability", *Arms Collecting, Vol. 29, No.4* (November 1991), p.115

26. House of Lords Record Office, London. *Select Committee on Small Arms. Reports Committee's Vol. XVIII-1854*, p.1

27. Ibid., pp.10-11

28. House of Lords Record Office, London. "Examination of Mr Joseph Brazier, 24th March 1854", *Select Committee on Small Arms. Reports Committee's Vol. XVIII-1854*, p.247 (285)

29. Ibid., p.246 (284)

30. Ibid., p.247 (285)

31. House of Lords Record Office, London. "Examination of Mr William Scott, 24th March 1854", *Select Committee on Small Arms. Reports Committee's Vol. XVIII-1854*, p.253 (291)

32. House of Lords Record Office, London. "Examination of Mr John Stephenson, 29th March 1854", *Select Committee on Small Arms. Reports Committee's Vol. XVIII-1854*, p.319 (357)

33. Op.cit., Brazier, p.251

34. Ibid., p.250

35. House of Lords Record Office, London. Letter from the Inspector of Small Arms, respecting the Disadvantages of the System pursued for obtaining Arms, George Lovell, 16th December 1848. Included under Appendix to Report from the *Select Committee on Small Arms. Reports Committee's Vol. XVIII-1854*, p.454 (492)

36. Op.cit., Bailey, pp.8-9

37. House of Lords Record Office, London. "Examination of Mr John Barnett, 30th March 1854", *Select Committee on Small Arms. Reports Committee's Vol. XVIII-1854*, p.339 (377)

38. Ibid., p.339 (377)

39. House of Lords Record Office, London. "Ordnance Estimates, 30th March 1854", *Select Committee on Small Arms. Reports Committee's Vol. XVIII-1854*, p.343

40. House of Lords Record Office, London. "Report from the Select Committee on Small Arms, 12th May 1854", *Reports Committee's Vol. XVIII-1854*, p.10

41. Ibid., p.10

42. India Office Reading Room, London. "Report of Colonel Bonner, 6th August 1839". Reference L/MIL/5/421. The reference to "musket No.4" suggests that Ordnance had sent the East India Company a number of sample weapons for trial and comment. Sending samples to different regiments was quite a usual occurrence within a weapon's evaluation phase.

43. Ibid.,

44. House of Lords Record Office, London. "Supply of the Musket", Report from the *Select Committee on Small Arms, 1st March 1854*, p.8

45. House of Lords Record Office, London. "Examination of Mr John Anderson, 13th March 1854", *Select Committee on Small Arms. Reports Committee's Vol. XVIII-1854*, p.27

46. Ibid., p.27

47. Ibid., p.29

48. House of Lords Record Office, London. "Examination of Mr John Anderson, 15th March 1854", *Select Committee on Small Arms. Reports Committee's Vol. XVIII-1854*, pp.64-5

49. Op.cit., Brazier, p.251

3. GEORGE LOVELL, THE BOARD OF ORDNANCE AND THE PRIVATE SECTOR

Examining the role of George Lovell and looking at his influence upon, and his relationship with the private gun contractors, particularly after he was promoted to Inspector of Small Arms in 1840, helps to explain the continuing problems experienced by government in the procurement of sufficient quantities of good quality small arms during the first half of the nineteenth century. Research suggests that Lovell was an exceedingly complex man, at times headstrong, with a burning desire to secure for the British soldier the best possible weapons to defend the Empire. To discover how Lovell was to achieve this goal will require the reader to follow his footsteps down a somewhat intricate path and be prepared to weave and change direction as different external influences come into play.

Enfield's developing role and Lovell the engineer

At this point it is worth pausing to remind ourselves of the early role of the Enfield manufactory, so that Lovell can be viewed against the background of the factory's development.

Prior to the introduction of the "American system of manufactures" at Enfield Lock in the mid 1850s, the factory's role was one of assembly, repair, refurbishment, development, and testing, of a range of muskets, swords, and rifles. A further part of Enfield's responsibility, that of monitoring the quality and cost of weapons supplied to Ordnance by the private gun trade, became considerably strengthened with the transfer of the remaining sealed patterns from the Tower of London after the devastating fire at the armoury and workshops on the night of 30th October, 1841.[1] Holding the patterns against which military arms were judged placed Enfield in a very powerful position, allowing them to determine and maintain strict standards of accuracy and finish. However, as we will learn, it was the appointment of George Lovell, the resident Storekeeper at Enfield Lock, to the position of Inspector of Small Arms in 1840, placing him in charge of all aspects of the manufacture of military weapons, which was to have a profound influence upon the development of the British military gun trade. Significantly the position of Inspector had been re-established, which probably indicates that at the time, not only did the Board of Ordnance hold Lovell in high regard for his inventive and technical skills, but it also suggests that they were becoming aware of the increasing variations and gathering pace of weapon development.

The Tower of London, where small arms patterns were held up until the fire in 1840

It was important for Ordnance to ensure that the growing and evolving technology was carefully monitored and managed by experienced personnel, making Lovell with his considerable knowledge of the gun trade the ideal candidate for the job. The fact that he had spent a quarter of a century at Enfield, taking him from the establishment of the plant to the perfection and development of the percussion cap, had no doubt helped Lovell's candidature. Lovell's promotion, apart from making him responsible for over-seeing the manufacture of military weapons, had effectively placed him in charge of all military small arms inspection, with responsibility for the superintendence of the Ordnance departments at the Tower, at Birmingham, and at the

Viscount Henry Hardinge,
Master General of Ordnance

manufactory at Enfield. His reporting line was direct to the Master General of Ordnance, placing him in a very powerful and influential position.[2]

Lovell's appointment, as we will learn, was to become an act of mixed fortune for the British small arms industry, although at the time it is probably fair to conclude that the major changes he was to inflict upon the gun trade could not have been foreseen. However, the occasion can be identified as one of the most important single contributory factors which was to account for far reaching improvements in the manufactured quality and standardisation of British military small arms. However, the path to this eventual goal was paved with many hazards.

Since his appointment as Storekeeper at Enfield Lock in 1816, a position akin to today's site director, Lovell had not only involved himself in purely organisational and operational matters, he had also taken a personal and active interest in the design, development, and improvement of small arms generally. He was responsible for and influential in the design and development of a wide range of Ordnance products, from the percussion lock system to bayonets and different forms of ammunition including experiments with various types of fulminating powder. De Witt Bailey has identified Lovell as being responsible for the design of at least 25 small arms, and if modifications are included he suggests this figure would be much higher.[3]

Brunswick pattern 44 rifle
designed by George Lovell

Largely under Lovell's direction a new smooth-bore musket received approval in 1841 and went into production. The model was to be known as "The Percussion Musket 1842", continuing in service with the British Army until being partially succeeded by the Minié rifle in 1851 which in turn was replaced by the "Enfield three-grooved Rifle" or "Rifle, musket Pattern 1853". This arm had the double distinction of being the first weapon to go into service with the British Army bearing the name "Enfield", and was also the first musket to be manufactured in Britain using the mass production techniques of interchangeable parts under the "American system" when the new purpose-built factory at Enfield Lock officially started producing in quantity in January 1857.[4]

What views did Lovell really hold?

Lovell's former role as Storekeeper at the government armoury at Enfield Lock had allowed him the opportunity to bring together and maintain a small group of skilled artisans. This encouraged him to hold the view that significant differences existed between the Ordnance manufactory, which he had nurtured from its inception in 1816, and the private gun trade at large, particularly that of the Birmingham district. In April 1852 (a time approaching the end of his career) he was prompted to write:

> At Enfield no workman is admitted unless he be of the first class in his trade, and of sober, moral, and regular habits. He has the assistance of the best machinery and works under the immediate eye of the viewer, who corrects any errors of work as they arise. He has a comfortable home, and receives his wages in full at a certain hour every week. Whereas at Birmingham, the first and ruling question is price; the man who will work at the lowest rate is entrusted with it, without much care as to capability or character; there is little or no tie between him and his master; he is

mulcted for the mill-power that he uses and for tools, and receives his wages often very irregularly. The consequence is, that the workmanship is inferior, and the men often resort to all sorts of shifts and tricks to evade the viewer's eye. The master complains of the injustice of the inspection, when it is his own fault for employing inferior workmen and screwing them down in price.[5]

Lovell's account which stressed the flawlessness of the government armoury compared to the workmanship of the Birmingham district was accepted as a clear indication of the "superiority of the Enfield manufactory" by the Master General, who was no doubt looking for ways to alleviate the political pressures placed upon Ordnance by the continuing lobby of Parliament by the private gun trade. The April Minute of the Master General when referring to Lovell's definition of Enfield suggests that this "would be of use to the clerk of the Ordnance in answering any attack in the House of Commons".[6]

There can be little doubt that Lovell harboured strong and lasting opinions regarding the inadequacies of the private gun trade, singling out Birmingham as a particular example. It is also abundantly clear that he favoured the notion of having government owned and run establishments for the manufacture of military supplies. In 1830 he had taken the trouble to write a lengthy critique on blank sheets opposite the main text of an anonymously published pamphlet on the *Observations on the Manufacture of Fire-Arms for Military Purposes* where he expressed the following vehement views:

> It is the first Duty of every Department entrusted with the details, to see that our Fleets and Armies be equipped at every point in the most perfect manner.-In all the essential parts this has been tried by competition in Private hands, and failed:-1st: Our ships of war, when built by Contract were notoriously unsound!-The Navy Board were obliged to increase the number of Publick Dock Yards. - 2nd: Our Gunpowder made by Private hands would not reach our enemies!-The ordnance Department established their own Powder Mills.-3rd: The Carriages of our field and Battering Guns when made by Private Carpenters were disgraceful!-The Royal Carriage Department was instituted.-4th: The arms of our Soldiers, made by Birmingham Contractors were as proverbially "bad as a Brummagen Halfpenny" and even to these the supply was deficient!-The Royal manufactory of arms was in consequence established. – These several Institutions have arisen and increased out of pure necessity:-The Government has positively been driven into the measures, and what are the results? – Our Ships, our Powder, our Artillery, our Arms, are acknowledged even by our enemies to be superior to all the world. – That System is good which works well![7]

While it is probably fair to say that some of these comments contain elements of emotion, nevertheless it is a particularly damming judgement not only of the private gun trade, but private industry generally. It is obvious from Lovell's exposition that he firmly believed that only properly administered government establishments were capable of turning out work of a satisfactory standard. Comparing these earlier opinions with those he espoused in 1852, suggest his views had not changed that much with regard to the private gun trade's quality of workmanship. However, in contrast, if one examines Lovell's evidence given before the 1849 Select Committee on Army and Ordnance Expenditure, a completely different picture emerges. Lovell was questioned by Sir James Graham on matters relating to the possible advantages of Ordnance having in-house production of small arms. Responding to the point put by Sir James "You do not concur in the opinion that it would be desirable to manufacture as the exclusive mode of supply?" Lovell replied, "Certainly not; we should then have no check upon our own men". Confirming the response Sir James continued; "You would prefer contract as the rule, with Enfield as the check?" To this Lovell replied; "Yes, Enfield is useful as a check". Making absolutely sure what Lovell had in his mind Sir James pressed home the point; "You would keep the establishment at Enfield as low as possible, keeping in view the necessity of it as a check?" Lovell replied; "Yes".[8]

On the face of the 1849 evidence, it would appear that Lovell had completely reversed the strong views that he had expressed in 1830 and accepted the role of Enfield as a minimum manufacturing establishment which would act as "check" upon the private gun trade. It is interesting to note that he volunteered the opinion that the private gun trade would act as a "check" upon his "own men", a complete contradiction of his earlier and later views. The example of Lovell's apparent change of direction to his erstwhile opinions can be seen in his report of April 1852, mentioned above. This illustrates that he was making a clear distinction between the superiority of the workmen employed at Enfield over those doing comparable jobs in the private sector. So, on the one hand Lovell is saying his workmen are superior to those in the private sector and now he is suggesting that the private gun trade would act as a "check" upon his own men.

While these later opinions appear less vigorous to those expressed in 1830, it does however suggest that he had not altered his original strongly held beliefs. Although Lovell's publicly expressed views seem a puzzling contradiction, one might speculate that because of the increasing pressure from the private gun lobby on Parliament, and in particular the many personal attacks by the trade upon his character, he may have considered discretion to be the better part of valour, deciding not to reveal all his true opinions. Perhaps there was a personal reason for his less forthright stance. At the time, an enquiry was in progress into the behaviour of Lovell's son Francis, the Assistant Inspector of Small Arms, who had compensated the French gun stock contractor Pierlot & Siminos for losses. The inquiry continued until July 1852, when Lovell junior was sacked. It is clear from the ensuing correspondence with the Master General that Lovell senior was deeply upset by the incident. Returning from leave he wrote to the Board on the 19th July, asking them to reconsider their judgement. In his letter, Lovell stated he "deeply deplores" the fact his son should have exposed himself to want of discretion, although in support he suggested the inquiry had found no "moral turpitude" in his actions. Lovell believed the incident had brought disgrace upon his house. His letter expressed the view that the "sentence" would weigh heavily on "a large family of brothers and sisters". The Board ignored Lovell's pleas, and did not reverse its judgement.[9]

A brave try?

The evidence placed before the 1854 Select Committee on Small Arms, included the debate carried on in correspondence since the early 1840s between George Lovell, the Master General and Board of Ordnance over Lovell's plan to break what the Board perceived as an endless cycle of poor quality and late delivery by the private contractors. Lovell had pointed out that the gun trade in London and Birmingham had joined in combination against Ordnance, therefore he concluded that it was impossible for the system of placing contracts to work as the competitive element had effectively been removed. Furthermore, he explained that the gun trade workers had in turn joined Unions and were acting in combination against their masters by striking for better wages. In spite of this, and his considerable reservations of the private gun contractors' ability to produce sufficient qualities of good quality weapons, Lovell advanced what would seem to be a very sensible and practical approach to ease the situation when he suggested:

> ...before I can propose any further orders being issued, it appears to me to be absolutely necessary for the security of the public interests, that a better understanding should be come to with gun contractors, and that the prices of setting up arms should be thoroughly investigated, and regulated upon a more fair and reasonable base than they have hitherto been.[10]

Considering Lovell's views of the private contractors, this was a revolutionary proposal. Lovell went even further by suggesting that the present situation could be remedied if he was allowed to call a meeting consisting of representatives from the London and Birmingham gun trades which he would attend with the Storekeeper from Enfield, R.W. Gunner. He also suggested that the Board of Ordnance should nominate a suitable person to be present. As Lovell explained, his reasons for calling the meeting was so:

> That every process in detail should be gone carefully through item by item, and that the prices that are to be paid to the workmen fixed and settled: taking the scale of prices paid in the Royal manufactory as a guide, but subject to such modifications as the differing circumstances of the private trade may point out as necessary; and when this has been done, that the percentage shall be determined upon, which the contractor shall receive for his outlay of capital, his risk, losses, time and trouble.[11]

Lovell went on to say "I would further advise, that the workmen's prices, when so fixed, for Ordnance work, should be printed and distributed, and that no contractor should be allowed to give more or less".[12] This was a brave and ambitious proposal and clearly shows that Lovell had a good understanding of the working of the private sector. It is doubtful if Lovell would have made such a proposal on the spur of the moment. It is more likely that he had taken time to carefully consider and formulate his ideas during his period at Enfield. Furthermore, it demonstrates that although Lovell was harbouring strong personal beliefs about how and where weapons should be made, he had astutely weighed up the political situation, probably judging that in the relatively peaceful inter-war period there was little opportunity for Ordnance to take outright control of manufacture. This would have been difficult to achieve, given the frequent questioning by vocal members within the House of Commons regarding the military public spending estimates.[13]

Lovell's way forward was to recommend to the Board of Ordnance a radical overhaul of the contract system, which if implemented would have helped to address the serious haemorrhaging of skilled workers from the industry in peacetime.

Quite soon after his promotion to Inspector of Small Arms in 1840, Lovell placed his plan before the Board of Ordnance. It is clear from the correspondence that Lovell's thoughts were focused on the survival of the British gun trade as a whole, as he had prepared his case with care by taking prior soundings in the private sector. Lovell explained, "I have mentioned this proposal to some of the leading contractors at Birmingham and in London, who are quite ready and willing to enter into such an agreement". In view of this bold initiative, it may seem somewhat ironic that Lovell was to come under an increasing number of personal attacks and criticisms by the gun trade at large, particularly for the strictness of inspection imposed by his viewers, when it would appear at least on the surface, that he was desperately trying to improve the overall conditions within the small arms industry. Perhaps the trade were becoming wary of Lovell, suspecting that he had an ulterior motive. On the one hand he was apparently trying to improve the conditions of the contractors and their workers, while at the same time he was tightening the quality screw.

Although the logic of his proposals seems to have been understood, Lovell received the following reply, "... the Master General and Board cannot of themselves interfere in any proceeding affecting the arrangements of the contractors with their workmen".[14] The Board's response does not appear to have put Lovell off from striving to achieve his objective, as he single-mindedly and courageously persevered with his ideas, writing some eight years later:

> I have since the year 1842, been enabled to bring about an understanding between the masters and workmen, and to establish a "List of Prices of Labour," by which every master has agreed to be governed; which the workmen themselves find to operate beneficially, and which has had the effect of doing away with "strikes" for wages ever since.[15]

However, Lovell does point out that while he considered the prices paid for labour in the gun trade generally fair and reasonable, he did feel that the profits of the masters should be brought into competition. As an example, he highlighted the trade's setting-up costs for the new percussion musket which he was able to measure quite accurately against similar work carried out at Enfield. From this he concluded that the masters by the method of payment, were regularly deriving an advance of 7 shillings and 5 pence (24.5 per cent) monthly against each gun. This sum, Lovell suggested can be turned over twelve times a year "without any risk of the bankruptcies or delays the mere private commerce brings with it".[16] He therefore reasoned that the 24.5 per cent was the sum more than any other, which the gun trade would be prepared to negotiate down in open competition, providing the number of contracts put out were strictly regulated by the Board and extended over periods of not less than three years.[17] It can be seen that Lovell has identified a major problem with the Ordnance contract system, that of its short-term nature. This observation has highlighted a further important point. Should Ordnance have offered the private sector long-term or guaranteed follow-on contracts, then initial tooling-up and other associated costs could have been amortised across a longer production run, resulting in customer benefit from a lower product price.

In achieving his plan, Lovell wrote "I have sedulously avoided lowering the quality of the musket either in workmanship or material; for in that I am convinced there would be no true economy". He concluded his letter of December 1848 in confident mood by drawing the Board's attention to the following current supply position of gun stocks:

> ...by the perfect success of the desiccating process for seasoning stocks, which is now in full operation at Enfield, and by the powerful assistance of the machinery for jointing and percussioning, which I have introduced of late years, and looking to the store on hand, I can be certain of providing in regular succession a sufficient supply of stocks, locks, bayonets, and all other materials, to whatever extent and for whatever period may be determined upon".[18]

It is clear from Lovell's proposals regarding the introduction of long-term contracts that he was trying to introduce a strong element of stability into the gun making industry. Over the years the gun trade had continually suffered from successive "stop go" policies in times of war and peace, with the subsequent loss of skilled labour to the industry. If the plan had been fully implemented (and as yet there is no evidence to suggest that it ever was, not even partially) it would have gone a long way towards solving the problems of gun makers poaching skilled workers from other gunsmiths in times of boom, and the workers themselves plying their trade between several masters at a time. All these movements of people were known to seriously affect the quality of the product, which in turn led to delays as Ordnance rejected deliveries of unsatisfactory weapons and parts.

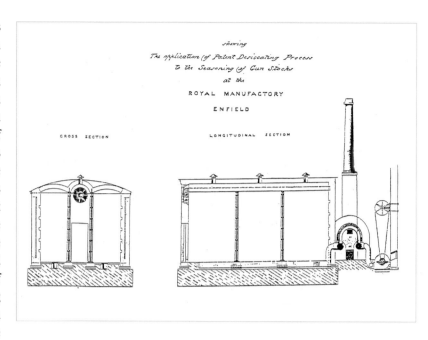

Diagram of gun stock seasoning plant installed by George Lovell

A change of tactics by Lovell?

Studying the well documented evidence of the 1854 Government Select Committee on Small Arms can be both fruitful and rewarding, particularly in teasing out subtle clues. One of the most revealing pieces of evidence to come before the Committee was from the Birmingham gun maker, Isaac Brentnall Sheath, who had contracted to set up a quantity of arms for Ordnance in 1851. The contract had not been completed on time. When questioned about the delay, Sheath gave two main reasons, these were "... not having materials", and "... the pattern was not decided upon by the Board of Ordnance to enable us to proceed with it". He was then asked, "have you not a proper pattern given to you at first?" Sheath replied, "no we never have patterns allowed us". This is quite extraordinary, as without a pattern for reference, it would have been almost impossible for the setting up contractor to ensure that the work being carried out was in accordance with the required Ordnance standard. From the evidence it is learned that the closest the contractor is able to get to the pattern is at the Ordnance viewing rooms. Sheath elucidates, "the pattern is placed in the viewer's hands, and we send a workman down to the viewer to have our jigs made in his presence, and then he explains the different points that he wants attended to".[19] The understanding of the consequences of this arrangement and its impact upon quality and standardisation is a crucial factor in explaining the differences which existed between mid century American machine-made weapons and their British labour-intensive counterparts. To have grasped the implications and significance of how the private sector had to cope with Ordnance small arms contracts under such unreasonable conditions of working, may have allowed some contemporary writers to be a little more generous towards the independent gun trade's manufacturing capabilities.

It is worth once more reminding ourselves of the evidence contained in the letter dated 12th September 1854, from Hollis & Sheath to Joseph Wood, Secretary Ordnance Office, discussed earlier, and comparing this with the revelations by Sheath to the Select Committee earlier that March regarding the 1851 setting up contract. This would appear to reinforce the notion that Ordnance had learned little from their earlier experiences of poor quality and

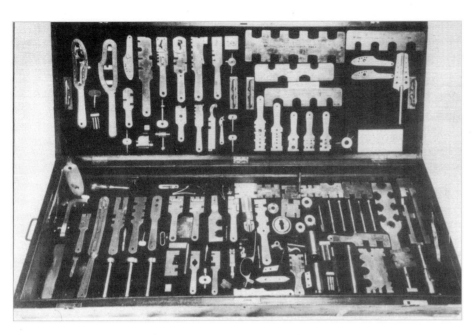

Set of measurement gauges for the Enfield pattern 1853 rifle

late deliveries. In the letter, the contractor suggests that "... we believe we can complete the 20,000 musket pattern 1853 in March next, providing we have the materials (less sights) issued to us at the rate of 200 each per week from this date." What is more revealing comes later in the letter when the contractor suggests that he will be able "... to keep pace with the setting up... as soon as the proper tools are prepared for viewing the sights...".[20] It is clear that the reference to "tools... for viewing the sights...", refers to measuring gauges. On the face of this information, it does seem incredible that after three years Ordnance were still not prepared, or were slow to let contractors have patterns or gauges to check that their work conformed with the standards they themselves had set. It will be recalled from the Hollis & Sheath letter that it was not absolutely clear who was responsible for making the gauges, the contractor or Ordnance. Neither is it clear when the later Pattern 1853 contract was issued, that Ordnance would be supplying contractors with master patterns on time. From the recommendations contained within the report of the 1854 Select Committee on Small Arms, "... that in future the contract should be understood to commence from the time of the delivery of the pattern...", one might conclude that old ways were slow to change.[21] Either way, it would seem Ordnance were at fault. If they had not supplied the pattern, then, without this essential standard to work from, it would have been impossible for the contractor to construct accurate gauges.

Therefore it is difficult to see how essential work on the weapon could have commenced. On the other hand, if it was the responsibility of Ordnance to supply the gauges, then we know from Hollis & Sheath's letter they had not done so. What is perhaps more surprising, particularly when considering the Master General and George Lovell's previous views of the private sector (with "the man who will work for the lowest rate"), is that it had still not been planned to ensure dubious quality was filtered out at source prior to the weapon or component being submitted to the Ordnance viewers. This could have easily been achieved by supplying contractors with duplicate sets of gauges and patterns. After all, it was as much in the financial interests of Ordnance as well as the contractors to get the article right first time. Delays and quality problems emanating from the inability of contractors to accurately check their work would no doubt have posed a grave risk to Britain's national security when demand for weapons increased in time of war.

Considering the many positive things accomplished by George Lovell in his long career, the notion that contractors were deliberately denied duplicate sets of gauges and patterns seem to go against all the very bench-marks he was trying to set in his quest for quality and standardisation. By effectively forcing the various contractors to make their own jigs (and perhaps gauges) from a pattern held by the viewer, it can surely not have escaped the attention of Ordnance that it would have been almost impossible to achieve uniformity of manufacture. Gauge making was carried out by the highest skilled craftsmen, some of these precision tools taking many months to make and perfect. If Lovell was genuine in his belief regarding the low level of competence of the private sector craftsmen, it would seem folly in the extreme to have trusted contractors to manufacture their own gauges and expect precision. Furthermore, if Ordnance were deliberately forcing the individual contractors to manufacture their own duplicate sets of gauges, then it must have been realised that the outcome would have been considerable delays in the military weapon supply chain. Moreover, it would have been difficult if not impossible for each individual contractor to meet a consistent standard of component tolerance, as it is highly unlikely that all the gauges could have been made to a precise specification in the different manufacturing establishments.

In Britain at the middle of the nineteenth century, concepts of manufacturing from a controlled single standard were known and understood. Much of the pioneering work had been done by eminent engineers like Henry Maudslay and Joseph Whitworth, who had both set national bench-marks for accurate measurement. Had Ordnance adopted a policy to supply patterns and gauges to the contractors they could have ensured that these tools complied with a single set of standards. After all, the viewer's gauges and patterns were already made by Ordnance, so the logical plan would have been to extend this work and make duplicate sets for the contractors. Although this action may have seemed costly in the short term, in the longer term the outlay could have been recouped by cutting the reject rate, saving material, reducing losses incurred through delays, and ensuring the army and navy were equipped on time. To ensure the system operated fairly, independent officers within Ordnance could have held master sets of patterns and gauges and act as arbitrators should a dispute over standards of acceptability arise. These are not the retrospective views of a twentieth-century writer, as Sheath had put forward similar ideas in his evidence to the Select Committee. If gauges and patterns had been made at Enfield, for the private gun trade the work would have corresponded with the role already adopted by the factory which functioned largely as a unit for specialist and experimental work. More than any other British establishment, Enfield was ideally suited to the task, particularly as one is mindful of Lovell when he said of the place "no workman is admitted unless he be of the first class in his trade". Had Ordnance taken responsibility for making and issuing all gauges and patterns, then they would have been in a stronger position to accurately monitor the work of the private sector with greater authority. Contractors would have had little room to complain of misunderstandings over manufacturing dimensions, and there could be no excuses for delays to finished product due to lack of measuring equipment. Therefore, one is left to speculate why such a system was not adopted.

A hidden agenda?

It is difficult to comprehend why Ordnance had not apparently considered issuing patterns and gauges to at least the major setting up contractors, when they themselves were continually complaining of high reject rates and late delivery. The necessity for a closer watch on accuracy and quality would have seemed an obvious precaution when the system of open tendering was first introduced in 1850. With the emphasis firmly on lower prices, this could have attracted inexperienced companies to tender for business in the hope of establishing themselves as Ordnance contractors. As the system of open tendering had been introduced when Lovell was Inspector of Small Arms, being brought about by his recommendations to the Board of Ordnance, one would have expected that a man of his intellect, desperately striving to achieve standardisation of parts and weapons, would have at least put the idea to his superiors of issuing patterns and gauges to the contractors. Research to date has not been able to uncover any evidence which might suggest that Lovell had discussed or recommended these fundamental principles to the Master General or Board. Could it be that Lovell was cleverly developing his own hidden agenda? If the private gun trade could be subtly denied the wherewithal to manufacture weapons to a satisfactory standard, then this would leave the way clear for Ordnance to take control of the production of military small arms, allowing Lovell to realise the ambition he had proffered in 1830. It might therefore be construed from Sheath's experience, that Lovell, by deliberately denying the contractors patterns and gauges for the 1851 contract (although this was never outwardly obvious from the evidence taken before the Select Committee) was trying to ensure that the private gun trade would fail in its attempt to supply Ordnance on time with good quality arms. If this was his hidden agenda, it would have allowed Lovell the opportunity to persuade the Board that the plans he had advocated earlier for setting prices and wages within the private sector, which the Master General had rejected, were worth reviewing once more. Had the Board then decided to accept an interventionist role, adopting a policy similar to Lovell's earlier proposals for the contractors, this compromise would have gone some way to meeting his 1830 aspirations, when he had advocated Ordnance taking total responsibility for the production of all weapons supplied to the military. Parliament on the other hand, who had been under pressure from the private gun trade not to expand the Ordnance capability of military small arms manufacture, would have no doubt have welcomed the financial benefits to be gained from such an outcome. This concession if implemented, would also have met Lovell's opposite view, expressed in 1849, when he agreed that he "would keep the establishment at Enfield as low as possible...".[22] In other words, if Lovell was unable to realise his main ambition, that of Ordnance taking over full manufacturing control of military weapons from the private sector, then the lesser option would have provided a face saver. Of course these suggestions are no more than speculation, but Lovell was a man of considerable intellect who wanted his ideas adopted, and as De Witt Bailey has pointed out, he wished "... to ensure that Britain's soldiers could defend their Empire with an unfailing supply of the best possible weapons which technology and experience could produce".[23] It is therefore conceivable that the suggestion of Lovell harbouring long-term plans for Ordnance to take control of the manufacture of military small arms, was his way of trying to ensure the British soldier got the best.

What was Lovell's motive?

While it is not intended to devalue Lovell's magnificent contribution to the British arms industry, research suggests that he was generally over ambitious with regard to the strictness of view. Of course it might be argued that by applying such rigid standards of inspection, it was Lovell's plan to force the private gun trade into employing more machinery. This was surely not his intention, as Lovell was fully aware of the gun trade's reasons for not investing in higher quantities of equipment, their reluctance being primarily due to the short and intermittent nature of the contract system, which gave little confidence or incentive to commit capital to machine-intensive programmes when the future was so unsure. It will be recalled that Lovell, as early as 1842, had recommended to the Board methods of regulating wages and prices within the private sector. He had also suggested that it would be advisable to offer the gun trade a minimum contract period of three years. Therefore, it is more likely that Lovell, frustrated by the reluctance of Ordnance to intervene in the private sector over wage and price structures, and unable to reduce the sector's influence upon Parliament, was preparing his own agenda to force the Board's hand to a greater manufacturing commitment.

From the evidence of the contractors given before the Select Committee on Small Arms in 1854, it is known that they had not each been issued with patterns. However, James Gunner (son of R. W. Gunner) had reported to the Committee that one pattern was supplied "as a guide" for all the manufacturers, which if correct was a most unsatisfactory way of working.[24] There is confirmation of this point through the evidence of Richard Aston who worked with his brother as a General Gun Furniture Maker (odd metal parts of the gun stock and elsewhere). Aston gave the reason for being late with deliveries of the 1851 bayonet because "... we were seven weeks before we got the pattern". When asked if he had ever applied for a duplicate? He replied "Many times; and Mr Lovell said that I should be the first to find fault with it". Asked what he had meant by this, Aston alleged that Lovell had said "they could not make six or seven near enough to view to".[25] This remark would appear extraordinary in the light of Lovell's boast that Enfield employed only skilled artisans. If this was the real position, it would have been hardly fair to have expected high standards from the private sector considering Lovell's low opinion of them. And of course, Lovell was well aware that he had been more than economical with the issue of patterns and gauges. As Enfield already produced a number of duplicate gauges of high accuracy for the Ordnance viewers to check the contractors work, the excuse offered through Aston would not seem plausible. More likely Lovell was offering Aston the least line of resistance, perhaps not wishing to reveal his innermost thoughts.

It is known from correspondence that George Lovell was signing letters as Inspector of Small Arms in 1853. This would confirm he still had overall responsibility for manufacture and inspection. From this one can only conclude that the responsibility for issuing the precise means of measurement to the contractors was entirely his. If he was somehow denying the contractors the ability to measure work accurately to assume manufacturing control, then as an employee of Ordnance he was taking a dangerous strategic gamble. Clearly, it would have been physically impractical for the different contractors in London and Birmingham to check the accuracy of their work from a solitary pattern held by the government viewer before submission to Ordnance. Such an arrangement would seem completely out of character with Lovell's enthusiastic drive towards improved weapon quality and standardisation. However, as suggested above, it is possible that Lovell's judgement may have been influenced by the incident concerning the Master General and the Board's treatment of his son Francis over the compensation of the French gun stock contractor. The influence of the gun stock episode upon Lovell's state of mind is probably no more than one would expect from a man whose health was failing, as can be witnessed by the shaky and deteriorating handwriting in correspondence towards the end of his career. Arms expert and historian Howard Blackmore, has implied that the incident lead eventually to Lovell's demise and described it thus. "Lovell himself was admonished and ordered to move to Birmingham where most of the new rifled muskets were in the hands of the contractors. He died in 1854, his achievements forgotten and largely blamed for the failure of the system".[26]

However, the argument suggesting faulty judgement due to Lovell's poor state of mind can only be upheld if his later life is taken in isolation, clearly an unsustainable proposition. As Lovell had been appointed Inspector of Small Arms in 1840, he would have had both the authority and the opportunity to have developed, and put in place, a strategy for issuing duplicate sets of patterns and gauges to contractors had he so wished. Therefore to argue that Lovell's downfall had somehow been caused by failing faculties later in life after the gun stock episode can confidently be dismissed.

The most likely reason for Lovell's final isolation, as suggested by the overwhelming evidence, was his single-minded devotion to the quest for small arms perfection by hidden agenda or otherwise. This analysis is outwardly manifest in his uncompromising adherence to the strictness of viewing standards, placing the independent gun makers in an impossible position. Support for this view can also be seen in the evidence of Joseph Brazier when he explained that viewing had become less strict when Richard Webb Gunner took over responsibilities from Lovell.

The evidence suggests that Lovell never gave up his quest for perfection. This therefore makes it difficult to fully understand why the private sector had not been issued with the necessary measuring tools to do the job. Under the circumstances, one would have expected the private gun trade to have been given the opportunity on at least one major contract to accurately measure their work, even as an experiment. Perhaps this denial implies that Lovell really did have a hidden agenda.

An impossible task

Because of the strictness of view, the private gun trade was unable to cope with the more exacting levels of inspection imposed when the new system of open tendering was introduced in 1850. Without standardised gauges or patterns, the private gun trade found it almost impossible to cope with the military contracts. Having only the traditional manual methods of manufacture to rely on the gun trade was trapped, unable to meet economically the new exacting standards imposed by the viewers under Lovell's authority. The effect upon the industry was chaotic, with contractors failing to meet their delivery dates and as a consequence, suffering financial penalties and also material loss. Once Lovell had set the standards for tighter inspection he could not easily have gone back, even had he wanted to. Apart from a loss of face had he reverted to former standards it would have created confusion amongst the viewers. If the harsh measures he had imposed were designed to force the private sector into failing, then Lovell had not succeeded. It is clear he had not convinced government that an Ordnance committed to full-scale military small arms manufacture was the only way forward. However, if Lovell was not operating a hidden agenda and was genuinely trying to organise the private gun trade into a first class British arms industry, then surely he could not have failed to recognise the most practical way of achieving his goal was to invite cooperation by developing a co-ordinated strategy for the industry, not by alienating the participants by denying them the wherewithal to check their work. After all, he had laid the foundations earlier by ignoring the Board's instruction when he unilaterally decided to discuss an improved price structure with both masters and men. Nevertheless, by his adherence to strict standards of tolerance and finish, and by withholding gauges and patterns, he had alienated a large section of the would-be participants. Therefore it was hardly likely that he would personally realise his passionate ambition.

*Flag of Master General
of Ordnance*

*Badge of Royal Army Ordnance
Corps, note the similarity to the
Board of Ordnance coat of arms*

*Board of Ordnance
coat of arms*

Had Lovell seen the report of the Select Committee published in May 1854, one month after his death, he may well have realised that there were other ways of improving the supply of good quality military arms through a more liberal policy of collaboration with the private sector. With his first rate knowledge of the gun trade, Lovell must have been well aware of the East India Company's methods of procuring arms from the private sector. While it is recognised the East India Company's methods were not perfect, they did however have an infinitely better customer supplier relationship, and were therefore more likely to mutually resolve difficulties with their contractors than Ordnance. Had Lovell approached his quest for perfection on a similar basis and secured the support of the Board of Ordnance, we may have seen a different outcome for the British small arms industry. Of course, one can be wise with the benefit of hindsight.

De Witt Bailey, in summing up Lovell's contribution to the British arms industry states, "Lovell was the most effective and successful standard-bearer in the struggle between the two opposing factions regarding the hotly contested question as to whether the Government or the private sector should control the manufacture of Britain's military small arms. Throughout his career Lovell was passionately dedicated to the concept that the central Government should control the manufacture of military small arms...".[27] While Lovell's passion to see an efficient well run military small arms industry cannot be denied, from the evidence so far uncovered he cannot really be classified as the "standard-bearer" in the contest for government control of the military small arms trade, as all his public statements do not support this view.

Lovell can rest in peace

Sadly, it was not until 1857, less than three years after Lovell's death that his innermost ambitions were to be fully realised. Provoked by the war in the Crimea, the government-controlled factory at Enfield Lock started production with the newly acquired machine tools from America. Now it was possible for Enfield to achieve levels of standardisation which Lovell could only have dreamed of. In a somewhat ironic way, it had been the continuing pressure upon Parliament from the private gun trade which had helped tie Ordnance hands for so long. Support for the private sector by politicians had remained firm. In a letter to the editor of the *Aris's Gazette* in March 1852, the Birmingham MP, William Schofield, added a conciliatory note to a dispute between the gun manufacturers and their workmen when he took the opportunity to warn of the possible dangers facing the trade:

John Bright, the Liberal MP who spoke about the concerns of the private gun makers in Parliament

Already it is understood that the Government has largely extended the operations of Enfield, and, no longer confining itself to repairs and experiments, has undertaken many processes of manufacture; and it is seriously to be feared that the Ordnance Office will not be slow to avail itself of any excuse for still further steps in this direction.[28]

Before the 1854 Select Committee on Small Arms had been appointed to consider the cheapest and most efficient way of providing weapons for her Majesty's service, John Dent Goodman was to observe:

Before this resolution was carried out the subject was warmly debated in the House of Commons, Mr Newdegate, Mr Muntz, Mr Geach, Lord Seymour, and other members strongly insisted upon the impolicy of Government entering into competition as manufacturers with the private trade of the country...[29]

Even as late as 1868, eleven years after Enfield had commenced full-scale production, the continuing influence of the private sector could still be recognised. John Bright MP addressed a deputation of Birmingham gun makers, when it was stated:

The object which these manufacturers had before them was to criticise the action of the Government in establishing manufactories at Enfield and elsewhere, and generally to condemn the policy of Government in undertaking such commercial or industrial operations as can be carried out adequately and safely by private enterprise.[30]

Had Lovell been allowed in the early 1840s to negotiate improved contracts with the gun trade, there may have been a different outcome as to how the military would be supplied in the future. Although the government eventually had to commit large sums of money to upgrade Enfield, it is probably fair to speculate that they would have preferred to have obtained their arms from the private sector, thereby saving vast amounts of public funds. No doubt politicians appreciated that once small arms manufacture had been taken on by government there would be a continuing requirement for a long-term financial commitment. Under the circumstances in which they found themselves, their hand forced by war, there was little choice but to take in-house control.

George Lovell's name remembered at Enfield Island Village

GEORGE LOVELL DRIVE

However, the Lovell period had helped shape Enfield, providing the factory with the necessary discipline which would be required in its future role as a major small arms producer, bringing it for the first time into unfettered competition with the private gun trade. Had George Lovell been alive to witness the scale of the new factory he would no doubt have been justly proud. While the strictness of inspection he had imposed was probably too ambitious for the day, he had nevertheless broadened the debate on precision and standards.

REFERENCES

1. National Archive, Kew. WO44/304
2. Bailey De Witt, "George Lovell And The Growth Of The RSAF, Enfield". Paper presented at MA Day School, Middlesex University

(4th July 1992), pp.5-24, also see for more information on George Lovell, House of Lords Record Office, *The Committees Army and Ordnance Expenditure Session, 1st Feb – 1st Aug, 1949. Vol.9*, pp.301-2. For further reading on Lovell, see: Blackmore Howard L., *British Soldiers' Firearms (1650-1850)*, (London 1961) pp.205-34. For the sequence of weapons developed at Enfield, see: Reynolds E.G.B., *Early Enfield Arms The Muzzle Loaders, Small Arms Profile No.14*, pp.24-8. The main product assembled at the Royal Armoury Mills, at Enfield Lock, as it was known in the early years, was the Brown Bess smooth-bore musket. This weapon had been the personal arm of the British soldier until the arrival of the flint lock Baker rifle with its barrel containing seven rifled grooves. The technique of rifling had been developed to improve accuracy of fire. This was achieved by spinning the projectile, giving it greater stability in flight, making the weapon's performance superior to that of the earlier smooth-bore muskets. Unfortunately the introduction of rifling to the inside of the previously smooth barrel of the muzzle loader, made loading more difficult because the grooves presented resistance to the ball. In an effort to overcome the problem, for a time a small mallet was issued with each weapon to assist the ramming of the leaden ball down the barrel. This crude method of loading often resulted in distorting and jamming the ball.

The Baker rifle was to be the last of the British military flint-locks. In 1831 a number of muskets were converted to the percussion system and in trials proved to be more accurate and reliable than their predecessors, giving less recoil and a greater rate of fire. Conversion was effected by replacing the hammer, spring and pan, the cock being substituted for a percussion hammer. A small pillar was fitted into the barrel to hold the detonating cap. After many experiments with both British and foreign designs in the late 1830s and early 1840s, George Lovell, prior to taking up his new appointment, was responsible for the introduction of the two grooved Brunswick rifle. The rifle fired a spherical lead ball with a raised belt around its middle, designed to fit the grooves in the barrel. This arm came next in the revolution of Enfield's weapon development. To improve the introduction of the ball into the barrel, a notch was cut across the muzzle, this modification assisted the belted area into the grooves. After trials at Woolwich the weapon was finally approved and a quantity issued to the Army. Under the guidance of George Lovell the rifle was later converted to side lock action in 1841. Although certain advantages were claimed for the Brunswick, it was still inclined to suffer from loading problems. It does seem curious that after being in service with the British Army for some 15 years, a Select Committee on Small Arms was to make the following severe criticisms: "The Brunswick rifle has shown itself to be much inferior in point of range to every other arm hitherto noticed. The loading of this rifle is so difficult that it is a wonder how the rifle regiments have continued to use it so long, the force required to ram down the ball being so great as to render any man's hand unsteady for accurate shooting".

3. Bailey De Witt op.cit, p.5
4. Reynolds E.G.B. op.cit, p.26
5. House of Lords Record Office, London. "Report from the Inspector of Small Arms, relating to the differences between Birmingham and Enfield, George Lovell, 3rd April 1852". Included under, Appendix to Report from the *Select Committee on Small Arms. Reports Committee's Vol. XVIII-1854*, pp.450-1 (488-9)
6. Ibid. Minute of Master General, p.451 (489)
7. The British Library, London. "Observations on the Manufacture of Fire-Arms for Military Purposes", *British Library Catalogue No. 08820 b25*, Longman & Co. and James Drake, (London 1829), p.158. Also see, Rosenberg Nathan, *The American System of Manufacture*, Edinburgh University Press (Edinburgh, 1969) p.38

8. House of Lords Record Office, London. "Examination of G. Lovell, Esq. 4th May 1849", *Reports from the Committees Army and Ordnance Expenditure Session: 1st Feb – 1st Aug, 1849. Vol. IX.*, p.308

9. National Archive, Kew. Correspondence and report concerning inquiry into the Assistant Inspector of Small Arms, Francis G. Lovell. WO 44/701.

10. House of Lords Record Office, London. Letter from the Inspector of Small Arms, relative to the Progress made in the Preparation of Percussion Arms, George Lovell, 10th September 1840. Included under, Appendix to Report from the *Select Committee on Small Arms. Reports Committee's Vol. XVIII-1854*, p.452 (490)

11. Ibid. p.452 (490)

12. Ibid. p.452 (490)

13. Public Addresses by John Bright MP, Edited by James E. Thorald Rogers, Macmillian & Co. (London 1879) pp.143-4

14. House of Lords Record Office, London. Memorandum from Secretary, War Office, J. Wood, 23rd September 1840. Included under, Appendix to Report from the *Select Committee on Small Arms. Reports Committee's Vol. XVIII-1854*, p.453 (491)

15. House of Lords Record Office, London. Letter from the Inspector of Small Arms, respecting the Disadvantages of the System pursued for obtaining Arms, George Lovell, 16th December 1848. Included under, Appendix to Report from the *Select Committee on Small Arms. Reports Committee's Vol. XVIII-1854*, p.455 (493)

16. Ibid. p.455 (493)

17. Ibid. p.455 (493)

18. Ibid. p.456 (494)

19. House of Lords Record Office, London. "Examination of Mr Isaac Brentnall Sheath, 29th March 1854", *Select Committee on Small Arms. Reports Committee's Vol. XVIII-1854*, p.323 (361)

20. National Archive, Kew. Letter to J. Wood, Office of Ordnance, from Hollis & Sheath (12th September 1854). Reference WO 44/701

21. Report from the *Select Committee on Small Arms*, op.cit. (1st March 1854), p.10

22. House of Lords Record Office, London. "Examination of G. Lovell, Esq. 4th May 1849", *Reports from the Committees Army and Ordnance Expenditure Session: 1st Feb – 1st Aug, 1849. Vol. IX.* p.309

23. Bailey De Witt op.cit, p.11

24. Report from the *Select Committee on Small Arms*, op.cit. 1st March 1854, evidence of J. Gunner p.286

25. Report from the *Select Committee on Small Arms*, op.cit. 28th March 1854, evidence of R. Aston p.297

26. Blackmore, op.cit. p.119

27. Bailey De Witt op.cit, pp.10-11

28. House of Lords Record Office, London. Letter to the Editor of *Aris's Gazette* from William Schofield MP, 11th March 1852. Included under Appendix to Report from the *Select Committee on Small Arms. Reports Committee's Vol. XVIII-1854*, p.453 (491)

29. Goodman John Dent, *Industrial History of Birmingham and the Midland Hardware District*, Ed. Timmins, Robert Hardwick (London 1866) p.397

30. Public Addresses by John Bright MP, op.cit. p.139

4. APPRAISING THE EFFECTS OF THE CRIMEAN WAR, ORDNANCE FAILINGS, THE TRADE UNION AND PUBLICITY UPON THE ENFIELD FACTORY

The mid 1850s represent one of the most critical periods in the history of British small arms manufacture, one in which apparently unconnected events have combined together to produce remarkable effects. By focussing attention on this period, we are able to identify not only early changes to manufacturing technology and work-place organisation but also the difficulties experienced by a nationalised industry overseen by incompetent or inexperienced government bureaucrats. Perhaps surprisingly, parallels can be drawn between some of these nineteenth-century events and those which have occurred in the small arms industry of today in the twenty-first century. A relatively recent example which occurred in the late twentieth century helps to illustrate the point. On this occasion, government bureaucracy interfered with the department responsible for the production of the Enfield SA 80 (Light Support Weapon) and caused confusion amongst the manufacturing staff. The action created a six-week production delay, as government officials, who had not properly investigated an isolated complaint of premature weapon discharge, prompted design changes to the gun.[1]

A confused picture

Prior to the expansion of the Ordnance factory at Enfield in the mid 1850s, the picture of the English gun trade is one of an industry lacking direction and severely stricken by turmoil and confusion. As the middle of the century was reached the mounting pressure from sections within Ordnance for control of the military small arms industry finally took hold, motivated in the main by the requirements of war.

Following the Great Exhibition of 1851, the continuing debate between the private gun trade and the Board of Ordnance over weapon deliveries and quality standards was becoming more acrimonious, the arguments spilling over into the evidence given before the Select Committee on Small Arms in 1854. As we have already discussed, many engineers and entrepreneurs had visited the exhibition held within the Crystal Palace and marvelled at such American exhibits as the Sharpe's rifle manufactured by Robbins & Lawrence and the revolvers of Colonel Colt made with standardised parts. However, there were some established gun makers, like Mr W. Scott of Birmingham, who would not entertain the idea that large quantities of machine-made products could be accurately produced without the involvement of skilled artisans.

When asked by the Select Committee if he thought it possible to produce parts by machines which could "fit into one another perfectly without a great deal of manual labour", he replied "Certainly not; by no means; it is impossible".[2]

Joseph Whitworth's fact finding tour of America in 1853, when he and George Wallis visited a number of diverse manufacturing establishments, and the subsequent visit by the Commission led by Colonel Burn in 1854, which placed substantial contracts for arms production machinery with American manufacturers, were all intertwined with Ordnance seeking ways to overcome the problems they were encountering with arms procurement. At the time the British private gun trade were allegedly falling behind with military deliveries and failing the quality standards set by Ordnance.

Mary Seacole was a nurse who attended troops at the Crimea

Lord Raglan (1788-1855), Commander in Chief of the British Army at the Crimea

The situation was further complicated by the introduction of the new pattern 1853 Enfield rifle to replace the existing service 1851 Minié and as already argued, there was evidence of Ordnance withholding the new pattern from which the contractors had to copy. Out of this chaotic state there was mounting pressure upon Ordnance to equip soldiers in the Crimea with decent serviceable weapons, not only rifles but also swords and bayonets. With the build up of hostilities between Russia and Turkey in 1853 and war between them eventually breaking out in October of that year, it was obvious that a major response would be required from small arms manufacturers. This came when Britain and France entered the conflict in March 1854 after declaring war upon Russia.[3]

Unprepared for battle

During what must be viewed as a critical period in the life of the British small arms industry, correspondence between military regiments and Ordnance for the years 1854 to 1855 exposes serious flaws in the Ordnance supply chain. These letters indicate quite graphically how fragile the position of Britain really was in arming her troops in time of war. It also illustrates that almost 40 years after the establishment of the government armoury at Enfield Lock in response to the parlous state of the indigenous military small arms industry at the time of the Napoleonic wars, Britain was still unprepared for conflict.

The position is clearly illustrated in a letter dated 14th July 1854 from Lieutenant Colonel Griffith commanding the Second Dragoons in Manchester to Joseph Wood the Secretary to the Board of Ordnance, complaining, it would seem not unreasonably, about the poor state of his Regiment's weapons. Griffith wrote, "The whole of the Carbines require to be replaced, most of them being worn out from long use. The Victoria Carbines have been mostly in use for 14 years being issued in 1840". Further complaints were made about the "unserviceable" state of the Regiment's swords.

In March 1854 similar criticisms had been raised by the 11th Hussars serving in Ireland. Soon Griffith and his men were to embark for the Crimea without replacement Carbines or swords, 180 new pattern swords finally being issued to the Second Dragoons at their Manchester barrack on 1st August after they had already sailed to the front. When the mistake was eventually realised, the swords were dispatched to the Crimea by the Cleopatra on 11th November. Sadly the error was a costly one, as a communication from the War Department dated 13th December to Joseph Wood, quoted Colonel Griffith as follows:

Florence Nightingale visiting injured troops at the Crimea. An image from The Illustrated London News.

Swords are very defective – as in our engagement, when our men made a thrust with the sword, they are all but useless, and would not go into a man's body, and many of our poor fellows got badly wounded and some lost their lives entirely from the miserable state of their arms. They were quite good enough for home service, but quite unfit for active service.[4]

Unfortunately this was not the end of the Second Dragoon's problems as Colonel Griffith was to write again on the 25th April 1855, reminding Joseph Wood that, before embarkation to the Crimea, the Adjutant General's letters of 18th and 22nd July 1854 had placed requisitions for carbines and swords. The Board of Ordnance correspondence dated 25th July clearly shows that they had no means of supplying this trivial amount of 286 carbines which Griffith had requested. A note scribbled on the back of Griffith's communication dated 26th April 1855 by an S. Roper, states "There is no longer any difficulty in supplying the 286 Victoria Carbines requested by 2nd Dragoons". This was nine months after the original order was placed.[5]

It is probable that it was Enfield which had responsibility for manufacturing this modest amount of arms, as it was probable that such a small contract would not have been worth putting out to tender. Had this been done, then the delay in supplying the weapons would no doubt have been longer. The competitive nature of the contract system would have required Ordnance to distribute and vet the various incoming bids from the private sector and this would have taken time to study and process. Interestingly, this episode also provides a clue to the time required for a factory to adapt to the manufacture of a weapon which was not part of the current production programme. Given the urgency of war, and remembering the weapon was not new and had previously been in production, the incident serves as a general indication of the length of time and the difficulties involved in organising men, mechanisms and material. The introduction of a totally new pattern would no doubt have taken considerably longer to organise and reach full-scale production capacity. New jigs and gauges would have to be made and, of course, machine operators and other personnel would take time to become fully proficient and familiar with the work.

The complaint relating to poor quality swords was investigated by R.W. Gunner, the Inspector of Small Arms at the Birmingham Ordnance office. He reported, "Soon after the introduction of this Pattern in the year 1822 it was found after a careful course of experimental trials that any of the tests beyond those above described was attended with excessive and unnecessary loss either from breakage or failure in elasticity in the fabrication of the blades".[6] Gunner went on to say that the "New Pattern" swords are subject to more stringent tests, the implication being that it was known the military were equipped with inferior weapons and nothing had been done in the forty years of relative peace to rectify the situation. The incident and other reports of poor quality provoked the Master General of Ordnance, Viscount Hardinge, to set up a committee of Cavalry Officers to look at the current stocks of swords in store and those in the process of manufacture both at Enfield and Birmingham. In addition to the standard tests, Gunner requested the Committee to test the weapons more severely. This they did by "proving the cutting on a bar of iron and the point against a brick wall, without injury in any case to the Swords". After taking evidence from the Inspector of Small Arms and the "Superintendents of the Royal Manufactory", the Committee reported, in January 1855, that, in their opinion, the whole of these weapons are made of the best possible materials and they consider them excellent Swords and fit for any service.[7] This statement was made after four of the Enfield swords and one from Birmingham (over two per cent of those examined), failed the test. The Committee concluded that in "each instance the fracture was not caused by flaw or softness of metal, but rather from being too highly tempered".[8] While technically the analysis may have been correct, it would be hard to imagine that soldiers in the heat of combat would be interested in the precise nature of the fault. Weapon failure for any reason would have been unacceptable; what soldiers required was reliable weapons in which they could have confidence. Perhaps, at the time, Ordnance officers had not appreciated the fact that battles are often won on the factory floor through the quality and quantity of weapons supplied to the troops. The Ordnance Committee, detached from the horrors of war, declared on completion of their investigation that the present swords were "fit for any service".

From researching the considerable correspondence on the Crimea, it is clear that soldiers had been sent to the front ill equipped for combat with old issue arms, tragically discovering the inadequacy of their weapons in battle. The failure of the swords in action might indicate that 100 per cent testing and inspection was not being carried out or perhaps some had escaped the view either deliberately or by accident.

Supply and weapon problems

From our discussion it can be seen that there was a whole catalogue of poor organisation, mismanagement and incompetence surrounding the procurement and supply of small arms to soldiers on active service. Furthermore, it would appear that there was a complete lack of understanding by members of the Board of Ordnance relating to the necessary time-scales required by the small arms industry to prepare and schedule the production of new weapons. Apart from senior Ordnance personnel in the business of arms procurement having little understanding of how a manufacturing facility operated, it was also apparent that there was a failure to grasp the simple logistics of supplying the troops at the front. The Army in the Crimea had wanted weapons of standard calibre to ease problems in the ammunition supply chain. This would have eliminated the confusion brought about through the issue of more than one size of ammunition. It can readily be deduced from the correspondence between Ordnance and the different regiments that at least three types of weapon were in service with the front line troops, all having different calibre bores.[9] Such a mix of weapons of incompatible calibre had introduced severe supply difficulties for the Army. The authorities had tried to resolve these problems on a makeshift basis by keeping batches of the 1851 Minié and Enfield pattern 1853 muskets separate. These were then issued to different regiments. By knowing where the various weapon types were, it was hoped that this would avoid mistakes of wrong ammunition being delivered to the regiments.

With the issue of the new smaller calibre (0.577 inch) pattern 1853 it would appear that some of the former strategic advantages of warfare had been lost. For example, Major E.G.B. Reynolds has argued that "It was considered an advantage to have a bore larger than certain Continental armies because, whereas captured ammunition could be fired from English muskets, English leaden balls could not be fired out of theirs".[10]

The 1851 Minié was not the ideal choice of weapon for troops in combat. This can be seen from the many regimental reports which originated from trials carried out in August 1854. Here it was concluded that the barrel of this weapon was too hot to hold after firing between thirty to fifty rounds. Twelve to thirteen minutes had to be allowed for the weapon to cool sufficiently, raising fears that the powder might prematurely explode in the barrel causing injury. Furthermore, the Minié was over one pound heavier than the Enfield pattern 1853, making it less than ideal to carry and handle.[11]

With the many logistical problems confronting the Army, ranging from the supply of equipment to suitability of weapons and ammunition it would not seem unreasonable to question the competence of the Board of Ordnance and the military authorities. If they were unable to accomplish those tasks which were more suited to their military backgrounds, then it would be difficult to see how they could cope with technical matters concerning the design, manufacturing, and scheduling of weapons.

Shipments of replacement arms from England were slow to arrive at the Crimea. This was primarily due to the problems already highlighted, ranging from the contract system and the strictness of view to the failure of Ordnance to supply an adequate number of patterns and tools to the private gun trade. By 3rd January 1855, research has shown, there were contracts (not all signed) outstanding for up to 160,000 weapons, mainly the Enfield pattern 1853. Although figures relating to the individual suppliers of weapons are not entirely clear, it can be deduced from the correspondence that orders for 100,000 guns had been placed with Birmingham contractors, 40,000 with Liège, 1,500 with London, and 1000 with Enfield. Ordnance had promised that 10,000 of these arms would be delivered to Balaklava by the end of January, with a continuing schedule of 4,000 per month until May and each rifle was to be supplied with 500 cartridges.[12] The grand plan was, by August or September, to have the Army in the Crimea, "entirely armed with rifles of one pattern – that of the 1853".[13]

The harbour at Balaklava

After all the complaints by Ordnance against the private gun trade, the above figures clearly show that they were the only sector of the arms industry capable of supplying reasonable quantities of weapons to the soldiers at the front, albeit behind schedule on occasion, and still by mainly labour-intensive methods of manufacture. However, as already pointed out, the delays were not entirely the fault of the private sector. Therefore, the establishment of the "Ordnance" factory at Enfield at the beginning of the century to secure adequate supplies of arms for the military without recourse to the private sector and the necessity of placing orders abroad, had clearly not achieved its goal. The successful lobbying of Parliament by the private gun trade had ensured that Enfield remained incapable of manufacturing large quantities of weapons. This had inadvertently brought foreign imports from Liège into the country when demand for arms increased. Here it might be argued that due to a failure by politicians to fully appreciate the technological requirements of a country with an Empire to police British interests abroad had been rendered vulnerable by the lack of a strategic weapon manufacturing policy.

Initially, it will be recalled, government had sought to develop a small arms strategy by setting up Enfield in 1816 but had bowed under political pressure from the private sector. However, we have seen that Ordnance had failed to heed George Lovell when he suggested a sensible method of working with the gun trade. No doubt a co-ordinated weapons manufacturing and development programme could have been advantageously cultivated between the private and public sectors based upon Lovell's recommendations. Failure of government to develop such a scheme in the relatively peaceful period after the Napoleonic conflict left Britain once again vulnerable when war loomed.

Failure of government to learn from experience

When the British Government decided to send a Commission to America in 1854 to investigate the possible purchase of suitable arms making machinery, the timing almost exactly coincided with Britain's entry into the Crimean War. Even after the Commission had left England, Parliament was still arguing over the amounts of money to be spent on re-equipping the Enfield factory. In fact the initial sum was reduced from £30,000 to the absurd amount of £10,000 but was later reinstated, the Commission being allowed an almost open cheque facility to purchase the necessary machine tools.[14] No doubt the outbreak of the Crimean conflict had persuaded Parliament to release its grip on the purse strings. By the lack of written evidence to the contrary, it would seem reasonable to conclude that Ordnance was not working toward a cohesive strategic plan for the British small arms industry with a view to securing future weapon supplies. Therefore, without the pressure created by the Crimean campaign it is unlikely that Enfield would have had the opportunity to become one of the world's leading small arms producers by the middle of the nineteenth century. This tends to reinforce the notion that the British Government and its advisers lacked a fundamental knowledge of manufacturing matters, particularly an understanding of the planning processes and the time-scales involved in preparing and equipping a small arms production plant. Although it has been shown in earlier chapters that the private gun trade's influence upon Parliament had been exceedingly powerful, by which the trade had successfully resisted Ordnance intrusion into their industry, there is no evidence to suggest that government had the political will or commitment to become involved in full-scale small arms manufacture on its own account. Of course, it might be argued that the long period of relative peace following the end of the Napoleonic Wars had lulled the British Government into a false sense of security. If this was the case, then it would appear naive in the extreme, particularly if one remembers the need for Britain to be alert at all times to the unpredictability of outbreaks of unrest in her possessions overseas. Under such circumstances one would have expected Britain to have been particularly vigilant, needing to be positioned to react quickly to restore law and order. Given such conditions, it would seem rational that Britain would require a plentiful supply of reliable arms to be called upon should such an emergency arise.

Evidence of Ordnance ignorance

At a time when there was a desperate need to supply the Army at the Crimea with weapons of standard calibre and type, research at the National Archives has uncovered a substantial amount of correspondence between Captain Manly Dixon, Superintendent of the Enfield manufactory and a number of defence agencies relating to mounting pressure to introduce new types of weapon. A letter from Dixon to Ordnance 30th May 1855, asked "whether it would be advisable to purchase 1,000 or 1,500 Sharpe's breech loading Carbines instead of issuing contracts for making the Victoria Carbine, a weapon which is all but useless". Dixon went on to suggest that the Sharpe's breech loader is "much superior to anything that has yet been invented" and he further pointed out that the Victoria Carbine "would take 6-7 months to manufacture". This figure would seem rather generous, as it will be recalled that just over a year before it had taken nine months to organise the production of only 286 of these weapons. In a reply from Ordnance to Dixon dated 5th June it was stated that Viscount Hardinge has inspected a Sharpe's breech loader and "considers a Carbine invented by Mr Prince to be superior". He also went on to suggest that "some of Prince's pattern be made and distributed for test to the Regiments with the Sharpe's". In the mean-time Dixon received an order for 4,000 Victoria Carbines to be delivered to General Beatson for the Irregular Turkish Cavalry. Dixon's reply exudes frustration when he states "there are no contracts for material for these arms, at present existing and there are no materials in store". Later in his letter he forcefully concluded "The question now is whether a contract shall issue for an arm for Cavalry purposes which hardly shoots straight at 100 yards, is cumbrous, and difficult to load on horseback and requires a different ammunition to any other arm in the British Army".[15]

This is a damming report by any account and is further evidence of how critical the arms supply situation had become. Not only is it an indication of the plight of the front line troops, but it illustrates the failure of Ordnance to recognise or understand the basic requirements of the small arms industry and the time-scales involved in implementing a new manufacturing programme. This latter point should have appeared particularly pertinent to Hardinge, particularly after Dixon had already explained in previous correspondence that the Victoria Carbine, a weapon which had already been in production "would take 6-7 months to manufacture". For Hardinge to propose that an entirely new weapon be manufactured and "distributed for test to the Regiments" would suggest not only that Dixon's former point had been missed or ignored but also that he was prepared to carry out experiments with an untried arm in time of war. This latter fact seems quite extraordinary and almost beyond belief, again emphasising that the military side of Ordnance had little idea of time-scales and were seemingly prepared to risk soldier's lives while they were trying to find an improved weapon.

In a further communication between Ordnance and Dixon it is suggested that "Viscount Hardinge is now of the opinion that Mr Leitch's breech loading Carbine be examined". From the correspondence it would appear that this weapon was being recommended for use with the British Cavalry. Dixon therefore suggests as an expedient that Colt's revolvers should be issued to the Cavalry in lieu of the Victoria Carbine. It will be recalled that Dixon had been highly critical of this latter weapon and, apart from it being an old design, there were no stocks available.

In a letter to Dixon from the War Department dated 11th July 1855 it was stated that Hardinge had now "re-considered his opinion and understands that the breech loader would be for the Cavalry only". Dixon was also informed that Hardinge did not want the Sharpe's or Colt's weapons purchased from America and he was given the news that a Leitch breech loader was being sent to him for evaluation after the weapon had already been examined by a Board of Cavalry Officers who apparently found it "excellent practice at 300 yards". This communication was followed by another letter dated 8th August, informing Dixon that Hardinge had "decided the best fire arm for the Cavalry is Leitch's breech loading rifle". The message went on to say "this improved arm will of course do away with the necessity of anymore Victoria Carbines being procured". By 15th August Dixon was replying in very strong terms in relation to his findings on the Leitch rifle. Dixon explained that Mr Leitch had been given the opportunity to fire his weapon at Enfield, "a model which he [Leitch] stated had been shewn to the Board of Cavalry Officers and approved by them and subsequently approved and inspected by Viscount Hardinge". The opportunity was taken by Dixon to report on how the rifle performed in the demonstration given by Mr Leitch, stating "The results showed that in our opinion the arm is less adapted for Cavalry purposes than any other which has been submitted". These views were also supported by Captain Warlow, an experienced Ordnance officer and one of the members of the 1854 Commission to America. Warlow found up to six areas of complaint with the weapon. These and Dixon's opinions received the support and backing of James Gunner, Storekeeper at Enfield. A communication to Dixon from Ordnance dated 15th August informed him that Hardinge:

Viscount Henry Hardinge,
Master General of Ordnance

... recommends that instructions be immediately given for the preparation of 15,000 of Leitch's breech loading rifled carbines in order that a sufficient reserve be at hand to meet casualties. His Lordship would be glad to learn how soon any, and what proportion of these weapons may be expected to be ready in order that the Regiments serving in the Crimea may be supplied at the earliest possible period.[16]

As the date of Hardinge's instruction coincided with that of Dixon's report on the Leitch rifle, is not obvious from the correspondence whether the former communication arrived at Enfield before or after the technical assessment took place. If it came before, this would indicate that the Board had already made up its mind and was therefore not prepared to receive a serious evaluation of the weapon by Enfield personnel. Had it come after, it would imply a large measure of arrogance on behalf of the Board, particularly as the technical advice had come from three of the country's leading experts on military small arms.

Had Enfield not possessed men of the calibre of Dixon and his colleagues who understood not only the intricacies of production and procurement time-scales but military requirements as well, and were also prepared to stand their ground and argue their case with high ranking Ordnance officers, it is difficult to contemplate what fate might have eventually befallen the British soldier. However, the whole episode and particularly the action of ordering Dixon to produce 15,000 Leitch breech loaders, illustrates the Master General's lack of manufacturing knowledge. This clearly demonstrates that Hardinge had no idea of how long it would take to tool-up and prepare for manufacture.

Explanations for Ordnance incompetence emerge

It should be recognised that the dialogue between Captain Dixon and in particular Viscount Henry Hardinge has been truncated for brevity. However, analysing the correspondence and noting the critical period during which the exchange took place has provided a fresh insight into behind the scenes actions of senior military and Board of Ordnance personnel. The investigation has helped uncover what is sometimes perceived as the mysteries surroundingcertain aspects of military decision making, the results of which are often viewed with incredulity. Those outside the process who question the reasons, which on occasion appear irrational, can begin to understand why certain actions were or were not taken. Historians researching the transfer of the "American system of manufactures" to Britain have failed to fully explore the Board of Ordnance comprehension of military supply chain requirements,particularly at the time of the Crimean War. By opening this line of enquiry it has been possible to demonstrate that certain military and Board of Ordnance officers with responsibility for supplying small arms to front line troops, lacked a fundamental understanding of the weapon manufacturing process and consequently the ability to appreciate development and delivery time-scales. The correspondence has shown quite clearly that there was considerable antagonism between the technical experts at Enfield and the military and Ordnance bureaucrats, further demonstrating that this latter group were not versed in a basic understanding of the problems caused by re-scheduling or re-planning production. Neither had the importance of maintaining long-term manufacturing stability through continuity of product design been grasped. It would also appear that the Board had little comprehension of the limitations of the gauges, tools and machinery which had been ordered from America to equip the Enfield factory. This equipment had been specifically designed to support large scale manufacture of one particular weapon, the Pattern 1853 rifle, and could not be expected to support any other pattern of arm. Perhaps the problems of a nineteenth-century government bureaucracy ignorant about manufacturing are best summed by G.R. Searle when he wrote:

> … the most important administrative appointments soon became the preserve of "gentlemen" who had benefited from a "liberal" university education, but who possessed neither practical experience nor knowledge relevant to their work. Yet partly because of the assumption that specialists were spendthrifts who needed tight curbing, public officials with technical qualification and attainments usually found themselves subordinated at all points to these "general administrators"[17]

The Snider breech loading modification to the Enfield pattern 1853

Of course, the lack of understanding by the Board and other military personnel may have been a question of poor communication by engineers but this argument can generally be discounted on the grounds that there had been almost forty years of peace during which good liaisons could have been developed had there been the will. Views of engineers had been expressed and recorded, some by famous and high-profile men like Whitworth, Nasmyth and Anderson, when they drew up reports for government agencies and gave evidence before the various Select Committees, so it was not as if information concerning engineering and manufacturing matters was unknown in high places. The lack of Ordnance understanding can again be seen after the adoption of the Enfield pattern 1853 rifle as the standard arm for the forces in the Crimea. It was hoped that the delivery of this weapon in quantity to the front line troops would overcome the potentially disastrous situation of having more than one type of ammunition in circulation. As pointed out earlier, problems had already been caused for the Army with the issue of a least three different calibre weapons to the front. However, from the correspondence between Dixon and Hardinge it can be seen that the Board and influential military officers were changing their minds almost daily, encouraging Enfield to introduce new weapon types, some of which, if accepted, would require additional designs of ammunition and training of the men, hardly a situation to be contemplated when war was raging. While these distracting communications between Ordnance and Enfield were taking place, it should be remembered that substantial contracts had been placed with the private sector for the Pattern 1853 and shipments of the weapon to the Army were already underway.

American soldier with Enfield pattern 1853

Investigating the correspondence between Ordnance and Enfield has helped to clarify the reasons governing the timing of the British Government's intervention into the traditional small arms manufacturing business of the private sector, bringing about for the first time the entry of Ordnance into large scale military weapon manufacture. In fact it is the clarification of the timing issue which has provided important information, showing how Enfield was catapulted into adopting revolutionary methods of mass production with new imported machine tools, rather than having a more sedate and evolutionary approach to large scale arms manufacture. Had the Crimean conflict not come about, then Enfield may well have retained its original role as a small scale manufacturing unit with responsibilities for weapon repair, research and development.

Some wives accompanied troops at the Crimean War

The Relief of the Light Brigade, a painting (1897) by Richard Woodville, Jr.

Playing a dangerous game?

Early in 1855 work on the new buildings began at Enfield to house the machinery on order from America, the task of construction being undertaken by the Royal Engineers under the command of Major General Collinson.[18] While preparation for the site's expansion was taking place a decision to alter dramatically the terms and conditions of the workforce was implemented. A memorandum dated 4th July 1855 explained that the current terms and conditions of workmen employed by the Ordnance establishment at Enfield would be suspended as of the 21st "when they will be considered as ceasing to belong to the factory – as it is hoped that many will be willing to re-engage under the new system". The new arrangements required "... old hands to be pensioned", and it was proposed that workmen "... such as receive it [pension] for long and faithful services shall be recommended for a gratuity". Furthermore, an abstract of the rules was to be hung in the factory telling the work-force that they would have to apply to the Superintendent before the 17th July to be re-engaged. The working hours were to be brought in to line with other private factories in Britain, 10.5 hours per day for the first five days and 7 hours on the sixth, bringing the total working week to 59.5 hours. Even senior craftsmen did not escape the changes. All the Superintendent Armourers were informed that, on the 23rd of July, they would receive their instructions from the Tower "under the immediate superintendence of Mr Phillcox but subject to the order and charge of Mr Turner". Time keeping was to be formally structured, gates to be opened at 5.45am, work commencing at 6am., workmen arriving 5 minutes late would be deducted 15 minutes pay, arrival after 6.15am would see 30 minutes pay deducted. Gates were to be closed at 6.30am, workmen arriving after this time would have to wait until the breakfast break at 9am, to be allowed in. There was to be a time book which would show the punctuality or lateness of the employees and this would reflect the amount of wages received by individuals. Wages would be paid before the Saturday dinner break.[19]

From the timing of the new working practices it would seem that management had taken a terrible risk. The act of introducing these fresh terms and conditions could have easily provoked a serious strike. With Britain deeply involved in the Crimean war, further problems with the supply of arms would seem to have been the last thing government wanted. It was probable, however, that Ordnance felt confident in taking this action, perhaps banking on the knowledge that memories of the 1852 "great lock out" were still fresh in workers minds. (This was the occasion (January to March 1852) when the Amalgamated Society of Engineers, Machinists, Millwrights, Smiths and Pattern Makers (ASE) made demands upon factory owners that every machine should be attended by a skilled Union operative.) The risk of industrial action may also have appeared slight, because, as the Enfield factory was a government establishment, the workers enjoyed better terms and conditions than their private sector counterparts. From the rapidly rising output of the Enfield factory after January 1857, it would seem fair to conclude that the changes went through relatively smoothly.

Membership card of the Amalgamated Society of Engineers

Birth of the Union

With the organisational changes taking place, it is probably no coincidence that on the 5th November 1855 the Amalgamated Society of Engineers (ASE) formed the Enfield Lock Branch. The inaugural meeting was attended by the Union's General Secretary, William Allan, who formally declared the Branch open. Unfortunately, the Union minute books for this important period in the birth of the Branch are incomplete and the early entries are erratic. For example, the second entry does not occur until 24th February 1857, the business being conducted is of a general administrative nature and sadly does not refer to the introduction of the new American machine tools at the Enfield factory.

From an examination of later entries in the minute books, it can clearly be established that the Branch was catering strictly for skilled craftsmen only. Membership of able bodied men was actively encouraged as this was thought necessary to maintaining high standards of craftsmanship but those with disabilities were excluded. At the time, skilled workers' jobs were under threat from the increasing number of machine tools being introduced into the Enfield factory. The following examples taken from the minutes give a clear indication of the measure of strictness being operated by the Branch in an effort to preserve and maintain a skilled membership:

> October 26th 1872 – That the sympathy of this Branch be conveyed to Mr Tuckey on his being disqualified to becoming a member of this Society through his loss of two fingers on one hand.

> January 17th 1874 – That Thomas Tanner be admitted a member of this Society. He having undergone an examination by Doctor J Hutchinson of the Ophthalmic Hospital, London, who certifies that his left eye is perfect, and that the right eye suffers from a congenital defect and that it will not be detrimental to his following his employment.

> January 31st 1874 – That our Secretary be instructed to write to the Council to know whether we are justified in admitting a member suffering from a rupture to the sick benefit of our Society.

> October 10th 1874 – That our Secretary be requested to write to Newcastle informing the Secretary that James Trigg was not working at this Factory as a mechanic he being employed while working here on the component parts of the gun.[20]

On reading these extracts one is left with the impression that a type of craft elitism was being operated. This may have accounted for the relatively small number of men belonging to the Branch. In 1855 the Branch membership was only 44 rising to 122 by 1880.[21] The work-force estimates of the RSAF Superintendent and historian G.H. Roberts, suggest that in 1858 "... about 1,000 unskilled or semi-skilled and 250 skilled men were employed, a considerable number of whom had come from Col. S. Colt's Factory at Pimlico".[22] Therefore, during the early years of the Branch, membership as a proportion of workers employed at the factory was less than four per cent.

A climate of mixed views-and uncertainty

After almost forty years of only partial manufacturing involvement, government had been forced by war to accept responsibility for the full-scale production of military small arms. However, the plan to expand Enfield was not shared by all politicians, some taking the view that a government owned armoury was not essential, believing that the private gun trade could provide all of Britain's military requirements without placing an undue burden on the Exchequer. Research has shown that, if Ordnance had sought to establish sensible long-term contracts with the private sector and taken the trouble to foster good relationships with the gun makers, supplying them with reasonable quantities of patterns and gauges, a reliable source of military weapons could have been developed with minimum reliance upon public expenditure.

The report of the Select Committee on Small Arms 1854 was able to present an objective analysis of the problems befalling the gun trade in the supply and manufacture of military weapons. In drawing up their report the Committee reached the following conclusions:-

> While Your Committee recommended the system of contracting for the supply of Small Arms should not be discontinued, they are, nevertheless, of opinion that a manufactory of Small Arms under the Board of Ordnance should be tried to a limited extent. This manufactory would serve as an experiment of the advantages to be derived from the more extensive application of machinery, as a check upon the price of contractors, and as a resource in times of emergency, and it should be arranged with a view to its economical working.[23]

While it is clear that the Committee wanted to retain the contract system and had not wished to give Enfield sole responsibility for the production of all military small arms, their recommendation had nevertheless allowed Ordnance the opportunity to keep their feet firmly in the manufacturing door. When Britain joined the conflict in the Crimea, followed by the purchase of machine tools from America, the chance for Ordnance to push the door fully open finally came.

It would seem unreasonable to assume that politicians were unaware of the high levels of expenditure required to fund a fully mechanised modern small arms factory on a continuous basis. Apart from the financial information coming before the various Select Committees, there was also the examples of factories directly under Ordnance control, like Woolwich Arsenal and Waltham Abbey Gunpowder Mills. Furthermore, from the haphazard and intermittent working of the contract system, it should have been obvious to politicians that there were no individual manufacturers outside of government who were big enough to have the confidence, let alone the finances, to risk investment in a large scale manufacturing plant. Many private companies had yet to be convinced of the superiority of the "American system of manufactures" over the traditional labour-intensive methods of gun production. This latter system had generally served them well over the years, allowing the private sector the flexibility to exploit different markets at minimum capital outlay.

Politics slow engineering influence

It was not only politicians who had appeared to lack the imagination and understanding of the needs of their armed forces at a time of a rapidly changing technology, after all many were under pressure from their gun making constituents. The collective responsibility of the Board of Ordnance was also found wanting. They had allowed the British Army to embark for the Crimea with inadequate and out of date weapons. Moreover, as research has shown, even the Master General was prepared to continue a time consuming and unhelpful dialogue with the technical and manufacturing experts over the introduction and trial of new weapons. This not only demonstrates a lack of understanding of the planning required in the manufacturing process but also an ignorance of the problems which would have undoubtedly been caused by issuing unfamiliar weapons to soldiers at the front (or perhaps it was naivety). Placing untried battlefield weapons in the hands of men in action, who had not been given the opportunity to train with them, would have no doubt resulted in disastrous consequences, not to mention confusion if new types of ammunition had to be issued as well.

The lack of Ordnance understanding of manufacturing issues would suggest that by the middle of the nineteenth century the voices of the engineers and technicians, although beginning to gain respect, had yet to be allowed to influence the decision making process. Perhaps Viscount Hardinge was still stirred by his earlier experiences of the former Inspector of Small Arms, George Lovell, as he had expressed the view, although possibly unfairly, that "The Inspector has an undue confidence in his own authority to act independent of the Board or of my own authority."[24]

The timing of the expansion and equipping of the Enfield factory when the Crimean War was in progress demonstrates clearly how unprepared the Board of Ordnance were for major conflict. In fact, the situation is even worse than it appears on the surface. A report, called for by John Anderson, Inspector of Machinery, and published in 1857 suggests that the new factory to house the machinery from America was originally planned for Woolwich. It was not until 2nd February 1855 (after Anderson's return from the United States) that the Board of Ordnance gave the order to commence building on the Enfield site. Naturally this caused further delays as plans had to be redrawn and the work put out to tender. The building was completed in 1856 but not before more costly delays were encountered due to "… the ground being a bog of peat…".[25]

As it has been shown, the whole episode surrounding government small arms production in the early to mid 1850s is one of general indecision, confusion and Ordnance incompetence. This would seem to have been an extremely serious state of affairs for the British nation to have been placed, particularly when considering the developing international scene. It were not as if politicians had suddenly realised that if Russia were to occupy Turkey, then India, the jewel in the British crown, would suddenly become exceedingly vulnerable. Russia had been expanding her Empire for years and there was more than enough intelligence information from British agents to have caused politicians considerable anxiety.[26] More than ever, the British Government needed an arms manufacturing strategy which would introduce stability to the supply of weapons to her troops. Would the incoming "American system", developed by engineers, based on new production and assembly principles, achieve this?

Time for change

The arrival of the "American system of manufactures" (as it later became known) in Britain was to show, by the early 1860s, that Enfield was in a position to influence dramatically and change totally the method of British small arms production. At the time it was probably not fully appreciated how this new system of manufacture might affect other industries in Britain. The change appears to have been influential on at least two levels. First, the publicity given to Enfield had made the factory highly visible. This had set other industrialists thinking and they began considering the installation of new plant and equipment. Secondly, the new factory processes had imposed different standards on contractors which by the 1860s meant external supplies of military arms would only be accepted by Ordnance if made with interchangeable parts. This caused suppliers like the London Gun Company and the amalgamation of Birmingham gun makers (by 1861 called BSA) to implement machine-intensive production.

Although not referring directly to Enfield, Clive Treblicock wrote in relation to his "spin-off" theory, "The intricacy of the new weapons, the excellence of the manufacturing equipment, the heavy commitment to research – as well as the advocacy of the trade journal – would strongly suggest that by the 1880s the British armament industry had reached a level of technical achievement from which it could profitably influence "civilian" industries".[27] Free of pressure from the private gun trade and without the need to play political games with the contractors, Enfield's role had changed from a small volume repair shop to that of a major international small arms manufacturer. By 1860 the annual production figure for rifles alone had reached 90,707 – 1744 per week.[28]

Enfield's growing fame

A visible consequence of the Enfield factory, after full-scale production commenced in January 1857 with the imported American machine tools, was the vast amount of attention it attracted, particularly from the national press. Articles appeared in newspapers and learned journals proclaiming admiration for the manufacturing system and extolling the "beauty" of the machinery installed at the plant. The reporting in some instances exuded such national pride that the reader might be forgiven for believing mistakenly that the factory and its equipment was a marvellous piece of solely British ingenuity. Being cynical, it could be argued that this was the government encouraging publicity for the factory as a way of justifying to the public the large amount of capital expenditure, rather than simply being a piece of Victorian pride.

In the period immediately following the cessation of hostilities in the Crimea much publicity was given to the new factory, highlighting its modern production techniques and machine tools. Although several articles paid tribute to American machine manufacturers Robbins & Lawrence and the Ames Company, the references were often glossed over as in the case of *The Mechanic's Magazine* of 23rd August 1861. The machinery designers are referred to as "our American cousins", implying that the writer was trying to claim credit for Britain through a family connection.[29] The fame of the Enfield

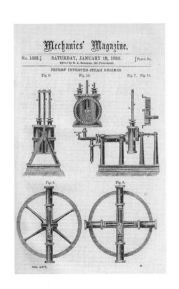

The Mechanics Magazine *that published an article praising the operation of American machine tools at the RSAF*

factory was not short lived, neither were the admirers confined to the world of adults. No doubt wishing to encourage the younger generation and perhaps to secure the craftsmen of the future, the *Boys Own Magazine* ran an article in 1860 entitled "Manly Exercises, Rifles and Rifle Shooting" which gave an account of weapon manufacture at Enfield. The writer, obviously overwhelmed by the experience of his visit to the factory, described the large machine room in the following florid terms:

> Let our readers imagine, if they can, a single room more than an acre in extent, lofty, and well lit, in which some thousand men and boys are increasingly employed in superintending machinery. The ear is pained by the hum of fly-wheels, which revolve in thousands till the eye is giddy with their whirl. Miles of shafting are spinning round mistily, with a monotonous hum; the room is almost darkened, and the view completely obscured, by some 50,000 or 60,000 feet of broad, flapping lathe-bands, which are driving no less than 600 distinct machines, all going together, on their own allotted tasks, with a tremulous rapidity and ease that seems to swallow up the work like magic, and the first sight of which is inexpressibly astonishing to the spectator. It takes some minutes before the visitor can subdue the over-whelming feeling of surprise which this scene of activity always excites, no matter how often entered on.[30]

John Anderson, the engineer from Woolwich Arsenal who had been a member of the 1854 three-man Commission to America, gave lectures to the Institute of Mechanical Engineers. In 1858 he read a paper in Newcastle on the applications of the *Copying or Transfer Principle in the Production of Wooden Articles* in which he described the sequenced operation of the new gun stock forming machinery at Enfield. A further paper in 1862 on the *Copying Principle in the Manufacture and Rifling of Guns* was given in Birmingham. Here Anderson described the levels of precision attained in machining and measurement at the government ordnance factories at Woolwich and Enfield. At the end of the lecture the chairman remarked that "members would have an opportunity to visit the works at Woolwich and see the whole of the processes described in the paper in the manufacture and rifling of guns and also of visiting the Small Arms Factory at Enfield, where the same principles had been carried out by Mr Anderson, and the same accuracy of workmanship attained".[31] While Enfield was enjoying the attention and prestige of a modern state of the art factory, there were remarks from members of Anderson's audience which suggested that Britain's manufacturing industries were suffering from under-investment. A Mr Richardson, who had previously visited the Woolwich factory, commented, "It would be a great advantage if the engineering workshops throughout the country would endeavour to approach to the same amount of perfection, by employing a better class of machinery and tools, which would produce an important advance in mechanical engineering".[32]

The increased productivity brought about by the introduction of the new machine tools coupled with the technology of interchangeability, gave Enfield a reputation as a centre of excellence. This point was emphasised by Howard Blackmore when he quoted William Greener the respected quality gun maker, a man apparently not given to generous comment, saying "Enfield, the seat of the Government manufacture of small arms, will become a celebrated place in future history; its productions being now one of the wonders of the present age".[33] Greener's view supports the notion that Enfield was seen more in terms of making a contribution towards production technology rather than having a role as a small arms design centre. The role of Enfield was more of a trial judge and weapon modifier rather than a design house.

The message spreads to the private sector

With the repeated enthusiastic coverage given to the Enfield factory by journalists and others, and the influencing of engineers and entrepreneurs through lectures within learned societies, the conditions were building up for a watershed within the British gun trade. Continually suffering shortages of skilled labour, yet encouraged by the sudden demand for arms brought about by the outbreak of war in the Crimea and later by the American Civil War in 1861, it had become clear to the private gun trade that if it wished to secure future orders for military weapons, manufacturing methods within its industry would have to change dramatically. No longer could the private sector expect to enjoy the same monopolistic conditions which prevailed prior to 1854 and which had effectively denied Ordnance the ability to compete for military small arms contracts. Now the private gun trade would have to compete with the much publicised and highly visible government factory at Enfield which was now able to dictate even stricter terms on which Ordnance would accept weapons and parts. In future, weapons would only be accepted if they conformed to a precise standard and were manufactured with interchangeable parts.[34] For generations the private gunsmiths had operated within a system of small shops employing mainly hand skills. If the private industry was to survive late into the nineteenth century and beyond, it would need to alter dramatically its method of production. The gauntlet had been thrown down by Enfield and the private gun trade was about to pick it up.

In 1861, four years after the RSAF commenced full-scale production with the imported machinery using the techniques of interchangeability, a group of midland firms came together to erect a new small arms factory at Small Heath in Birmingham. The plant was similar to the installation at Enfield and purpose-built, modelling itself on the "American system" using the techniques of interchangeable production. Over the coming years, the conglomerate known as the Birmingham Small Arms Company (BSA) would demonstrate how the lessons learned from the manufacture of standardised weapons would be transferred to the mass production of consumer products such as the bicycle.

Perhaps the most significant change for the private sector came from a complete reversal of government policy which moved from a position of obstruction and arms-length dealing to one of close cooperation. Instead of

An artist's impression showing the growth of the former BSA works from 1862

A photograph of the former BSA factory Small Heath, showing an extensive garden area around the plant

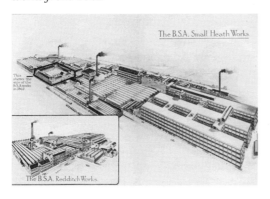

withholding patterns and gauges as they had in the past, Enfield was actively encouraged to assist BSA in making weapons which were compatible with their own production and therefore interchangeable between factories. The following statement by a grateful Birmingham Small Arms Company shows just how far Ordnance had moved from its earlier position:

> Every assistance has been rendered to the directors by the War Dept. of H. M. Government. The experience of Enfield has been freely placed at their disposal; free access has been granted to the Royal Manufactory with permission to make drawings of machinery. Models and gauges have been supplied which have effected for the company an incalculable saving.[35]

This was a far cry from the denial of the means of measurement which had occurred during Lovell's time as Inspector of Small Arms.

Greenwood & Batley of Leeds, who supplied machine tools to the RSAF and BSA in the mid nineteenth century

Government encourages industrial investment

Although it is true that BSA took delivery of specialist gun stocking machines from the Ames Manufacturing Company of Chicopee, Massachusetts similar to those supplied to Enfield, the pattern of machine tool acquisition was beginning to change. Roger Lumley has concluded from his research that claims suggesting the majority of the early machinery installed at BSA had come from the United States of America were false. During the 1860s, out of a total of 430 machine tools purchased, only 65 came from the USA, the original order for American equipment being cancelled at the outbreak of the Civil War of 1861. Of the 2,324 machines purchased by BSA in the nineteenth century, less than seven per cent came from abroad.[36] The Leeds based company Greenwood and Batley, which was only founded in 1856, were rapidly becoming recognised both at home and abroad as a quality producer of machine tools for the manufacture of small arms. Prior to supplying BSA this manufacturer had already equipped the London Armoury Company, giving it an output capacity capable of reaching 900 complete arms per week.[37] So in a way the machine tool story relating to self-acting mass production methods had come full circle. The ideas transferring to America from Portsmouth and elsewhere at the beginning of the century, returning to Enfield at an advanced state of development by the middle of it, to be taken up by British machine tool manufacturers, who spread the technology within Britain and abroad. Ironically and by default, the British Government, by its ability to place large orders for small arms, had broken the mould of the private sector's small workshop culture, forcing investment in capital equipment through the formation of larger manufacturing units. Looking from the position of the twentieth century, it can be seen that the act of importing specialised machine tools from America was an extremely influential component in a cocktail of many ingredients which helped to shape British light engineering. Although the introduction of the machine tool into the small arms industry influenced the spread of mass production technology in Britain, eventually transferring to other industries and encouraging greater size, it also had the effect of reducing the ability of industry to be flexible, thereby limiting the individuality of the product. Therefore, standardisation of parts came to mean standardisation of product.

Popular evidence and complexity reassessed

There is little doubt that a significant part of the subject under investigation, that of a longer reliance by the Board of Ordnance on labour-intensive methods of small arms manufacture in relation to their American counterparts, is an issue which is multifaceted and highly complex. In

Gunstock turning lathe manufactured in USA by the Ames Manufacturing Company

actuality, not all the procedures of small arms production were labour intensive in the first half of the nineteenth century. For example, the gun trade in Britain had successfully applied machinery to some of the processes in the production of rifle barrels. While apart from operations such as drilling, grinding and stamping, high levels of labour were used in the manufacture of locks and stocks. It is therefore probable that due to these, often conflicting, pieces of evidence that the debate surrounding the method of early arms manufacture looks set to continue and why the subject has held scholarly interest for so long.

As an example of subject complexity, Nathan Rosenberg, when including the *Report of the Committee on the Machinery of the United States of America* (published in 1855) in his book *The American System of Manufactures*, has in a way helped complicate (not deliberately) the debate surrounding the interpretation of what is meant, or what is considered acceptable in our understanding of nineteenth-century component interchangeability. Rosenberg and many of his contemporaries when quoting from this report focus considerable attention on the section which describes the Committee's visit to the Springfield National Armoury in 1854. When there, and by way of experiment, the Committee arranged for ten weapons made between 1844 and 1853 to be stripped and their component parts mixed together. The Committee then selected components at random and passed them to a workman where it is reported, he was able to assemble them with the "use of a turnscrew [screwdriver] only, and as quickly as though they had been English muskets, whose parts had been carefully kept separate". This often quoted section of the report has been used by writers in many standard works as a powerful example to illustrate how far American technology had advanced towards standardisation and interchangeability. However, it would appear from the unquestioned acceptance of this section that none of the authors had actually physically examined the weapon under discussion. Had they done so, this may have resulted in clearer definitions today of what constitutes interchangeability. For example, can interchangeability be defined as having different levels of tolerance, or is it purely taken to be parts that must transfer between every weapon in a mechanised production run without further adjustment by hand tools? One might further ask, were the strict standards of tolerance absolutely necessary to allow all the parts to interchange between weapons? These questions will be debated in the light of physical evidence obtained from the examination of Enfield pattern gun locks. Here it will be demonstrated that a crucial part of the Committee's report has been successively misinterpreted by many leading commentators. By a re-examination of the primary source material, and relating this to the new physical evidence it will be shown how this mistake occurred.

Rifle barrel boring machines

However, this oversight by scholars who have written about the interchangeability of components in early small arms may cause later researchers who also uncover the error to approach other standard works with a degree of caution. A further example of complexity which requires addressing can be seen in the work of David Hounshell. Here Hounshell has probably inadvertently misled the reader by implying that John Anderson was the leader of the 1854 Committee on the Machinery of the United States of America and that he was also author of the 1855 report. While not denying that Anderson was part of the Committee and did indeed contribute to the writing of the report, it is hardly accurate or fair to write, "In his report, Anderson indicated..." or; "Anderson and his committee..." when the leader was in fact Lieutenant Colonel Burn, Royal Artillery. While this may seem a minor point to make, it does however illustrate the type of problem occasionally encountered by the researcher when referring to secondary source material which can further complicate the subject under investigation. In fact, Hounshell cites Rosenberg as his reference, showing how easy it is to continue a mistake which can eventually become part of accepted belief. These points have been deliberately highlighted to help illustrate that in the pursuance of truth there is a need where practicable to refer back to primary sources, otherwise there is a danger of perpetuating a mistake or an error of interpretation. However, the questioning of concepts formerly taken to be solid and stable must be considered part of scholarly research. Therefore it is hoped that those researchers who take the trouble to read this investigation will avail themselves of the opportunity to re-examine the sources of the author, who for practical reasons has not been able to investigate every reference by referring to a primary source.

Throughout the already covered narrative there have been many references to " skills" which may have raised questions in the reader's mind of whether there were any clear-cut differences between those possessed by British and American workers. If so, was this another factor in delaying progress towards automated machine production on this side of the Atlantic?

Springfield National Armoury, USA, now a museum

REFERENCES

1. Kirby, Charles, "Service Rifle SNAFU", *Handgunner, No. 34* (June 1986), pp.19-22. The article gives a classic illustration of how confusion between a government manufacturing plant (RSAF) and a government body (MoD), over the alleged accidental firing of the SA80 when dropped, caused production delays by bureaucrats insisting on modifications to the weapon which were probably unnecessary.

2. House of Lords Record Office, London. Report from the *Select Committee on Small Arms, 12th May 1854, Reports Committee's Vol. XVIII-1854*, p.257

3. Holt, Elizabeth, *The Crimean War,* Wayland Publishers (London, 1974), pp.117-19

4. National Archive, Kew. Correspondence between Lieutenant Colonel Griffiths, J. Wood, Ordnance and War Department, 1854 -1855. Reference WO 44/701. It is worth noting that from the closeness of the dates on this correspondence, that is to say, sent 25th April, note on back 26th April, suggests that the message had been telegraphed. As a point of information, there was in fact considerable telegraph activity at the Crimea. The Gateshead firm of Newell & Company took part in laying a marine cable under the Bosphorus and the French had established a link to Paris. This therefore corrects the statement of the American Historian, F.W. Foster Gleason, when he suggested that the Civil War of 1861 was the "first telegraph war". National Archive, Kew. Telegraph Information Crimea, 1854, Reference WO 33/2A Gleason, F.W. Foster, "Arms For Men", Ordnance, July/August 1961, pp.62

5. Ibid., WO 44/701

6. Ibid., WO 44/701

7. Ibid., WO 44/701

8. Public Record Office, Kew. Circular, 27th January 1855, Reference WO 44/701

9. The Victoria carbine had a calibre of 0.733 inches, the Minié 0.753 inches and the Enfield pattern 1853 0.577 inches

10. Reynolds, E.G.B., "Early Enfield Arms – The Muzzle Loaders", Small Arms Profile No. 14, pp.26-7

11. National Archive, Kew. Reference WO 44/701. Report, August 1854, concerning trials by different regiments regarding 1851 Minie.

12. National Archive, Kew. Ten page Memorandum, 3rd January 1855, Correspondence, 2nd March 1855, 10th March 1855, 31st March 1855, Reference WO 44/701

13. Ibid., WO 44/701

14. House of Lords Record Office, London. "Report of the Committee on The Machinery Of The United States of America, Presented to the House of Commons in Pursuance of their Address, 10th July 1955", pp.543-4

15. National Archive, Kew. Correspondence between Captain Dixon, Ordnance and War Department, 1854 - 1855. Reference WO 44/701

16. Ibid., WO 44/701

17. Searle, G. R., *The Quest for National Efficiency*, Basil Blackwell (Oxford, 1971) p.21

18. Ministry of Defence Pattern Room, Nottingham. Roberts, G. H., CBE M. INST. C. E. (Superintendent RSAF 1922-1931), "Notes on The History Of The Royal Small Arms Factory, Enfield Lock". Unsigned typed manuscript (c1931), p.C10

19. National Archive, Kew. Memorandum 4th July 1855, Work Rules – RSAF, Reference WO 44/701

20. AUEW District Office, Edmonton, London. *Minute Book of the Enfield Lock Branch – ASE 1855-1865*, (First minute book).

21. Ibid., Books 1,2 and 3. See also, The First 80 Years, Some Account To 1935 of the Enfield Lock Branch (founded 1855) of the Amalgamated Union Of Engineers and

Foundry Workers, Formerly the AEU Originally the ASE p.4

22. Op. cit., Roberts, p.Cl1

23. House of Lords Record Office, London. "Report from the Select Committee on Small Arms, 12th May 1854", *Reports Committee's Vol. XVIII-1854*, pp.10

24. Bailey, De Witt, "George-Lovell And The Growth Of The RSAF Enfield", paper presented at MA Day School, Middlesex University (4th July 1992), pp.8

25. National Archive, Kew. WO 44/701. General Statement of the Past and, Present Condition of the Several Manufacturing Branches of the War Department, as called for by a letter dated May 8th 1856 by John Anderson, Inspector of Machinery.

26. Richards, D. S., *The Savage Frontier, A History of the Anglo-Afghan Wars*, Macmillan (London, 1990), pp.1-16

27. Treblicock, Clive, "Spin-Off In British Economic History: Armaments and Industry 1760-1914", *Economic History Review, 2nd Ser. XXII* (1969), pp.481

28. Op. cit., Roberts, p.C12

29. "The Enfield Small Arms Factory", *The Mechanics Magazine, Leviathan Workshops. No 11* (23rd August 1861), pp.110-11

30. "Manly Exercises, Rifle and Rifle Shooting", *Boys Own Magazine, Vol. 6* (1860)

31. Anderson, John, "On The Application Of The Copying Principle In The Manufacture And Rifling Of Guns", paper given before The Institute Of Mechanical Engineers Proceedings. Published by the Institution Birmingham 1862, pp.125-45

32. Ibid., pp.125-45

33. Blackmore, Howard L., "Military Gun Manufacturing In London And The Adoption Of Interchangeability", *Arms Collecting, Vol. 29, No. 4* (November 1991), p.121

34. Lumley, Roger., "The American System of Manufacturer in Birmingham: Production Methods at the Birmingham Small Arms Co. in the Nineteenth Century", *Business History, Vol. 31* (1989) p.37

35. Ibid., p.36

36. Ibid., pp.36-7

37. "Birmingham Small Arms Factory", *The Engineer Vol. 16* (25th December 1863), p.375

5. THE GREAT SKILLS DEBATE – BRITAIN VERSUS AMERICA!

Over the years there has been a considerable level of debate amongst engineers, historians of technology and economic historians as to what effect the introduction of the system of interchangeability by standardised machine-made parts had on the traditional skills of the artisan. Arguments range from the complete deskilling of the workforce to the opposite extreme of improving and enhancing skills and status. To discover the validity of these arguments and arrive at a balanced view, it will be necessary to analyse and assemble the fragmented evidence which is liberally scattered throughout a variety of documents and articles including a range of Select Committee Reports.

The skills debate

Skills were learned and developed in a number of ways. Some came about by formal training through apprenticeships which typically took five to seven years to complete. Usually there was a contractual element to the arrangement where the signing of a legal document (an indenture) took place and so the apprentice was said to be indentured. In most cases the newcomer would be under the experienced and watchful eye of the master or foreman for his formative years with the company until he became fully proficient at his trade. Less formal arrangements evolved through other types of on the job training where the employee perfected his skills by carrying out particular tasks. In the case of sons following fathers into the family business it was usual for the trainee to work through all the various departments and processes eventually to be in a position to take over on the father's death or retirement. The introduction of machine tools into manufacturing was to cause a division of labour which encouraged employers to take on low paid unskilled workers from a variety of backgrounds to act as machine minders and feeders. While this would have reduced the necessity for time-served apprentices, it has been argued that in the early years of machine tools, before repeatable tight tolerance standards were reached, some workers skill levels actually increased, or at least were in high demand. It is this latter area, coupled with the debate surrounding the system of interchangeability, which has led to the greatest controversy among those studying the effect of machine tools upon artisan skills.

The artefactual evidence

Robert B. Gordon, professor of geophysics and applied mechanics at Yale University, by studying in great detail the material evidence of nineteenth-century gun lock parts, and in particular the tumbler, has argued that American artificer skills had, with the introduction of interchangeability, increased rather than decreased. Gordon has found evidence to suggest that bringing lock parts to gauge by skilful hand filing continued in the national and the better private armouries at least until 1884. He further argues that "the tool marks and dimension measurements show that by 1850

Robert B. Gordon, professor of geophysics and applied mechanics at Yale University

artificers using hand files had learned to bring rough forged and machine parts of complex shape to final dimensions specified by gauges to an accuracy of a few thousandths of an inch in routine production".[1] Gordon's detailed analysis has found that as the accuracies of machine-made lock parts increased, so did the skills of the artificers, who by the 1870s could judge by feel and fit to gauge, measurements to better than 0.001 inch.

Mid nineteenth-century skill in Britain

Comparing the work of Gordon on mid nineteenth-century American lock parts, most of which seem to have required a high level of skilled labour in construction and finishing (he suggests 54.5 per cent hand work on a tumbler in 1864), with the evidence of eminent engineers given before the 1854 Select Committee on Small Arms, raises doubts regarding the level of skill applied in Britain within similar areas of manufacture. The evidence alluded to falls into two groups of engineering opinion. There were those who believed that almost any intelligent labourer could be turned into a mechanic in a relatively short period of time capable of taking on the work previously carried out by skilled time-served men. Then there were those who held a contrary view, believing it was only skilled artisans who were capable of bringing work to an accurate state of finish. James Nasmyth, who had once worked for Henry Maudslay, a greatly respected and skilful engineer, was a devoted advocate of employing unskilled labour. His main reasons for this would appear to be Union breaking, keeping wages low, and improving productivity. Nasmyth informed the 1854 Select Committee on Small Arms, "the most trustworthy men I have were originally agricultural labourers; people taken from the fields in my own neighbourhood".[2] He then went on to explain that he first put these new workmen "through a kind of apprenticeship before that in serving as labourers in the shop". Nasmyth further explained that by selecting the "most intelligent", he was able to get them "producing three or four times the amount" of work in a week above what he described as his "legal hands". To illustrate his point Nasmyth gave the example of sacking one of his experienced craftsmen whose job it was to tend a self-acting cylinder boring machine, a process which he described as requiring, "very great accuracy and care". The workman had apparently refused to take responsibility for looking after a second machine while minding the first. Nasmyth took the labourer who assisted in loading the work into this machine and put him in charge, telling him, "for every additional machine you manage I will give you an additional shilling a week". We are told that the man "manages six machines and has plenty of spare time".[3] Looking further at Nasmyth's evidence it is discovered that he pays his "leading men £2.10s per week" and some of his more recent recruits 18.s.[4] Assuming that the labourer Nasmyth put in charge of the machine was earning 18.s. and was paid an extra 5.s. "for the additional machines" he managed, then his total weekly wage would amount to £1.3s. Therefore, Nasmyth would have saved £1.7s. per week on this operation while increasing his output five fold. When Colonel Colt, the American arms manufacturer, opened his pistol factory opposite Vauxhall Bridge in London in 1853 he was eventually forced to take on and train unskilled labour. Colt in evidence to the Select Committee on Small Arms explained how he employed, what the Committee had described as, "your men of ignorance", by stating:

> they first come as labourers at 2s. a day, and if I find them expert and honest I employ them as watchmen, or to weigh metal. In a little time if there is a

Henry Maudslay (1771-1831), the highly respected engineer who set exacting precision standards

machine vacant, I put them on it. They would improve from 2s. in the first few months up to 4s. or 5s., and by and by they become masters. One half of my masters are Englishmen now, and they fill vacancies of Americans who become dissatisfied, from ill-health and from other causes and go home. The best get 8s. a day, and at last they become masters too. Do not bring me a man who knows anything, if you want to teach him anything.[5]

What Colt meant by this last remark was that he required men who had not already been subjected to learning particular mechanical skills as it would be difficult to release them from their old habits. As Colt succinctly put it, he required "good brains and little knowledge".

The evidence of Colt was independently corroborated by Nasmyth who informed the Committee of his delight, when on one of his visits to Colt's factory he had seen "men who had been butchers, bakers, and tailors, not because they had so been, but because they were steady, intelligent young men, or old, as the case might be, where there was a free opening given to them, able and willing to apply their intelligence to the accomplishment of a given result".[6]

However, when examining the evidence of Gage Stickney, an American engineer who had been brought to England by Colt, and up until recently had been superintendent of Colt's London factory, a different picture begins to emerge relating to the level of workforce skills. Stickney was adamant that about two thirds of the factory workforce were of medium class skill, and the remaining third were first class, remarking, "... and the highest price is paid for it".[7]

What now begins to emerge out of the contradictory evidence between Nasmyth and Stickney is the debate concerning interchangeability and how closely machine-made parts were finished. Nasmyth as a machine builder, and as might be expected, when asked, "Do you suppose that those parts that come from the machine would be fit to put together in the state they are?" –

James Nasmyth (1808-1890)

answered "yes". Incredibly, after making this clear and forthright statement, Nasmyth, almost immediately under close questioning admitted that when parts came off the machine in Colt's factory they were passed to the "finishing-shop". .8. It would appear therefore, that Nasmyth was stating what he believed could be achieved, rather than what was happening in reality. Even Colt admitted that he had to rely on manual labour for "... taking the burr off and passing the parts from one machine to another, finishing and assembling the work".[9]

In discussing with the Committee the manufacture of Colt's pistols, Gage Stickney explained that the individual parts were prepared by machinery, but they were finished "by first class mechanics". Stickney was quite uncompromising about this point when he explained, "I have never known any cheap labour capable of finishing any lock; with skilled workmen it requires long practice, so much so, that the first-class gunsmiths are not doing half the work".[10] These remarks would seem to authenticate the scientific findings of Robert Gordon when he discovered evidence of hand finishing on lock tumblers as late as the

*Samuel Colt's factory, Pimlico,
London, mid nineteenth century*

1880s. Joseph Whitworth (later Sir), one of several influential British engineers
in terms of precision measurement and a machine builder, also expressed
strong views to the Select Committee which did not totally agree with those
of Nasmyth. Whitworth, like Nasmyth, had interestingly been a former
employee of the late Henry Maudslay and for many years had been deeply
involved with the development of accurate screw threads, particularly in
relation to the lathe. No doubt influenced by his mentor's continuing quest
for greater accuracy, Whitworth developed a new measuring system which
was gauge based. In this he used a method of measuring from end-standards
which amounted to a series of precision bars made with flat parallel ends.
These bars were used in conjunction with a Whitworth designed measuring
machine, something akin to a bench micrometer. It was claimed that by using
a combination of these devices accurate measurements could be obtained
down to 0.000001 inch.[11]

An example of how great respect for Whitworth was in the field of precision
measurement can be gained from the evidence of the Birmingham engineer,
Richard Prosser. When giving evidence before the Select Committee he
related an account of how he had been able to solve a problem of
standardisation at long range, by sending his American customer a set of
Whitworth's gauges, while keeping a duplicate set himself. Prosser told the
Committee that he was making tubes in England for the boilers of his
American customer. Apparently the holes to accommodate the tubes were
bored in the United States. From the evidence it is clear that Prosser's
customer had experienced considerable difficulty in trying to marry the tubes
to the holes. As Prosser explained that it was not until he despatched a "... set
of Mr Whitworth's gauges, we know what an inch is".[12] Given this example
it would seem that Whitworth's credentials can be trusted when it comes to
the early debate on hand finishing after machining. Also, further research has
shown he was held in high esteem by many of his contemporaries, largely
for his dedication to precision measurement and the setting of standards. A
monument to Whitworth's achievements which has survived to this day is
his classification for screw threads. This has now become part of our
engineering vocabulary.

Joseph Whitworth (1803-1877)

A time of anxiety

In evidence to the Select Committee, Whitworth acknowledged that some days earlier he had listened to the opinions of James Nasmyth who had expressed the view that machine-made musket parts could be taken at random and fitted together without recourse to finishing by hand labour. While Whitworth agreed that the parts would probably fit, he suggested that this would be "badly". Here we have opposing views voiced by two prominent engineers, which is probably a microcosm of mid nineteenth-century engineering opinion as a whole, reflecting in a sense the doubts and fears of an industry which is about to undergo the painful transition from the old to the new technology. Also, it would seem reasonable to speculate that some of these anxieties would have trickled down to the shop floor causing concern amongst the workforce. After all, most would have heard of the recently established factory of Colonel Colt in London and the sometimes exaggerated claims made for his American method of automated pistol production and the use of unskilled labour. It is also conceivable that further claims for the coming revolution in machine tool use would have been reinforced by the Great Exhibition of 1851 where American technology and products were on display for all to see. So it is probably fair to assume that artisans and small gun makers were concerned that traditional skills were under threat.

Gun trade unease in Britain

Research has shown that for many years the private gun trade had been highly suspicious of Ordnance, a powerful department of government, suspecting that it was secretively planning the expansion of the Enfield factory to take control of military small arms production. Therefore, it is not too difficult to understand the unwillingness of some time-served gunsmiths to believe that machines could replace skilled labour. Perhaps in their hearts they knew it, but were reluctant to openly admit it, hoping that they could convince Ordnance and others that their skills were still needed. It is also possible that those in the traditional gun trade may have been overcome by an early form of "techno-fear" which would eventually manifest itself to twentieth-century workers at the introduction of Computer Numeric Control (CNC) machines. Here computer programmable machinery has removed the job of the machine setter and shown improved machine setting consistency. This translates into improved levels of component accuracy which relates to greater levels of productivity.

While this later CNC technology has taken away many machining operator skills it has, on the other hand, brought in new skilled jobs like software programme designing and machine operator programmer.

A belief in skill

Whitworth had stated that when he made a new machine or tool by machine methods, it was always necessary to perfect it afterwards by hand labour. When asked by the Committee why he used this means of manufacture, he explained, "Because wherever we want great perfection of parts we must do it by hand labour; there cannot be a more striking instance of that than what I have mentioned to-day".[13] Questioned about his visit to the Springfield Armoury in 1853, Whitworth was asked whether he had seen men working by hand as well as by machine, to which he replied, "yes". However, he was unable to say what type of workmen he had observed, but nevertheless expressed the view that he thought they were a "high class of labour". He further confirmed that he had not seen one boy employed. Later, when describing the workmen who were attending the machines at Springfield, he suggested that he was unable to tell if they were mechanics, but stated that "...they were men of great intelligence". [14]

Differences of finish

From Whitworth's evidence it is clear that by the middle of the nineteenth century machine tools had still not reached the pinnacle of their development. This supports the proposition that satisfactory standards of product quality could not be achieved without further refinement or finishing by hand. On a cautionary note, it is possible that the researcher, when referring to the many documentary references of finish, if not careful, might confuse this as meaning the hand filing of parts to mechanically fit the gauge after coming off the machine. In this respect, and on a number of occasions, both Whitworth and other witnesses (during Select Committee questioning) are alluding to the surface finish of a weapon or part. That is to say, its aesthetic appearance and not the fit. This particular aspect I have already researched in some depth and have been able to show that the one time Ordnance Inspector of Small Arms, George Lovell's rigid insistence upon maintaining high standards of finish on product and parts, caused considerable problems for the private gun trade. In fact it is this insistence to produce almost sporting gun finishes on military grade weapons which helps to explain the difference in the arms procurement philosophy between the British Board of Ordnance and their American counterparts. From the evidence it would appear that British Ordnance had adopted a policy which meant not only had the arm to match the pattern, but it had to look good as well. On the other hand, American national armouries favoured a more practical approach, showing concern for how the arm functioned, not to how it looked. This view is supported by the testimony of Colonel Samuel Colt, when he stated that he could get an extra £1 for one of his engraved pistols, suggesting that the British "... pay often more for pretty than for useful articles". [15]

Nasmyth voiced very strong views to the Committee on finish, as he believed it destroyed the character of the work. He explained that:

> It is like taking a fine carving, and rubbing it down with sand-paper till the sharpness and precision and truth are gone. Even Colonel Colt's manufacture, (sic) after he had attained remarkable precision in the parts, in order to meet the views of the public as to burnish, gloss, shine, and sparkle, they were obliged to be set up to be worked with emery-paper, so that all the beautiful sharp corners that a mechanic would admire were rubbed away and rounded. In fact, the work attained the maximum of perfection up to a certain point, and beyond that, by applying the finish, it began to deteriorate very decidedly. [16]

Tell-tale physical clues

Ironically the quest for niceties of finish to make the arm look good, as objected to by Nasmyth, can often mask important evidence when examining early artefacts for clues of how they were manufactured. The use of emery-paper and polishing wheels to improve surface finish can often remove tool marks in the process, and in some instances that is precisely what they were designed to do. Tool marks on the work-piece can provide important indicators to the scientific historian when studying such factors as the continuing use of hand tools after the introduction of machine-intensive production methods. Fortunately, from the physical evidence available, nineteenth-century engineers did not find it necessary to make the internal parts of the gun lock mechanism as aesthetically pleasing as those on the outside by removing all the machine tool abrasions. This has left a considerable wealth of pictorial data for examination and interpretation allowing scientific historians like Robert Gordon to challenge the conclusions of Fecelia Deyrup that "the development of machine tools was clearly recognised at the time as a factor of major importance in the reduction of skill". Through Gordon's findings it is possible to challenge the views of David Hounshell when he suggests that well before the middle of the nineteenth century "virtually all the fabrication of the musket (except barrel welding) was carried out by machines...".[17]

By referring to Gordon's detailed laboratory studies of different sets of tool markings found on lock parts taken from the Springfield Armoury, it is learned that "tumblers made through the 1870s and 1880s,... are always found to have edges that have been filed".[18] Therefore the evidence gained from the physical examination of artefacts by Gordon, in contrast to the largely documentary evidence of Deyrup and Hounshell, suggest that manual skills did not completely disappear with the introduction of machine tools, but stayed alongside them for much longer than had earlier been suspected. These findings would seem to confirm the views of Whitworth in 1854 (discussed above), when he agreed that parts made by machine would fit, but probably "badly". From Gordon's findings we know that hand finishing of lock parts in the United States lasted for approximately twenty years after the American machine tools were installed at Enfield Lock. While the Enfield machine tools were the latest to be manufactured they still had to go through many years of development and refinement before consistently tight levels of precision could be achieved. Apart from machine operators and setters having to learn new tricks of the trade, through on the job experience, they had to take account of the improvements in cutting tool materials that were evolving along with the product.

Given this background, it should be remembered that the lock of a muzzle loader, which is activated by the trigger, is the only moving mechanism on the gun. Therefore until machine tools reached a standard of repeatable precision, there would be a requirement to finely adjust the tumbler and sear of the lock by skilful hand filing to achieve a correctly weighted trigger pull (typically 8lbs for an Enfield 1853 rifle).[19] This mechanism functions by having just the right sliding contact between the surfaces of the sear and tumbler. To achieve this, considerable skill and expertise was required. The sensitivity of this particular adjustment was necessary so that soldiers could be issued with weapons which not only had a similar feel, but could easily be exchanged, particularly in battle, without being vastly different to use. If the trigger pull was too heavy, this could affect the soldier's aim, and if the pull was too light, the weapon could be prematurely or accidentally discharged. These crucial factors would seem to lend support to the argument which suggests that the use of skilled hand finishing did not immediately diminish upon the introduction of machine tools, making Gordon's findings perfectly plausible. Until early machine tools had gone through several years of shop floor development, with operators and engineers learning by experience how to "fine-tune" product and machinery to reach closer tolerances, it would seem the logical rule rather than the exception that hand finishing continued until machines were perfected. These conclusions have been reached not by accepting all which has been written, but through interviewing and watching engineers and craftsmen who are currently in the gun trade, many practising the traditional skills.

Examining remaining hand skills

To ensure that the research carried out for this chapter assumed not only a documentary investigation but also a practical one, and to become more familiar with the level of skills which may have been possessed by early artisans, the author decided to seek interviews with prominent gun makers and visit their establishments. The purpose of adopting this approach was two-fold. Firstly, it was reasoned that certain skills amongst those craftsmen making the current range of sporting guns (fowling pieces) by hand would have probably changed little from those employed by nineteenth-century artisans. And secondly, the author wished to ensure that the chapter was more than just a desk-top exercise. However, all companies contacted were not always willing to cooperate in this investigation, some arguing they had insufficient time, while others said it was for the protection of trade secrets. Those who did collaborate have been able to provide sufficient information to allow a better understanding of their industry.

Skilled craftsmen grinding gun barrels and making judgements by eye and feel

One of the most interesting findings emanating from the research was to discover how many of the skills had survived from the nineteenth-century gun trade. In some cases these could be traced back to source through previous generations of craftsmen. Sadly only a handful of private gun makers are left, but like their predecessors they are often supported by small independent craftsmen working alone. Apprenticeships are still common within the larger companies and the selection of trainees appears to be on the basis of a bright and uncontaminated intellect rather than academic qualifications. This would seem to agree with Colonel Colt's philosophy of training unskilled people who had "good brains and little knowledge". To explain their training policy the Chief Executive of James Purdey & Sons wrote, "the Apprentice training time is 5 years in one particular skill, namely, Barrels, Actions, Ejectors, Stocking, Engraving and Finishing. When the boy has completed his course he stays with that particular skill all his working life, and his initials are placed on the part he makes for each particular gun".[20] This initialling of the part by the craftsman is reminiscent of the traceable system of marking which was operated by Ordnance under George Lovell, the Ordnance Inspector of Small Arms. The viewer would only stamp those parts which he considered good enough to pass inspection with his individual mark allowing the item to be traced if it subsequently failed.

A further example of a nineteenth-century practice finding its way into the twentieth century was that of skill transfer between the many metal-working industries. It is a commonly held belief that one of the main reasons why Birmingham became so successful in the manufacture of small arms was because skilled workers could be drawn from a range of allied industries which were traditionally located in the surrounding districts. In times of high weapon demand Birmingham was generally able to respond to the need more quickly, with men and material, than other districts of small arms manufacture in Britain. When discussing the events surrounding the American Civil War, John Goodman, a Midlands small arms manufacturer, refers to "... the wonderful elasticity of the Birmingham trade, when called upon to put out its full power...".[21] This "elasticity", to a certain extent helped prevent the complete loss of gun making skills to the trade by allowing artisans to seek employment locally in times of slackness in weapon production. In a similar

Apprentice training at the RSAF in 1947. For many years the RSAF training programmes had been the envy of the industry

way it was learned through an interview with the proprietor of Turner Richards, Gun makers that he had served time in the machine tool industry before setting up as an independent maker of sporting guns. Therefore it can be seen that once basic metal-working, or for that matter, wood-working skills had been thoroughly learned in one particular industry, it would have been less difficult to transfer to another branch of industry. However, it will be appreciated that this practice within the gun trade would mostly apply when skilled hand labour was still required. It would not have suited either Colt or Nasmyth who wished to hold down labour and other costs by employing people with "good brains and little knowledge".

When carrying out research within the independent gun trade it was interesting to discover that a network of mutual support existed between many present-day gunsmiths and a number of specialist out workers and restorers. It would appear that this unofficial "network" has evolved over many years with some of the participants having direct links back to the nineteenth century. Specific pieces of work often flow within this grouping between different establishments according to individual levels of skill and expertise. It was also found that gun companies with household names would often place work with individual craftsmen who in some instances had set up on their own after leaving or retiring from one of the larger firms. Although this practice is not the same as the nineteenth-century contract system which operated between Ordnance and the independent gun trade, one is however able to recognise certain similarities.[22] For instance, a firm using a skilled out-worker when needed would save on a regular salary and other job entitlements, effectively reducing the company's overhead costs. However, if there is too much reliance on individual out-workers there can come a time when those craftsmen eventually die and the company are unable to produce quality arms. With the larger prestigious company a balance has to be struck between apprentice training and out-worker use.

To further improve understanding and also to help determine if the introduction of machinery completely removed the necessity for skilled craftsman, the writer has been in communication with the Navy Arms Company in America. For a number of years this company has been involved in the manufacture of a replica Pattern 1853 Enfield rifle. This weapon is made to a pattern measured from an original set of Ordnance gauges. With a view to gaining information in relation to how lock parts were finished, particularly the tumbler and sear, the author posed the following question to the company, "did any of the piece parts require bringing to gauge by filing?" The company President responded with the following explanation; "Regarding the lock parts, if they fit in the gauge, they are totally interchangeable. Regarding the tumbler and sear on every gun this must be touched up by hand".[23] While we have little idea of all the methods that this company employs to manufacturer its weapons, the President did commit to writing that "The guns that we make have total interchangeability". Again, this evidence would seem to support the material findings of Gordon's study of artefacts which suggests that skills did not immediately disappear with the introduction of machine-intensive methods of manufacture. In the light of this modern-day evidence it would seem reasonable to conclude that, although hand skills had considerably diminished as machine tools developed and achieved tighter production tolerances, in the mid nineteenth-century hand finishing of lock parts actually complemented the introduction of machine tools and sustained them through their factory period of "on the job" development and refinement. At least this would seem to be the logical interpretation arising from the results of Gordon's investigation of tumblers taken from American weapons. However, the picture is not as clear when researching the mainly documentary evidence during a similar period at the Royal Small Arms Factory, Enfield.

Machine tool processes and skill

One of the most comprehensively documented accounts of the different machining processes involving the production of the Enfield pattern 1853 rifle was published in a series of six articles in "The Engineer" in 1859. Here the author has described in some detail the different manufacturing operations surrounding each part of the weapon. By studying this information (which is the best account we have of Enfield's production processes in engineering terms) it was hoped to discover how reliant (or not) the various operations were on skilled hand labour in bringing the part in question to gauge. Since Gordon had concentrated his investigations upon how the tumbler was manufactured it was therefore felt that a useful comparison could be made with his findings if research was focussed upon this particular part. As debated earlier, the tumbler along with the sear form a crucial part of the lock mechanism which experts suggest (even today) requires careful finishing by hand. In the article the manufacture of the tumbler is described thus:

> The first process is to place the rough tumbler in a carrier and cause it to revolve between two stationary cutter-blocks; by this means the spindles are rounded, and the plate is thickened down and made perfectly square with its uprights; the spindles are the more accurately finished in another machine. After this it is requisite to take another slight cut off the upper side of the plate, so as to form a friction boss; this effected by another hollow-cutting spindle, which leaves the required boss. Then the spindle's points are cut to their exact length, and after this the swivel hole is drilled;...Having now two points by which the tumbler can now be secured in position, that is to say the pivot and swivel hole, it is by this means fixed upon a plate, and the outside edge is shaped by a system of forms and circular cutters; to effect this it is fixed in four separate machines. When this is done, the hole for the screw is made in the large end of the spindle, and this is tapped to receive the screw for holding on the hammer; then the end of the pivot is rounded with a small concave cutter-block, similar to that used in No. 3, and the slot formed in the side of the plate to receive the swivel, by means of a thin cutting plate milled on the edge; after this the bottom of the spindle or large pivot is squared by fixing the tumbler upright upon a moving plate, and feeding it between two revolving cutters, which form two parallel sides; and then by giving the plate a right-angle turn, and again passing the tumbler between the cutters, the other two sides are shaped and the end is squared. But to complete and perfect the work, the square is pressed into a die, which so compresses and draws the sides as to make the square fit the hole in the hammer perfectly. Its edge is then completed in the copying machine. It will be seen by this description, that the tumbler, in its act of manufacture, passes through fourteen different processes.[24]

The opportunity has been taken to reproduce the complete description of the manufacture of the tumbler and as the reader will see there is no mention whatsoever with regard to hand finishing. Of course it could be argued that the author omitted to mention that hand finishing had taken place. This could have been deliberate as the operation was considered of little consequence,

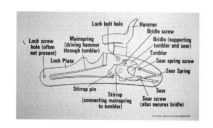

A drawing of the Enfield pattern 1853 lock, naming the various parts

or perhaps it was just an oversight. However, these two arguments on balance can probably be discounted, as immediately below the description of manufacturing the tumbler there is an account of how the sear is produced. After describing the machining operations for this component the author states quite clearly, although unfortunately not in detail, "... after this process the sear is finished by hand".[25] Also there are other references in the article to hand finishing, for example the main spring, which "is filed to gauge". The sight spring, which is "filed", the little sear spring, "filed to gauge", the ramrod groove, "touched up with file", the upper band spring, "filed, polished, blued", and the trigger, which is "filed and polished".[26]

There is only one other reference in the 1859 article to hand finishing. This refers to the production of the stock when it states, "... a slight friction with a piece of glass paper, placed upon a cork rubber, is all that is required, after the machine is complete, to leave a surface so smooth that nothing more requires to be done to them before they are handed over to the assembler".[27]

Out of a total of 719 manufacturing processes these are the only eight references in the article to hand finishing. However, it is possible that the author, concentrating specifically upon the various machining actions, deliberately did not report the component parts of the lock being assembled and tested as a sub-assembly. Although there has not yet been any documentary discoveries to say precisely how this operation was done it is suspected that any adjustment of the tumbler and sear could only be achieved (to give the required trigger pull) after the lock had been assembled and the necessary inspection weight attached to the trigger. If it was then found that the trigger pull was out of specification it would require an experienced and skilful filer to make the adjustment. Obviously the lock would have to be dismantled for this to take place.

Looking for further evidence of hand finishing in later publications has not provided an overwhelming amount of evidence on the subject. In 1861 an article was published in *The Mechanic's Magazine* on Enfield manufacturing processes, after a factory visit by the article's author. It would seem that the writer had been suitably impressed with the production of lock parts as he reported, "The lock plate leaves this tool in such a state as to require no hand touching, save engraving...". Directly after this account the following passage is written, "The various parts of the lock, such as the tumbler, the sear, the sear spring, swivel, bridle, and mainspring, are all forged and finished by machines fitted with steel cutters or "mills" and most of them arranged on the copying plan, which begets uniformity of size and shape".[28] Unfortunately there is no further evidence to provide clues of how the tumbler and sear may have been adjusted. There are just two references in the article to slight hand finishing, one refers to the stock and mentions "... a little touching with glass paper...", and the other relates to the back sight fitting, "... after a little touching with a smooth file...".[29] However the author comes tantalizingly close to identifying artisan skills when he reports:

> Much skill has been displayed in the performance of the various little operations necessary to the finishing of the trigger-plate, and to Mr Hague, of the furniture [mechanical accoutrements for the stock] department, just credit is given for it. It would be quite impossible, however, in the limits of the present paper, to particularize the minute points in which mechanical ability has been displayed.[30]

Interestingly, in an article published in *Engineering* in August 1886, and written after a visit by members of the Institute of Mechanical Engineers to the Enfield factory, the author, when discussing the manufacturing processes of a later weapon states, "Out of all these there are only four hand processes, the rest all being done by machine tools".[31] Unfortunately we are not told the total number of processes the weapon was subjected to, or whether hand finishing of the lock parts had been included. However, it would appear from the information gleaned, that almost 27 years since the 1859 article, the number of hand skill operations applied to a weapon at Enfield, although minimal, had hardly altered. Until such times as the discovery of more detailed documentary evidence, or a careful examination of the Enfield pattern 1853 lock parts can be carried out, particularly an analysis of the tumbler, (to compare with Robert Gordon's work) one cannot be completely certain that hand finishing at Enfield complemented for a time the introduction of machine tools as it seems to have done in America (see following section for more information). If it is confirmed that the writers of the above articles reported accurately what they had seen in the manufacture of the tumbler, that is to say no hand finishing, this would suggest that the parts coming off the American machine tools installed at Enfield, were more accurate than from those machine tools in the United States. However, it must be remembered that there is no evidence within the three articles to suggest that authors witnessed assembly and inspection of the lock mechanism. If they had, and were able to describe the operation correctly, then we would have a better understanding of machine accuracies in Britain at the time. From this information, the level of skilled hand finishing could have been assessed.

Gordon was able to study twenty American tumblers. Thirteen of these were manufactured between 1844 and 1855.[32] Therefore it can be deduced that the machine tools which produced these components were themselves manufactured earlier than those installed between 1855 and 1856 at Enfield. This being the case, one would expect these later machines to be more refined and therefore more accurate than their earlier American counterparts.

If future research is able to confirm these points, it could show that hand finishing skills in American arsenals like Springfield, were more intensive and perhaps lingered longer than they did at Enfield after the introduction of the later model machine tools.

A physical examination of the Enfield pattern 1853 tumbler

Gordon's research into the manufacture of tumblers has enabled him to determine that the introduction of machines with formed cutters (for milling the sides and edges of parts), at the Springfield National Armoury, date from 1841. This might lead one to conclude that having the ability to mill profiles would have significantly reduced the work of the filer. However, by examining tables relating to the labour content in a Springfield rifle musket of 1864, Gordon claims that "eighteen operations and seven types of power-driven machinery were used in making a tumbler, but one operation, hand filing by "... first class mechanics," accounts for more than half of the man-hours required".[33] It will be recalled that the author of the 1859 article in *The Engineer* reported fourteen operations in making the Pattern 1853 tumbler. This particular part being similar in both dimension and profile to the Springfield version described by Gordon. Given Gordon's thorough investigation of nineteenth-century American machining accuracies and the lingering use of hand skills it was decided to approach the Custodian of the Enfield small arms collection housed in the Ministry of Defence (MoD)

Pattern Room then located at Nottingham, to see if permission could be obtained to examine similar pattern tumblers from British weapons. It was reasoned that if the necessary authorisation could be obtained, the results of the study, although not having the laboratory treatment of Gordon's work, would nevertheless provide the basis for an objective comparison with the evidence he had produced. The prospect of such an exercise presented a unique opportunity to discover if similarities could be detected of hand filing in British machined specimens. From the results of the findings it was hoped to discover information that would improve our understanding of attainable machine accuracies and the level of interchangeability. As the artefact collection within the MoD Pattern Room is unique and a request for such a detailed examination had never been made before, the writer was fortunate in gaining permission to inspect a representative sample of three tumblers, the Custodian selecting them from three Enfield pattern 1853 rifles dated 1853, 1856, and 1869. The choice of these dates was quite deliberate to ensure that the samples represented different periods of manufacture; before, at the beginning, and several years after the introduction of the American machinery at Enfield Lock. While it is appreciated the quantity of tumblers examined was particularly small, one is mindful of the fact that the researcher is dealing with irreplaceable artefacts removed from a priceless and unique weapons collection. Although every care was taken by the Custodian to select samples of tumblers from weapons that were clearly dated, it would be impossible to know if these parts were original, and had not been replaced during the weapon's lifetime by an armourer. It is also probable that in Gordon's experiments he was unable to be absolutely sure that the tumblers which he examined were definitely the originals fitted when the weapon was first manufactured. There is nothing in his report to suggest otherwise.[34] In such circumstances, one can only trust the experience and the instincts of the experts to provide the required parts.

Subjectively examining and comparing the three tumblers, even the untrained eye could detect the finish of the 1853 sample was considerably cruder than the 1856 and 1869 versions. On the 1853 sample the flats of the arbour when placed against a straight edge and held up to the light revealed the four surfaces to be untrue. This was not the case on the two later samples where it was found the flats did not deviate from truth. The coarseness of tool marks and the irregularity of shape on the early sample, these being clearly visible when viewed through an optical microscope, suggest that there had been a significant decrease in the amount of hand filing on the two later specimens. This would support the view that the introduction of machinery had improved the mechanical accuracy of the tumbler, lessening the amount of handwork required to bring the part to gauge. If this were the case, then it could mean only the most skilful filers were retained to complete the smaller amount of work and therefore one cannot conclude (as Gordon was able to) from this relatively small sample that the skill of certain artisans increased with the introduction of machine tools.

The three samples were independently examined by a retired RSAF tool-maker who had worked at Enfield Lock for 34 years, completing his service as tool room foreman, making him a highly skilled man. He concluded that (with the exception of the 1853 arbour) each tumbler had been brought to size mainly by machining, although it was observed every sample exhibited evidence of hand filing. The "bents" (referred to by Gordon as notches) on all samples appeared to have been milled and hand filed. It could not be conclusively ascertained, even after examining the samples under magnification, whether the bents had been filed to meet the gauge. Neither could it be ascertained if they were filed to standardise the trigger pull with the friction surface of the sear or neatly touched up to remove burrs. Having discussed all three possibilities with the retired tool-maker it was felt that as the machine tool marks had not been completely removed from the bents in all cases by the action of filing, it was the case that a small degree of manual adjustment had taken place.[35] In the case of the 1856 and 1869 tumblers the amount of filing observed would not appear to equate to Gordon's discoveries on samples manufactured at Springfield within the same period as having "more than half of the man-hours" attributed to hand filing. However, in spite of the small sample, the exercise, if taken cautiously, suggests two things; firstly, the finished quality of Enfield tumblers improved dramatically with the introduction of the American machinery and secondly that hand finishing continued to at least 1869.

As the American machines shipped to Enfield were made to order specifically to accommodate the pattern 1853 rifle they would have been the most up-to-date, incorporating the latest modifications. Therefore this might suggest that they were capable of bringing the parts of the weapon to greater perfection than the machines employed at Springfield. These we know from Gordon's findings had been constructed and installed some years earlier. This could have accounted for the suggestion of reduced hand work on the Enfield samples when compared to the information supplied by Gordon. However, a more comprehensive and detailed study of a greater cross-section of tumblers would be required before this evidence can be taken as conclusive.

Discussing the question of skill with a number of time-served RSAF engineers it became evident that there was a collective understanding within the workforce that certain groups of workers were considered more skilful than others. First came the gauge-makers followed by the tool-makers. These two groups stood out from the rest. It was considered at least by their twentieth-century peers that the expertise of those workmen who had hand filed the bents, although skilful, would be classified as semi-skilled today. This opinion of skill as viewed from the artisans' perspective may shed some light on the views of engineers like Nasmyth who believed that any intelligent man provided that he was "well selected" could even be taken from the "plough-tail" and trained within twelve months for most of the general engineering functions within a machine shop. However, he did concede that it would require some "guiding men to initiate them".[36]

An exercise with gauges

Due to the possible risk of damage to artefacts from the MoD Pattern Room collection which might have occurred when stripping down an antique Pattern 1853 lock mechanism to its individual component parts, it was decided to look for an alternative method of testing measurement by gauge. Fortunately the author was able to acquire a machine-made pattern 1853 lock mechanism from a Birmingham Small Arms Company (BSA) Snider rifle manufactured in 1875. This lock, after the liberal application of a freeing agent, was duly stripped down to its individual component parts by the resident MoD Pattern Room Weapon Conservator. From the difficulty encountered in dismantling the lock it was concluded that the mechanism had not been taken apart for some considerable time. When the individual component parts were finally removed, they were soaked in a container of turpentine substitute and cleaned with a paint brush to remove what appeared to be hardened deposits of linseed oil. The parts were then subjected to ultrasonic cleaning in a heated

THE GREAT SKILLS DEBATE – BRITAIN VERSUS AMERICA!

bath to remove any remaining contamination before the gauging exercise took place. This latter process restored the surface "bluing" to areas of the metalwork.

The next part of the exercise was to borrow the boxed set of pattern 1853 gauges (manufactured in 1856) held in the MoD Pattern Room. Some of the gauges are designed to measure a component's dimensions by acceptance into an accurately defined aperture. These are known as receiver or acceptance gauges. All gauges thus constructed are of a single type, each having a sample component made accurately to size supplied with each device. This enables the operator to obtain a precise friction feel of how the component should slide in and out of the aperture. The plug type gauges (normally constructed in pairs) for judging the calibre accuracy of the rifle barrel, operate on a slightly different principle, that of a "go" and "no-go" basis. One plug is so dimensioned to pass closely down the barrel while the other is designed to be just over-size and unable to enter freely. If neither plug could enter the barrel the component would be classified as undersize but could be brought to size by further reaming. However, if both plugs could enter the barrel it would be clearly oversize and rejected, as metal could not be put back to make up the discrepancy.

In contrast, the lock receiver gauges worked by allowing the operator to finely judge the correct fit by eye and feel. By this method the part was either right or it was not. An oversize part could of course have the offending area "chalked" then adjusted to gauge by file. Of course an undersize component could drop into the aperture of the receiver gauge, but it would be quickly rejected by a skilled viewer who would note not only the friction feel of the part against the gauge wall, but judge the amount of peripheral gap by eye. Like the rifle barrel an undersize part could not have metal added. These findings would tend to support the notion that much of the " Ordnance inspection" in George Lovell's time relied very much on the preferences of the individual viewer which could therefore account for the private gun trade's accusations that different viewing standards were in operation between Enfield and Birmingham. In general it was alleged that the Birmingham viewing standards were stricter. A possible reason for this might have been because the Ordnance viewers in Birmingham were responsible for overseeing the private setters-up and only allowed parts through which were strictly to gauge. The Enfield Ordnance viewers, on the other hand, would be responsible for overseeing government employed workmen and, perhaps being closer to a factory environment, might have taken a slightly more practical approach. A clue to this possible anomaly might be gained from the evidence of the Birmingham leading gun lock maker Joseph Brazier (mentioned earlier) who had exhibited his work at the 1851 Exhibition for which he had won prizes. When appearing before the 1854 Select Committee, Brazier gave evidence that the viewers had rejecting his work because it had not met the gauge to a "hair's breadth".

Further gauge testing

Within the pattern 1853 gauge collection there were two types of receiving gauge for measuring different aspects of the lock plate mechanism. Both were equipped with sample lock plates. To test the interchangeability of these sample plates, one dated 1858, the other 1871, the items were swapped between the two gauges and judged to fit equally well in either position. The lock plate from the sample 1875 BSA Snider lock was then tried and found not to fit either gauge, the item being oversize. Research has shown that after the installation of the "American system" at Enfield, Ordnance imposed standards upon the private gun trade of only accepting parts that fully interchanged. John Goodman, the Chairman of BSA, when writing of the company in 1865, stated "In this factory the interchangeable system is carried out in full integrity. The machinery is of the highest class, containing all the improvements which a longer experience has suggested. Every assistance has been rendered by the War Department of her Majesty's Government. Models and gauges have been obtained from Enfield, and full permission granted to inspect that establishment whenever information was required".[37]

This therefore begs the question, how could BSA, who we know from Goodman's report were operating by the mid 1860s a similar production system to Enfield and using Ordnance manufactured patterns and gauges, produce a part which would not interchange?

While it is recognised that it not possible to judge a complete manufacturing system on the evidence gained from only one sample lock, the fact that the BSA lock plate was oversize would have meant that the aperture in the stock would have needed to have been larger than the Enfield pattern to accept the mechanism, making the stock incompatible too. However, based on such a small sample it would be unwise to speculate why by the mid 1870s, some two decades after the "American system" came to Enfield, and spread elsewhere, standards of interchangeability had not remained compatible between companies which were seemingly working to the same levels of specification. Nevertheless, it will be seen from the following account of the measurement exercise that other parts of the lock did in fact fit the gauge quite precisely. Continuing the exercise, further parts of the BSA lock were checked against the Enfield gauges. The double ended screw gauge turned in all four holes of the lock plate freely, but the gauge for measuring the distance between the lock plate hammer hole and the main spring pin locating hole showed the BSA lock to be out of tolerance, the hole centres being too far apart. When testing the lock saddle, this part fitted the gauge profile perfectly and the screw holes aligned correctly with the gauge pins. However, when the saddle diameter was tested through the gauge dimension gap it jammed half way through. Interestingly this was not because the part was faulty or oversize, but due to the indentations in the metal caused by the viewers pass mark which is customarily stamped on the piece after gauging to indicate acceptance.

It will be remembered that the action of stamping had raised the surface of the metal in one small area causing the piece not to pass through the gauge. This observation raises an interesting issue which might help clarify the difficulties experienced by the private gun trade when trying to resolve disputes with Ordnance over standards of acceptability. If the whole of the saddle face had been raised to the level caused by the stamp, which the author estimated to be not much more than one thousandth of an inch, the part would have been rejected for failing the gauge test. As the marked surface of the saddle when assembled into the lock is in "free air" and does not constitute a functional problem, it could have accounted for the point Brazier made when giving evidence before the Select Committee of 1854 regarding the inspection of locks, when he suggested "... it ought not to be viewed to a hair's breadth".[38]

Much of the interpretation of how the gauges were used has been accomplished by the author working practically with the artefacts and discussing the results of the experiments with the MoD Pattern Room Weapon Conservator. Unfortunately, by the deficiency of writing on the subject, it has not been possible to established if feeler gauges were used to judge if a part could have a certain tolerance pass when placed in a receiver gauge. Further work in this area is beyond the scope of this book but an in-depth investigation could prove an interesting exercise for a future researcher and provide more information on the use of nineteenth-century gauges for mechanical measurement and inspection generally. However, the exercise has highlighted a number of important issues. Firstly, it is not always necessary for a part to conform in every detail to the gauge to be interchangeable, as has been proved by the measurement of the saddle. Secondly, it may be necessary in future to qualify what is meant by the term interchangeability. For example, some writers have given the impression that this means the parts are produced so accurately that they can come directly from a machine, or group of machines, without requiring further adjustment by hand. From parts so made it is suggested that it is possible to place them in a box from which they can be taken at random for easy assembly. However, it would appear that in the case of the gun lock assembly, hand adjustment was necessary to ensure the trigger pull was correctly weighted. This does not detract from the overall concept of interchangeability but suggests there were slight differences between individual weapons. It should not be forgotten that over a period of time machinery wears and the cutting tool will require sharpening. If these aspects are not quickly detected by the operator during the production process it is possible to amass a large number of incorrectly sized parts. In the reality of manufacturing it is quite likely that these parts could be salvaged by hand finishing, providing the exercise is cost effective. Again this example would suggest that there is a need to define what is meant by interchangeability. Thirdly, it can be seen that care must be taken when arguing that the introduction of machine tools increased the work of skilled filers. In such circumstances, allowances must be made for the age and modernity of the machinery.

In conclusion

From the evidence produced in this chapter it shall be left for the reader to decide whether the introduction of component interchangeability into the manufacture of small arms produced a different outcome for the hand skills of artisans in Britain to their counterparts in America or whether on balance there was little to choose.

REFERENCES

1. Robert B. Gordon, "Who Turned the Mechanical Ideal into Mechanical Reality?", *Technology & Culture, Vol.29, No.4* (October 1988), p.766
2. House of Lords Record Office, London. "Examination of Mr J. Nasmyth, 17th March 1854", *Select Committee on Small Arms. Reports Committee's Vol. XVIII-1854*, p.113
3. Ibid. p.113
4. Ibid. p.118
5. Ibid. Colonel Colt, pp.89-91
6. Ibid. James Nasmyth, p.113
7. Ibid. Gage Stickley, p.421
8. Ibid. James Nasmyth, p.116
9. Ibid. Colonel Colt, p.85

10. Ibid Gage Stickney, p.421

11. L. W. N. Nickols, "The Measurement of Length", *The Charted Mechanical Engineer* (July 1964), p.390

12. House of Lords Record Office, London. "Examination of Mr R. Prosser, 21st March 1854", *Select Committee on Small Arms. Reports Committee's Vol. XVIII-1854*, p.178

13. Ibid. Mr J. Whitworth, p.146

14. Ibid. p.146

15. Ibid. Colonel Colt, p.92

16. Ibid. Mr J. Nasmyth, p.112

17. Robert B. Gordon, "Material Evidence of the Manufacturing Methods Used in Armory Practice", *The Journal of the Society of Industrial Archaeology, Vol. 14, No. 1* (1988), p.23

Gordon discusses on page 31 an examination of a Tower musket tumbler manufactured in England in 1862 and shows pictorial evidence of "relatively coarse file work", suggesting that the quality of handwork, "is of a lower standard than that carried on at any of the American armories (sic) studied here". This is not really surprising, as the Tower mark was placed upon many rifles and muskets that were made by a number of general arms contractors. In 1862, the only factory in England capable of manufacturing rifles or muskets by mainly machine methods would have been Enfield, which stamped the lock plate with its name. The BSA Company in Birmingham, although founded in 1861 did not start producing small arms by mechanical means until 1865, even then, as suggested by Roger Lumley, the factory initially used a mixture of hand labour and machine methods. For further reading see, Roger Lumley, "The American System of Manufactures in Birmingham: Production Methods at the Birmingham Small Arms Co. in the Nineteenth Century", *Business History, Vol. 31* (1989), pp.30-43. However Gordon does acknowledge that the tumbler was not manufactured at Enfield. He also goes on to explain that there is, "no evidence of hollow milling on the sides". This further confirms manufacture by a general contractor who at the time would still have been using mainly hand methods of production.

18. Ibid. p.31

19. *The Engineer*, June 17, 1859, "The Royal Small-Arm Factory Enfield", p.423. It should be noted that the diagram of the Enfield pattern 1853 lock contained under Fig.2a on page 204 on the March 25th edition of this journal is incorrectly shown as a mirror image.

20. Letter in possession of author from Hon. Richard Beaumont (Chairman), James Purdey & Sons Ltd, London (20th December 1993)

21. John D. Goodman, "The Birmingham Gun Trade", *Industrial History of Birmingham and the Midland Hardware District, A Series of Reports,* Timmins Ed., Published by Robert Hardwick (London 1866), p.418

22. Interview with Robert E. Turner, proprietor of Turner Richards Gun makers, Bromsgrove, Worcestershire, 13th January, 1994. Coincidentally Mr Turner had used lathes which had been manufactured in the nineteenth century. In a way this might be viewed as partially bridging the skill and technology gap between the two epochs.

23. Letter in possession of author from Val J. Forgett, President & CEO, Navy Arms Company, Inc., Ridgefield, New Jersey, United States of America (March 16th 1994)

24. "The Royal Small-Arm Factory Enfield", *The Engineer* (3rd June 1859), p.385

25. Ibid. p.385

26. Ibid. p.385. Also see, "The Royal Small Arm Factory Enfield", *The Engineer* (17th June, 1859), p.422

27. "Leviathan Workshops. No.11. The Enfield Small Arms Factory", *The Mechanic's Magazine* (6th September 1861), p.144

28. Ibid. p.111 & p.127

29. Ibid. p.144

30. "The Royal Small-Arm Factory Enfield", *The Engineer* (29th April 1859), p.295

31. "The Royal Small Arms Factory Enfield", *Engineering* (27th August 1886), p.218

32. Robert B. Gordon, "Who Turned The Mechanical Ideal into Mechanical Reality?", *Technology & Culture, Vol.29, No.4* (October 1988), p.761

33. Ibid. pp.752-3

34. Ibid. pp.754

35. Interview with Ken Robinson, retired tool room foreman at RSAF Enfield Lock (1995)

36. Op.cit. Nasmyth, p.118

37. J. D. Goodman, "The Birmingham Gun Trade", in S. Timmins, (ed.), *Birmingham and the Midland Hardware District: A series of reports*, Robert Hardwick, (London 1866) pp.403

38. House of Lords Record Office, London. "Report from the Select Committee on Small Arms, 24th March 1854", evidence of Joseph Brazier, p.251

Note.
The Ministry of Defence Pattern Room moved to the Enfield Building at the Royal Ordnance Factory, Nottingham after the closure of the RSAF Enfield Lock site in 1987. The Pattern Room Curator, the late Herbert Woodend MBE, moved with his beloved world-famous weapon collection to the new address. In 2001 the Royal Ordnance Factory, Nottingham closed and the Pattern Room collection transferred to the site of the Royal Armouries at Leeds.

PART TWO

6. FROM THE CRIMEAN WAR TO THE GREAT WAR

Once the American machine tools had been installed at Enfield, there was a dramatic increase in small arms production. This is the first example of a British factory using mass production techniques, as defined by the manufacture of standardised machine-made parts that interchanged completely, rather than those which are made to fit on an individual basis, usually by hand finishing.

Officers and men relaxing at the Crimea

The new system of manufacture was so successful that by year ending 30th June 1860, as we have seen earlier, the output of rifles alone had increased to 90,707, an average of 1,744 per week, later to go up to 1,900. By the year 1861 1,700 men were employed at the armoury and it is recorded that the large machine room (currently part of the Grade II listed building with the clock tower) was driven by two 40 horse power steam engines with Fairbairn expansion gear, while in the barrel mill a 70 horse power steam engine was employed along with the existing water wheels.

The private gun trade had yet to respond to the challenge of producing military weapons with standardised and interchangeable parts by the extensive use of machine tools. In later years, and forced by government contracts that specified only interchangeable parts to be supplied, the Birmingham gun manufacturers banded together to form the Birmingham Small Arms Company (BSA) which went on to become a famous arms producer in its own right.

However, the purchase of mass production machinery from America, which had been specifically ordered to supply the troops at the Crimea (1853-1856) with large quantities of the Enfield pattern 1853 rifle, had failed miserably in its intention. By the time the armoury had got into production the war in the Crimea was over. The reader will no doubt recall that when the Enfield Lock armoury was first set up in 1816 under a government initiative to provide arms to fight Napoleon, the Napoleonic wars had ended the year before. These incidences, which were set over forty years apart, demonstrate how successive governments seem to learn little from past experience.

The period to the turn of the century

While the Enfield Lock armoury missed the opportunity to supply the troops at the Crimea there was a very large quantity of rifles produced by the private contractors in support of the conflict. Soon the number of the Enfield pattern 1853 in circulation reached in excess of 800,000 weapons. Having so many rifles in circulation presented the War Office (which in 1856 had taken over the responsibility of weapon procurement from the Board of Ordnance) with a major financial headache and ways would need to be found to recover some of the costs associated with this over production.

By what would seem to be a fortunate quirk of history the British Government appears to have benefited from another conflict which ironically took place in the country that had just supplied Enfield Lock with its new mass production machine tools!

In 1861, after the Southern States in America had refused to abolish the system of slavery, the American Civil War began. This gave the British Government the opportunity to off-load large quantities of the Enfield pattern 1853 to the armies of both north and south as the conflict took hold.

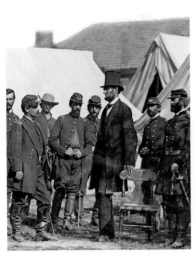

Abraham Lincoln posing with soldiers of the Northern Army

African American soldiers of the Northern Army during the American Civil War

American soldiers with the Enfield designed M1917 rifle

Enfield pattern 1853. These weapons were sold to the armies of the north and south

By the time Enfield Lock finally got into production with the Enfield pattern 1853, it had become patently obvious that Ordnance were now producing large quantities of what was essentially an outdated weapon. However, lady luck seems to have smiled once more on the Enfield armoury.

For some years muzzle loading weapons like the Enfield pattern 1853 had been losing favour with many armies around the world as the breech loading rifle was gaining popularity for its ease of loading and also for its superior rapidity of fire-power.

The Lee Enfield Rifle begins its long-term development

As we have already learned, the Pattern 1853, a muzzle loader, first saw service with the British Army at the Crimea but did not go into full-scale production at Enfield Lock until January 1857, almost a year after the war had ended. Muzzle loaders had distinct disadvantages for the soldier as in the heat of battle the ball and charge had to be rammed down the barrel with a rod (ramrod). This meant it was usual for the soldier to stand upright to accomplish the task, presenting the enemy with a relatively simple target.

With muzzle loading becoming old technology as the method of breech loading increased in popularity, it became clear that something needed to be done with the substantial stocks of the Enfield pattern 1853 held by the British Army. Rather than go through the costly and long-winded process of scrapping all the weapons and re-tooling the armoury for a new design, it made economic sense to have them converted to the new breech loading system.

In August 1864, following the recommendations of the Committee on Breech Loading Arms, the War Office placed an advertisement inviting gun makers and inventors, by open competition, to submit plans to convert the Enfield pattern 1853 from a muzzle loader to a breech loader, calling for two main criteria to be met. Firstly, the cost was "not to exceed £1 per arm" and secondly it was a requirement that "the shooting of the converted arm [should] not be inferior to the Enfield rifle" (un-modified muzzle loader). On completion of the modifications the weapons were to be assessed for accuracy, penetration, initial velocity, recoil, rapidity of fire, liability to failure, simplicity of management, fouling and exposure to weather.

The advertisement attracted 50 different applicants for the work, which after careful examination were whittled down to the eight most promising candidates. Over the coming months extensive trials were carried out where more than 5,500 rounds were fired with only one misfire. This not only gave the Committee faith in the breech loading system, but also the confidence to recommend the Snider method of conversion.

Apart from the improved way of loading, the Snider had also been designed to accept the revolutionary rolled brass cartridge developed by Colonel Boxer at Woolwich. Now it was possible for the soldier to load his weapon with comparative ease and safety, while lying prone on the ground.

Over the years, the improved weapon was to go through a long evolutionary process of development when different inventors' systems were tried (Martini-Henry, Enfield-Martini, Lee-Burton, Lee-Metford, to name but a few) and the best features of these weapons were incorporated. However, great emphasis was placed by the War Office upon having a design which would always function reliably under the severest of battlefield conditions (exposure to weather and mud). In 1895 the forerunner of the weapon which was to serve the Allied Forces throughout two World Wars and beyond emerged. This was the highly acclaimed Lee Enfield magazine rifle Mk I. But how did the name Lee become associated with the weapon? It had nothing whatsoever to do with the name of the waterway that flowed through and powered machinery at the Enfield Lock armoury as some commentators have wrongly suggested.

James Paris Lee was born in Hawick, Scotland in August 1831. In 1836 his family emigrated to Canada where he grew up and developed an interest in

Enfield pattern 1853 converted to a Snider breech loader

The Enfield-Snider breech loader was used extensively by British troops

Bullet used in Snider breech loader designed by Colonel Boxer

James Paris Lee seated, and brother John. James was responsible for the design of the Lee Enfield rifle's magazine and bolt action

Boer marksmen with Mauser rifles

firearms. After serving an apprenticeship in his father's clock and watch-making business he moved to Ontario where he set up on his own account in 1850. While there he married Caroline Chrysler (an early relative of the now famous car manufacturer). In 1860, with the addition of two sons, Lee moved with his family to Wisconsin in America. Here he experimented with a range of his own and some standard weapons, converting the famous Springfield muzzle loader to a breech loading system in 1861.

Lee persevered with his obsession of creating a repeating weapon and after years of experimentation and carrying out work for two of America's famous weapons companies, Sharp and Remington, his ideas for a bolt action magazine rifle were taken up by the British War Office. Manufacture of the now famous Lee Enfield rifle commenced in its Mk I format at the Royal Small Arms Factory, Enfield Lock in 1895.

The Great War 1914 – 1918

At the time of the Great War the Enfield Lock armoury had been established almost 100 years and during this time the factory had remained in State control. It would seem likely that during this period the government bureaucrats may have learned some very important lessons.

By the turn of the twentieth century, and probably provoked by the success of the German designed Mauser rifle which the Boer marksmen had used to good effect against the British troops during the Anglo-Boer Wars, Enfield began to develop a range of small arms that were more efficient and accurate than their predecessors. This technological leap was also helped by the introduction of new and improved materials. Accommodating these changes suggest that the organisation of the factory had improved and if this were the case it might further suggest that government had adopted a less intrusive role in the running of the factory.

As we have already seen, by 1895, after years of experiment with a range of different manufacturers' rifles, the Lee Enfield Mk I, which in its later guises was to become world famous, was born. In 1902 the short magazine, Lee Enfield (SMLE) bolt action Mk I (0.303 inch calibre) was introduced into service. Between the years 1905 and 1907 Enfield developed four Marks of the SMLE. The Mk III became the standard weapon adopted by the British Army and continued as the rifle of choice throughout the Great War. During the war the Enfield factory manufactured a staggering 2,007,119 rifles and bayonets and also produced large quantities of the Enfield Mk II (0.45 inch calibre) revolver.

Magazine Lee Enfield Mk I

It is interesting to note that by the outbreak of the Great War the RSAF at Enfield Lock had also designed a new rifle that fired a smaller high velocity round of 0.276 inch. However, with the production of the SMLE Mk III, Enfield lacked the capacity to manufacture a new rifle and it was also felt that a weapon of smaller calibre should not be introduced alongside the standard 0.303 in time of war as confusion over ammunition supply and use could occur. This is precisely what happened at the time of the Crimean War when at least three different calibres of weapon were issued to the British forces. Perhaps government and the military hierarchy had finally learned another important lesson!

The design for the new weapon, now known as the Pattern 1914, was adapted to the standard 0.303 inch round and sent to manufacturing companies in America where it was produced in the thousands. The Winchester factory produced 545, 511 rifles, the Remington factory 545,541 and the Eddystone factory a staggering 1,181, 908. However, due to slight differences between these manufacturers, presumably in the way machines were set up and also due to the fact that the Pattern 1914 was really a weapon in development rather than a drawing board design (fully dimensioned engineering drawings did not exist) meant that components between the three factories were not 100 per cent interchangeable.

Lee Enfield Mk III. These were the standard weapons of the Allied forces

The Winchester Repeating Arms Company that manufactured over 0.5 million Enfield designed rifles

Eddystone Rifle Works, where over one million Enfield designed pattern 1917 rifles were manufactured

The Remington Arms and Ammunition Company that produced over 0.5 million Enfield designed rifles

When the American army entered the Great War in April 1917 the Pattern 1914 was modified by the US Ordnance Department and chambered for the standard US 30-60 bullet, becoming known as Model 1917, sometimes called the M1917 Enfield. Production of the weapon was carried out by the same three manufacturers that produced the Pattern 1914. The scale of production was such that it overtook the quantities produced by the Springfield Armoury. Springfield was a supplier of the standard weapon to the American forces. By the end of the Great War it was estimated that around 75 per cent of American soldiers in Europe were equipped with the M1917, a figure which no doubt made the RSAF development engineers exceedingly proud of their achievements.

While the large number of weapons produced at Enfield during the Great War may at first seem surprising, considering the factory's past record under the Board of Ordnance, research in the 1990s by Professor Tim Putnam and Dr Dan Weinbren of Middlesex University suggest that by the start of hostilities things had dramatically changed at the factory. They wrote:

> Overtime working began immediately and crews for twelve hour day and night shifts were set up before the end of the month, to work from six to six. From 2nd September day shift men worked on Sundays from 7:30 to 5:30. Soon a thirteen day fortnight became compulsory. Factory Act constraints on the working time of boys were suspended until August 1916. Boys under 16 were restricted to a 60 hour week and others to 65 and boys working overtime excluded from night shift.

The Lewis light machine gun

In 1911 an American Army Colonel, Isaac Newton Lewis designed a light machine gun that became known as the Lewis gun. The weapon was adopted by the Allies and was manufactured under licence in Britain by the Birmingham Small Arms Company (BSA). It was also produced on the continent for the Belgian Army by manufacturers in Liège. Both the Belgian and British versions of the weapon were built to accept the standard 0.303 inch British round. There were two models of the Lewis gun, one with a magazine holding 47 rounds and an aircraft version with a 97 round magazine. The gun was a favourite with the Royal Flying Corps as it only weighed 12kg and was lighter than the Vickers machine gun. Also, the gun being air-cooled made it ideal as an aircraft weapon. Removing the gun's cooling jacket and fins when installing it in an aircraft reduced the overall weight of the weapon by a further 3kg.

To date no documentary material has come to light that suggests the RSAF were "manufacturing" Lewis guns during the period of the Great War but it would appear, from the photographic evidence, that they were certainly "assembling" the weapons in a building on the Enfield site. There are three different photographs of Lewis guns which all appear to have been taken around the same time in what seems to be an assembly shop at the Royal Small Arms Factory. Ray Tutill, a former engineer at the RSAF and President of the RSAF Apprentices Association has, after considerable detective work, identified the assembly shop as a building that once stood at the north end of the Enfield factory site. We also have evidence that the Lewis guns in question are aircraft versions. They were identified as such by the late Herbert Woodend MBE (Bert or Herbie to his friends) an internationally acknowledged weapons expert who was once in charge of both the Enfield and Nottingham Pattern Rooms. Bert has written the details and added his signature to the back of one of the photographs, which, for the author, is the best confirmation of authenticity that one can have.

A front mounted aircraft Lewis gun

View of Lewis guns being assembled at the Royal Small Arms Factory

However, it is possible that the photographs could have been taken after WW1. After the war new contracts for small arms were not being placed by the War Office which would mean that the Birmingham Small Arms Company, which held the British licence to build the Lewis gun, would have been left with a large quantity of parts and machine tools and these eventually came to Enfield Lock. So it would seem reasonable to assume that the Lewis gun assembly line shown in the photographs are, in fact, post-war. Should any reader have a different theory that can be corroborated by documentary evidence the author would be pleased to hear from them.

Lewis Gun Assembly at the Royal Small Arms Factory, Enfield

REFERENCES

Lewis, Jim, *From Gunpowder to Guns the Story of Two Lea Valley Armouries*, Middlesex University Press (2009)

Putnam, Tim & Weinbren, Dan, *A Short History of the Royal Small Arms Factory Enfield*, Centre for Applied Historical Studies, Middlesex University (1992)

Skennerton, Ian D., *The Lee Enfield Story*, published by Ian D. Skennerton, (Australia, 1993)

Personal conversations with Ray Tutill (former RSAF engineer) and Glen Chapelle (curator of Royal Ordnance archive, BAE Systems, Glascoed) (December 2013)

Lewis James H., "The Development of the Royal Small Arms Factory (Enfield Lock) and its Influence Upon Mass Production Technology and Product Design C1820-C1880", unpublished PhD thesis, Middlesex University (December 1996).

House of Lords Record Office, London. "Subject: The Trials of nine descriptions of Breech-loading Rifles accepted for competition in accordance with the terms of the War Office Advertisement of 22nd October 1966. " *Reference, Reports Commissioners 1886-68, XVI*, pp.32-4

Note. 1. By 1856 the War Office was responsible for weapon procurement for the armed forces. Formerly this role had been performed by the Board of Ordnance.

Note. 2. During the Great War the RSAF, Enfield was responsible for repairing large quantities of Vickers Machine Guns.

7. THE INTER-WAR PERIOD

As usually happens after most major conflicts armament workers at the ordnance factories, particularly those under government control, that had sustained the troops at the front, became some of the first to face redundancy as orders for weapons and equipment were scaled back. Women workers who had taken the place of the men who had been conscripted or volunteered to join the armed forces also suffered a similar fate. However, the women's plight would eventually have a society-changing outcome as the opportunities brought about by war-work demonstrated they were capable of mastering any task formerly carried out by men. There were further pressures on women to make way for men returning from the front as some men had been told by their pre-war employers that their jobs would be kept open until they returned from military duty. This policy forced women back into domesticity, which after almost four years of independent living, was not cherished by all. Years of war-work had given women newfound skills and this had shown many employers that the so called 'weaker sex' had a range of hidden talents and abilities which had never before been recognised. While war-work had allowed many women to experience a taste of domestic freedom real emancipation would be a long time coming! Even as I write, almost one hundred years later, women have still not reached wage parity with men.

Women ambulance drivers (WW1) from the British Red Cross Society Voluntary Aid Detachment

Women ambulance drivers in France during WW1

Women machinists working in a munitions factory. After WW1 women had to make way for men returning from war

Women workers constructing Sten guns

Women workers at the Royal Ordnance Factory, Fazakerley, near Liverpool during WW2

During the inter-war years the RSAF management had tried to maintain a skilled core workforce at Enfield Lock by introducing a programme of machine tool refurbishment and also by obtaining contracts for the repair of rifles and machine guns, but by 1922, with work running out, the establishment had been cut to around 1,200 personnel. This figure compared poorly with the armoury's wartime peak of over 7,000 men, 1,100 boys and 1,500 women. The reduction in personnel brought considerable hardship to the local "Lockie" community. Between 1921 and 1923, to help retain a shrinking workforce, different sorts of work were secured. Contracts were obtained to make automotive parts for the short-lived British company ABC Motors (1920) Limited, hand tools were produced for the General Post Office (GPO), wireless sets were constructed for the military and even the repair and manufacture of railway carriages was undertaken.

Towards the 1930s

Following the Treaty of Versailles in July 1919 strict conditions had been imposed on Germany by the Allies. Under the Treaty it was "forbidden to maintain or construct any fortification either on the left bank of the Rhine or the right bank to the west of a line drawn fifty kilometres to the east of the Rhine". The terms of the Treaty made it abundantly clear that if a violation " in any manner whatsoever" of this Article took place, this "will be regarded as committing a hostile act…and as calculated to disturb the peace of the world".

In October 1925 the Locarno Treaties were signed jointly by Germany, Italy, France, Belgium and Britain which stated that the area designated as the Rhineland under the Treaty of Versailles should maintain its demilitarised status permanently. Under this agreement if Germany were to attack France then Britain and Italy would come to France's aid. And if France attacked Germany then Britain and Italy would be obligated to come to the aid of Germany. Although such treaties were in place Germany had covertly been building up her military strength almost before the ink on the Treaty of Versailles had dried.

In 1933, Adolf Hitler and the Nazi Party came to power in Germany and six years later the world would find itself entering the second major conflict of the century. By 1935 Germany had unilaterally cancelled the terms of the Locarno Treaties and in 1936 Hitler dispatched his troops to occupy the

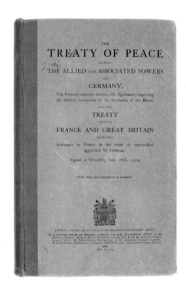

English translation of the Treaty of Versailles

THE GOOSE-STEP
"GOOSEY GOOSEY GANDER,
WHITHER DOST THOU WANDER?"
"ONLY THROUGH THE RHINELAND—
PRAY EXCUSE MY BLUNDER!"

The English translation of the Locarno treaties

A Punch cartoon depicting Germany breeching the Locarno Treaty

Rhineland. While this was clearly an act of aggression, with Hitler testing the Allies resolve, Britain, France and Italy stood by and did nothing. Later, in 1938, Hitler, having got away with his first challenge to the Allies tried his luck once more and annexed Austria, the incursion becoming known as Anschluss and again this aggressive act went unchallenged. Weeks later Hitler's troops crossed into the northern and western regions of Czechoslovakia (the area becoming known as Sudetenland) and in 1939 his troops occupied the rest of the country.

Hitler's European incursions appear not to have gone completely unnoticed by the War Office and others within the British Government as by 1935 it was announced that a replacement, through competition, had been found for the ageing American-designed Lewis light machine gun. The new weapon of choice was to be known as the Bren, designed by the talented Czechoslovakian engineer Vaclav Holek who worked at the Zbrojovka Brno Factory in Moravia. The name Bren was derived by combining the first two letters of Brno with the first two of Enfield. Apart from being lighter and more portable than the belt-fed machine guns of the day, the weapon also had the advantage of an air-cooled barrel that could easily be replaced after it became hot from rapid firing.

A licensing arrangement to manufacture the gun in a modified form, to accept the British standard 0.303 round, was agreed with the Czechoslovakian company. Once this was done the Enfield armoury had to start taking on staff once more as there was a desperate need to quickly build up weapon stocks. Hitler's illegal territorial gains in Europe had made government agencies extremely nervous as the shadows of a second world war began to darken the horizon.

Once the decision had been taken to manufacturer the Bren, other weapons, which had their design origins outside the Enfield Lock armoury, would be incorporated into production programmes as Britain began the belated task of quickly making up lost ground in its race to equip her armed forces.

A mounted anti-aircraft Bren gun

Anschluss; German troops make their way into Austria

Map showing closeness of Germany and annexed Austria to Czechoslovakia. Germany moved into Sudetenland in 1939

Adolf Hitler inspecting his troops after Germany annexed Austria in 1938

8. WORLD WAR TWO

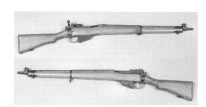

The Short Magazine Lee Enfield (SMLE) No.4 Mk I became the standard weapon of the British in WW2. This weapon had been in development since 1926!

Today's researchers might think it remarkable, given Hitler's territorial grabs in Europe, that during the inter-war period the now famous armoury at Enfield Lock had not developed any new weapons. There was really only one piece of development at this government-controlled armoury that had begun in 1926 with a long and drawn out programme of trials and upgrades of the latest version of the Lee Enfield rifle. This upgraded weapon was finally approved in November 1939 (the same month that Britain declared war on Germany). The weapon became known as the Short Magazine Lee Enfield (SMLE) No 4, Mk I. Ironically the rifle was never mass-produced at Enfield Lock as the design was shipped out to other factories to be manufactured, although some of these weapons found their way back to Enfield Lock for correction and inspection by skilled armourers.

Australian newspaper headlines 4th September 1939, when Britain and Australia declared war on Germany

The Prime Minister Neville Chamberlain, declaring war on Germany in a BBC radio broadcast, 3rd September 1939

Under-prepared and under-equipped

As has already been shown, during the inter-war years, the British Government had taken its eye off the ball and had seemingly ignored the increasing popularity, by armies around the world, for automatic weapons over the traditional bolt-action magazine rifle. For many years there had been debates in British military circles, going back as far as the mid nineteenth century when the single shot breech loading Snider rifle was introduced (remembering that this weapon was a modification of the muzzle loading Enfield pattern 1853). Here traditionalists in the military had argued that troops at the front would fire away too much ammunition because the weapons had superior loading power to what had been available before. This outdated point of view seems to have prevailed for some time and may have been partly responsible for government's reluctance to allow the Enfield Lock armoury to develop the latest series of automatic weapons. There was also the problem of treasury officials holding tightly onto the purse strings of government as they wished to keep a cap on spending within State-owned companies. So this was the unsatisfactory state of play at the beginning of the Second World War, which forced Britain to quickly purchase vast quantities of Thompson submachine guns from America to bridge the weapon gap so that her poorly equipped troops could at least be given a fighting chance. Later, in 1941, when America entered the war, the supply of the Thompson submachine gun became scarce as the manufacturers in the USA came under government pressure to equip her own military.

Winston Churchill with Thompson light machine gun

Canadian soldiers loading a Sten gun

Women assembling Sten guns

Winston Churchill, Prime Minister 1940-1945, firing Sten gun

The Sten gun

The Sten gun, a family of 9mm submachine guns, was designed by Major Reginald Shepherd and Harold Turpin. STEN derives its name from the first letters of the designer's surnames and the first two letters of Enfield. Shepherd had been Inspector of Armaments at the Woolwich Arsenal and Turpin was a Senior Draughtsman at the RSAF at Enfield Lock, so both men had first hand experience of arms design and production.

For over one hundred years, arms in the government ordnance factories had been made from first class materials to exacting quality standards but due to the government's unpreparedness for war the British armed forces had been left ill equipped. Now there was an urgent need for large numbers of an automatic weapon that could be manufactured quickly in small workshops, virtually anywhere, from a range of cheap materials by a less skilled workforce – the Sten gun fitted the bill perfectly. Shepherd and Turpin's gun was made from simple stamped metal parts and had a 32 round magazine that was horizontally mounted. The weapon had been specifically developed for troops engaged in close combat so there was no need for extensive trials to test long-range accuracy.

Over the years there were many different versions of the Sten manufactured and modified, some having a butt that was no more than a length of pipe with a curved welded piece designed as a shoulder support. Others were produced with an open curved butt made from metal, while a deluxe version sported a wooden butt.

The Sten entered service in 1941 and saw extensive use with the British and Commonwealth forces. In the mid 1940s, during the Battle of Dunkirk and in the subsequent troop evacuation, the Allies had lost considerable numbers of small arms. The timing of the Sten's introduction could not have been more opportune as the gun helped replace some of the weapons that had been lost or abandoned on the beaches of France when the flotillas of assorted craft arrived to take the exhausted troops to safety. The small craft mostly took the soldiers to bigger ships.

Sten Mk II

Sten Mk II, this was an Enfield designed weapon by Reginald Shepherd and Harold Turpin

Note the different shoulder butt of this Sten gun, this is the type being fired by Winston Churchill

Hispano cannon

By the mid 1930s it was realised by officials at the Air Ministry that due to the increasing speeds of new fighter and bomber aircraft there would be little time for aircrews to successfully and accurately fire the then current aircraft armament when attempting to engage the enemy. The Ministry's solution was to issue an order to install a six or eight gun system in operational and new fighter aircraft. While issuing such an order was a relatively easy task, the practicality and difficulty of installing such a weapon system in the different types of aircraft in service was another matter entirely. Because the current aircraft had not been designed with these particular weapon systems in mind it would mean that quite substantial and expensive modifications would have to be made. This in turn would inevitably cause delays while fitting and testing took place at a time when it was essential to get planes airborne to attack the enemy. The fitting of a multi-gun system to the new breed of fighter aircraft like the Hurricane and Spitfire would mean mounting weapons in the wings away from the engine which presented design engineers with a raft of new and difficult challenges. For example, it was found that at high altitude guns would freeze which meant that special lubricants and heating systems had to be developed to keep the guns firing.

Armourers fitting a 20mm Hispano Canon in a Spitfire Mk V

A Spitfire fitted with Hispano cannons

There was also a further major problem. During the inter-war years Britain had not kept abreast of, or invested in, new aircraft weapon technology and so would have to turn to foreign suppliers to obtain armaments off the shelf. This again would incur further costly delays as modifications would be needed to incorporate these new incompatible weapons, not only in re-chambering them for the British 0.303 round, but also to ensure that the aircraft was structurally strengthened and streamlined to cope with any added vibration that a new gun system might bring. This is a further example of a lack of awareness on the part of our politicians to devise long-term strategies to keep our country safe, leaving our engineers to try and make the best of a bad job in times of conflict.

In 1936 British officials attended trials of an early version of the 20mm Hispano-Suiza cannon (HS 404) at the Paris subsidiary of European Hispano-Suiza S.A. (a company originally manufacturing luxury cars and aircraft engines). Eventually a licensing agreement was signed to manufacture the weapons in Britain and, to relieve pressure on the RSAF at Enfield Lock, a production facility was set up in Springfield Road Grantham which became the British Manufacturing and Research Company (BMARC). However, during the war, the RSAF manufactured and tested 5,650 of these weapons.

As mentioned above there were normally several problems associated with fitting foreign weapons to the current range of British fighter aircraft and the Hispano-Suiza cannon was no exception, as the gun had originally been designed for mounting on an aircraft's solid engine block. When fitting the weapon to a Spitfire, for example, engine mounting was out of the question and the cannons had to be fitted into the wings. The Hispano came with a bulky sixty round magazine and this meant the cannon had to be mounted on its side to squeeze the magazine into the wing section. Mounting the cannon this way caused the gun to jam frequently and, as a result, a belt feed system had to be designed to replace the magazine. Unfortunately the belt feed did not become available until 1941 which meant it arrived too late to assist the RAF at the Battle of Britain.

Wartime production at Enfield Lock

In spite of the lack of government foresight and planning the Royal Small Arms Factory at Enfield Lock seems to have been able to design, develop, manufacture, repair, modify and test an outstanding number of small arms. Skilled personnel from Enfield also helped train the workforce at other government armament factories like Fazakerley and Maltby and supplied them with the essential patterns and jigs so that products could be uniformly manufactured across the group. Without these contributions by the Enfield workforce it would be difficult to imagine what would have been the final outcome of the Second World War.

The quantity of weapons manufactured at Enfield during the war period is as follows:

Over 225,000 Bren guns

Over 258,000 Sten guns

Over 275,000 Mk I 0.38 inch revolvers

      5,650 Hispano-Suiza HS 404 cannon

      2,700 Polsten cannon

      3,600 Vickers machine guns

The quantity of weapons repaired at Enfield during the war period is as follows:

Over 1,050,000 rifles of different patterns

Over 35,000 Bren guns

Over 11,000 Vickers machine guns

Over 36,500 Revolvers

Over 24,400 Signal pistols

Over 4,000 American Hotchkiss machine guns

Over 12,000 Lewis guns

Over 78,000 Thompson machine guns

Decisions, decisions, decisions – what to do after the war?

In the aftermath of WW2, with the rapid reduction of arms orders, the Enfield Lock workforce fell to around two thousand and by 1950 this number had effectively halved. In this post-war period the world had been left with many new economic and social problems to solve as the former Eastern and Western Allies developed into two distinctive power blocks. International relationships that had been important in the fight against Hitler had soured as political tensions grew, the period becoming known as the Cold War. The Middle East with its vast oil reserves now became a centre of tension as the British-Zionist crisis in Palestine took hold. Further afield the Indian sub-continent, part of the old British Empire, was seeking independence and on top of this several British protectorates began petitioning for self determination.

Enfield revolver Mk II

These post-war stirrings were an indication of the fragility of many places around the world. The war had created problems right across the globe with many countries suffering food shortages and a lack of basic materials for construction and manufacture. It would take time for struggling countries to rebuild their economies and get back on their feet. With so many countries having to look inward it is understandable that international relationships would change.

The major world powers had grown suspicious of one another during both wartime and post-war negotiations; the eastern and the western blocks each believed they had the magic formula to create societies that would make them stronger and self-reliant. This allowed the ideologies of communism and capitalism to split the east from the west and sadly the legacy of mistrust and suspicion is alive and flourishing to this day.

However, even with this level of world instability it is doubtful if the post-war British Government could have predicted just how many wars and skirmishes Britain would become involved in up until 1988, the time of the complete closure of the Enfield Lock small arms manufacturing facility. While personally not advocating a policy of developing and manufacturing weapons to overpower those countries or governments with whom you do not agree, the following list of conflicts in which Britain was involved, might seem to suggest that in a world where passions can quickly become inflamed and rapidly escalate out of control, there might be an argument for maintaining a government-controlled in-house arms production facility.

- (1945-1948)   British-Zionist conflict in Palestine
- (1946-1947)   Greek Civil War
- (1946-1990)   Cold War period
- (1948-1960)   Malayan Emergency
- (1950-1953)   Korean War
- (1952-1960)   Mau Mau Uprising in Kenya
- (1955-1959)   Cyprus Emergency
- (1956)   Suez Crisis
- (1962)   Brunei Revolt
- (1962-1975)   Dhofar Rebellion in Oman
- (1963-1966)   Indonesia-Malaysia Confrontation
- (1963-1967)   Aden Emergency
- (1969-1990s)   Northern Ireland Troubles
- (1975-1976)   Cod War Confrontation
- (1980)   Iranian Embassy Siege
- (1982)   Falklands War

Of course Britain has been involved in several wars and conflicts since closure of the RSAF at Enfield Lock and in these rapidly changing times the country has seen (and currently faces) terrorist threats from both without and within. Interestingly Britain today is in a similar situation with regard to the ability to arm itself as she was at the time of the Napoleonic wars when the country had to turn to arms makers in Liège, Belgium to supplement supplies from the private UK gun makers.

Post-war weapon development at the RSAF

With a lack of orders for weapons and a greatly reduced workforce there was an urgent need to ensure that the remaining staff were kept occupied and motivated. Elsewhere in Britain the Blitz had left its destructive mark on many towns and cities. One priority for the post-war government was to introduce

An early picture of the Belgium arms-making quarter in Liège

a massive rebuilding programme. This fortunately allowed the Enfield Lock factory to make a contribution by manufacturing a range of carpenters' tools and other essentials like household plumbing equipment and engine components.

By the start of the Korean War in 1950 Enfield's carpenters' tool manufacturing days and other work for the home market were over as the episode of diversifying was deemed not to have been a success. It has been suggested that although the tools produced were of high quality, senior factory personnel lacked the necessary marketing skills and experience to challenge the competition commercially. This lack of commercial know-how had not gone unnoticed in government circles and the Royal Ordnance Factories were made to adopt commercial practices by installing Boards of Management which included directors from the private sector. When the time came to re-arm the British and Commonwealth troops fighting in Korea it provided little extra work for the Enfield Lock factory as there were already stock-piles of arms remaining from WW2.

The immediate post-war period had created major problems for the British small arms industry which would eventually lead to its demise. It had been obvious that the British Army would soon need equipping with a self-loading rifle to keep pace with its recently formed North Atlantic Treaty Organisation (NATO) partners. The setting up of this military alliance in April 1949 had begun without a properly co-ordinated command structure. World events rapidly focussed minds on this omission when in August 1949 the Soviets detonated their first atomic bomb and in June the following year the communist North Korean People's Army invaded their independent neighbours in the South. A United Nations force led by America joined forces with the armies of the South. However, China, supported by the former Soviet Union, fought on the side of North Korea.

In 1951 NATO headquarters became quickly established in the Hotel Astoria, Paris on a temporary basis until a permanent structure could be built. The experienced WW2 veteran, General Dwight D. Eisenhower was appointed Supreme Allied Commander Europe and he would now oversee the setting up of a co-ordinated command structure. These rapidly world-changing scenes so soon after WW2 would have a profound effect on the British small arms industry.

Over the years, one of the major drawbacks to British industry growing and prospering has been the difficulty, or perhaps the reluctance, to develop and design products that conform to common specification and measurement standards with other countries. This has occurred across the electrical, electronic and mechanical sectors of industry and has resulted in the loss of export opportunities. Now the Enfield Lock factory was about to be caught up in the latest round of the small arms standardisation argument as the new NATO alliance was looking for, amongst other things, compatibly of weapons and ammunition across its armed forces.

The new NATO headquarters building, Brussels completed in 2017, a far cry from the Hotel Astoria, Paris, 1951

Following WW2, Britain had established a committee to determine the optimum calibre for future small arms and cartridge design. After much deliberation it was concluded that the new standard should be a rimless cartridge with a lead core and the weapon chambered for an 0.280 inch calibre round.

In 1950 Britain did not have the means of equipping its army with a self-loading small arm when it entered the Korea War. However, there was pressure to adopt, at least temporarily, the American MI semi-automatic rifle and the 0.30-60 inch Springfield rifle round which would have at least brought about some battlefield weapon compatibly between the Americans and the British. The British Army Council dismissed the idea outright as it probably believed that its earlier assessment for a new weapon calibre was correct. They may have also concluded that to place orders, even temporarily, with a foreign manufacturer would seriously affect the prospects of Britain's small arms industry and this could have cost the military the power to influence future weapon designs.

The American MI Garand rifle chambered for the standard US 30-06 round. Used by American forces during WW2 and Korean war

Small arms designers at Enfield Lock had already taken ideas gained from the battlefield experiences of WW2 troops and had probably "borrowed" ideas from Russian and Polish weapons engineers when they came up with two 7mm prototypes. These were built in what was known as the "bullpup" configuration. However, development of the weapon was halted after the Churchill government came to power in October 1951. Churchill, apart from being Prime Minister, had also taken on the role of Minister of Defence which no doubt increased his power when it came to choosing new weapons. By January 1954 the government announced the adoption of the FN FAL 7.62mm rifle designed by the Belgian company, Fabrique Nationale de Herstal (FN), for Britain's armed forces.

With post-war tensions between the eastern and western blocks growing, the Belgian weapon design was adopted by many countries across the world (some of these manufacturing under licence) and became one of the most widely used small arms in history and the backbone of NATO during the Cold War period, although it was not used in the USA. However, weapon parts interchangeability could not always be guaranteed for the Belgian small arm across all the NATO countries as measurements for Britain, Canada and Australia had been transposed from metric to imperial.

Note. The origins of the term bullpup are unclear but are thought to have come from America. When referring to a weapon of bullpup design it normally means that the weapon's action and magazine is situated in the gunstock and behind the trigger grip. This has the advantage of reducing the weapon's length and also its weight.

Enfield's Future

It is clear that adoption by the British Government of the Belgian weapon had placed a question mark against the future role of Enfield Lock as the site had a long tradition of designing, developing and manufacturing the complete weapon along with the various sets of jigs and measuring gauges.

However, the post-war development of faster jet aircraft for the RAF and Fleet Air Arm was about to bring a welcome boost for the Enfield workforce. New aircraft would need to be armed and Enfield found itself nicely placed to take up the challenge. Fortunately, by the late 1940s Enfield's weapon developers and Britain's Armament Development Establishment designers had been working on a replacement for the ageing Hispano-Suiza 20mm aircraft cannon. The outcome was a 30mm aircraft cannon known as the ADEN after the first two letters of Armament Development and the first two of Enfield.

An ADEN 30mm gun-pack being loaded into a Belgian Air Force Hawker Hunter

This weapon first went into service with the Hawker Hunter in 1954. The ADEN was developed in several different marques and installed in a number of post-war jet aircraft including the English Electric Lightning, the Gloster Javelin, the Supermarine Scimitar, the Saab Lansen and many more. Remarkably the Fleet Air Arm Sea Harriers retained the ADEN cannon right up until 2006.

The mid 1950s became an uncertain time for Britain's Royal Ordnance Factories as government appeared not to have developed a joined-up arms manufacturing strategy to address the rapidly changing international scene in the wake of WW2. To many observers it had become patently obvious that Britain was no longer a world power and was rapidly losing her ability, both economically and militarily, to influence the countries of her Empire. Several of these were now calling for self determination and armed struggles were breaking out in British territories across the globe.

Relations with the Soviets were becoming more fractious by the day as each side built up its spying and espionage activities, particularly in the light of Russia's first testing of an atomic bomb in 1949 followed by further tests of nuclear devices in the 1950s. British scientists, who had been involved in America's Manhattan project, detonated their first atomic bomb in October 1952. The following year the Korean War ended with the armistice of July 1953 when the regions of the North and South established a nervous peace with their respective armies dug-in either side of the 38th parallel dividing the country between communism and capitalism, a line maintained until this day (2018). While these events were taking place Britain still faced the monumental task of rebuilding a country that had been damaged both structurally and financially by the ravages of WW2. However, while wars have never solved mankind's problems, for Britain to ignore the mounting global tensions by leaving her military ill equipped and weak would seem foolhardy in the extreme.

Britain's adoption of the Belgian FN small arm had, by the mid 1950s, brought orders of 100,000 weapons for two of the Royal Ordnance Factories, Fazakerley, near Liverpool and Enfield Lock. The boost in production saw Enfield's workforce climb to 1,800 by 1958, an increase of 300 over the previous two years. However, the overall future of the Ordnance Factories, many of which had hurriedly been established just prior to WW2, was looking decidedly bleak, with five closures in 1957 alone.

There was still little sign, certainly from the public perspective, of a government long-term defence strategy emerging, especially with regard to the indigenous small arms manufacturing industry. Britain's recently acquired nuclear capability had probably confused government thinking as it was believed by many that possession of the atomic bomb was the ultimate deterrent to future wars and so conventional defence measures could be scaled back. By 1957 the end of National Service had been announced and by the early 1960s it was planned to massively reduce Britain's armed forces from 700,000 to 165,000 (current predictions are that by 2020 the figure will be 147,000).

The 1960s saw further cutbacks of Royal Ordnance Factories when Fazakerley closed. As Enfield Lock was now the only government-controlled small arms manufacturing establishment with a design facility left standing, the factory had benefited from Fazakerley's closure as outstanding orders,

A Fox FV 721 armoured fighting vehicle fitted with a RARDEN cannon

machinery and tooling were transferred to its southern sister. Also, at about this time, Enfield Lock was handed the design of small arms and related ammunition when responsibility and key personnel were transferred from the government's Armament Research and Development Establishment. While these changes provided a temporary boost for Enfield's fortunes it was not long before work began tailing off with the inevitable reduction in personnel.

By the early 1970s, while still manufacturing the ADEN aircraft cannon and the Belgian FN (L1A1) and its sister the General Purpose Machine Gun (GPMG) under licence, another weapon design was added to the Enfield production schedule. This was an Enfield designed 30mm auto-cannon, known as the RARDEN, after the first letters of Royal Armament Research and Development and the first two of Enfield. The cannon had been developed for a series of British armoured vehicles such as the FV721 Fox armoured car, the FV107 Scimitar tracked reconnaissance vehicle, the FV510 infantry fighting vehicle and also for a number of variants.

Soldier with an Enfield designed L85A1 now in service with the British Armed Forces

RARDEN cannon

Soldiers on exercise in West Germany in the 1960s, carrying a version of the Belgian FN FAL rifle

The SA80 Mk I, familiarly known as the EWS, Enfield Weapon System

A woman MoD police officer with SA80

From the start the cannon suffered a range of manufacturing problems which were caused by mistakes made in engineering drawings and this had a knock-on effect for measuring gauges and also individual weapon parts. There were also problems of compatibly when fitting the RARDEN to some of the armoured vehicles, causing modifications and, as a consequence, delivery hold-ups. In the mid 1970s a serious mistake occurred after the cannon had been fitted to the FV432 armoured personnel carrier. This armoured vehicle variant was designed to carry ten army personnel on two bench seats in the back. However, it was discovered that when the cannon and its turret were fitted, there was not sufficient room for all ten personnel. It is difficult to comprehend how such a simple mistake like this could have been made and one might speculate it was due to poor communication between the vehicle manufactures and Enfield Lock engineers. If this were the case it would suggest that an inter-disciplinary liaison team had not been established from the onset of this project, otherwise how could such a fundamental error occur? Unfortunately mistakes of this magnitude tend to result in bad publicity and this would not have helped Enfield Lock's long-term survival.

The Enfield Weapon System (EWS)

From the late 1960s Enfield's design department had been engaged in a novel weapon concept that was based around the newly developed 4.85mm calibre ammunition. Out of this development programme two types of "bullpup" (see earlier explanation) configured small arms materialised; an individual rifle type XL64E5 and a light machine gun type XL65E4. From these two weapons would emerge a family of variants that would be classified under the heading the Enfield Weapon System (ESW). Separate weapons from this family have now become more familiarly known as the SA80. These weapons had been designed without the traditional barrel mounted mechanical sights and now sported optical devices.

In comparison to the ageing Belgian 7.62mm FN, then in use with NATO forces, the SA80 was lighter, had a shorter barrel and was considerably cheaper by £100. Also the weapon's 4.85mm ammunition produced less recoil and was approximately half the weight of the current NATO round allowing troops to carry more ammunition into battle.

In May 1974 the Royal Electrical and Mechanical Engineers (REME) were given the new weapon to assess for ease of maintenance. From these trials a range of real and potential problems were highlighted. Enfield engineers listened to the criticisms and implemented design changes in the hope that the SA80 would eventually replace its Belgian rival to become the standard NATO weapon.

In 1977 NATO proposed that a series of trials should take place that would include the Enfield Weapon System and its new calibre ammunition and would also include weapons manufactured by other NATO countries. These trials were scheduled to last around two years. When the trials concluded NATO made the decision to adopt 5.56mm ammunition rather than the 4.85mm calibre that Enfield had proposed.

As the majority of weapons that took place in the trials, and in particular those manufactured in America, were chambered to take the 5.56mm round it is hardly surprising that NATO settled on this particular calibre. The standard weapon of the American armed forces, particularly during the Vietnam War, was the M16 rifle, chambered for 5.56mm ammunition. After the war there were in excess of 790,000 of these weapons effectively stockpiled and one might speculate that there could have been some behind the scenes lobbying by the Americans' to ensure that NATO adopted the 5.56mm calibre. If this were the case, then it would seem to be an example of politics winning the trials over technical superiority. It should be remembered that throughout the lifetime of a small arm the cost of the ammunition fired by the weapon will considerably outweigh the cost of the weapon many times over. This would give the country that manufactured both weapon and ammunition an added incentive to succeed when bargaining with a potential customer.

The American M16 assault rifle was used by US troops in the Vietnam war

Given the above mentioned circumstances Enfield had little option but to re-chamber the EWS to the 5.56mm NATO calibre. Had it not taken this step it is unlikely that the factory could have found markets for a weapon which had a unique calibre.

By now the current NATO weapons stock was reaching the end of its useful life and would need to be replaced by the 1980s. Therefore, the early re-chambering of the EWS to 5.56mm could put Enfield in a strong position when NATO countries began placing future orders for new weapons. However, Enfield's re-chambering of the EWS had a serious knock-on effect and, as a consequence, further modifications were required that caused an increase in manufacturing costs and also production delays.

In January 1984 a Provisional Acceptance Meeting was held within Whitehall under the chairmanship of Brigadier C.W. Beckett. Here it was recognised that there were still outstanding problems that had to be rectified with the EWS but it was nevertheless agreed that the weapon system was "safe and suitable for service". In June 1985 the Ministry of Defence (MoD) placed an order with Enfield Lock for 175,000 weapons and in October of that year the first weapons were handed over to the 1st Battalion, Worcestershire and Sherwood Foresters at a special ceremony.

To an outsider the order to manufacture thousands of weapons might be seen as a massive boost for the future of the Royal Small Arms Factory that would also signal a bright and secure outlook for the loyal Lockie community. However, behind the scenes, politicians seemed to be harbouring other thoughts and were busily at work!

Margaret Thatcher had become Prime Minister in May 1979 and by 1980 her Conservative government had lost no time in setting up a study group to explore ways of selling off government assets and amongst these were the Royal Ordnance Factories. Interestingly, the sale of State-owned assets is still very much a feature of government policy today (2018). In October 1986 the MoD began the bidding process which by April 1987 had culminated in the sale of the Royal Ordnance Factories to British Aerospace at what was seen by many as a knock-down price of £188.5 million, ending Enfield's 170 years of government ownership. Shortly after the purchase British Aerospace announced the closure of the Enfield Lock site and in 1988 all machinery was auctioned off and production of the EWS was transferred to Royal Ordnance plc, Nottingham (this factory has since been demolished along with the purpose-built Enfield Pattern Room).

In a way Enfield Lock with its sister factories could be looked upon as a bit of a curate's egg. There were good parts that were acquired as Enfield's

The ARWEN an anti-riot weapon designed at Enfield Lock. This weapon has a rotary magazine that holds five non-lethal baton rounds

engineers had been working on a number of encouraging new weapon designs and development projects. One of these was an anti-riot weapon that fired a non-lethal round (ARWEN) – the name originating from the first letters of anti-riot weapon system and the first two of Enfield. There was considerable commercial interest in this weapon from a number of police forces and other agencies. The not so good parts of the EWS, even after all its military trials and modifications, was that the system still carried a considerable number of unresolved technical problems, many not immediately coming to light, like failure to perform in arctic and desert environments. Allegedly these particular problems did not materialise until the weapons had been used by troops on active service or during authentic combat exercises.

When speaking with former RSAF engineers, all of whom defended the design of the EWS, many accusations emerged of constant changes to the specification from interfering bureaucrats. Also there were other stories of on-site army liaison officers insisting that certain parts of the weapon had to be modified, and then when these changes had been made, other army liaison officers, insisting the original designs be reinstated. If such stories are true they are a recipe for production disaster and also a good reason for ensuring government agencies and other outsiders are kept well away from interfering in the manufacturing process. From personal experience I know that re-working any product by putting it back through the manufacturing process can create quality assurance problems and costly product delays.

The episode was probably best summed up by Dr Dan Weinbren when he wrote in a letter to the author in January 1994:

> The EWS was, like much else in the baroque arsenal, expensive and thus designed to do too many jobs, fulfil too many briefs. It failed. The RSAF workforce and management were not to blame, though possibly management kow-towed to the MoD more than it should – those were pre-privatisation times. Almost certainly closure was not very closely related to this particular cock-up. I think the land value of the site was of greater importance.

It would be a humiliatingly cruel end for the Royal Small Arms Factory after a long tradition of engineering excellence.

I would suggest that there is a great opportunity for an inquisitive academic, or perhaps a research group, to carry out an in-depth study into the way that government historically procured its small arms. This should then be compared to current procurement systems and the methods by which government monitors a modern weapon, or other armament, development programme. In this way it should be possible to discover if lessons in good development and procurement practice have been learned. Perhaps, more importantly it might lift the stigma that has surrounded the last RSAF design team.

REFERENCES

Birchmore, Graham and Burgess, Roy, *The Lads of Enfield Lock*, Libri Publishing (2011)

Ezell, Edward, *Handguns of the World*, Barnes & Noble (1992)

Laidler, Laidler, *The Sten Machine Carbine*, Jeremy Tenniswood, (Colchester, Essex, 2000)

Low, Alfred, *The Anschluss Movement 1918 – 1919: and the Paris Peace Conference*, American Philosophical Society (1974)

Putnam, Tim and Weinbren, Dan, *A Short History of the Royal Small Arms Factory Enfield*, Centre for Applied Historical Studies, Middlesex University (1992)

Pam, David, *The Royal Small Arms Factory Enfield & Its Workers*, published by the author (1998)

Shirer, William, *Rise and Fall of the Third Reich: A History of Nazi Germany*, Simon & Schuster (1990)

Steininger, Wolf, *Austria, Germany and the Cold War: from Anschluss to the State Treaty 1938 – 1955*, Berghahm Books (New York, 2008)

9. THE WORLD-FAMOUS PATTERN ROOM COLLECTION

The former purpose-built Enfield Building, Nottingham. When the RSAF closed at Enfield Lock the pattern room collection was housed here

After a serious fire occurred at the Tower of London in 1840 the entire weapon content of its Pattern Room was transferred to a specially prepared building at Enfield Lock. In the early years, before the days of proper engineering drawings, it was customary when a new small arm was designed for skilled engineers to make an exact replica of the weapon which would then be sealed. This represented the "pattern" from which all future arms of that particular type would be made. Having a sealed example allowed contractors and others to visit the government establishment where the pattern was held to take precise measurements which would be transferred to machine or manmade parts before full-scale weapon manufacture could commence. When the complete weapons were checked by the government ordnance viewers for acceptance it was against the sealed pattern that they were measured. The term "sealed pattern" originates from the practice of fixing a red wax seal to an approved sample weapon to verify it was fit for service.

Over the years, particularly at the time of the late curator Herbert Woodend MBE, the Enfield Pattern Room collection grew to over 14,000 weapons. Several of these extremely important examples had been acquired from around the world. Amongst the artefacts were a number of handmade guns that had been captured from criminal gangs and terrorist groups. These have remained a unique research resource for military and police personnel. Much of the collection remains of considerable interest to those agencies charged with keeping us safe as the weapons are original and have never been deactivated. When the Royal Small Arms Factory was sold to British Aerospace, the Pattern Room collection transferred to the Royal Ordnance Factory, Nottingham and was housed in the purpose-built Enfield Building.

A chance meeting, in 2011, with a former intelligence Mandarin has uncovered a fascinating story about this world-famous RSAF Pattern Room

The late Bert Woodend on the right, discussing the working of a machine gun. Picture taken in the ground floor display room, Enfield Building, Nottingham

collection. This tells of how the officer prevented the collection from being broken up and sold off. It took a considerable amount of time to persuade the story teller to finally commit the details to paper. As someone who has carried out research into the dark arts of intelligence gathering, I find the story credible. The following indented paragraphs are the Mandarin's account of what happened.

> In the mid-1980s a young civil servant (who has asked to remain anonymous) was attached to the Defence Sales Organisation; his responsibilities included liaison with the UK defence industry. As part of this, he visited the Royal Small Arms Factory at Enfield Lock and was shown around the Pattern Room. He was totally blown away by this unique compendium of small-calibre weapons from the very earliest to the very latest. He regarded this as a national treasure, equivalent, in its way, to the British Museum reading room, where he had studied as a post-graduate student.

> Fast-forward to the mid-1990s, when the young civil servant had reached the middle ranks of the upper civil service. His responsibilities included the analysis of terrorist weapons and the Pattern Room was one of the resources used by his staff. Imagine his horror when the Ministry of Defence, still in the high tide of Thatcherite privatisation ideology, decided that the Pattern Room collection, now owned by BAe Systems, was scheduled to be sold off item-by-item, so breaking up the best (and indeed only) comprehensive collection of small-calibre weaponry in the Western world. He decided that this must not happen.

> Over the next few years he deployed all the weapons in a civil servant's armoury to fend off the hounds of the Treasury. The Pattern Room was a unique source of material for his staff – sell it off and they could be blind-sided in the event of terrorist attacks. It was part of the Ministry of Defence's historic legacy (albeit now sold off to a private company) – how would it look if this sale became public knowledge? Above all, he used the bureaucrat's key weapon of entangling all concerned in a web of

The upper floor of the former Nottingham pattern room. Now the collection is housed at the Royal Armouries, Leeds, and also stored in warehousing

correspondence where every contribution to the exchange triggered off a new wave of letters and emails, to the point that no one felt able to make a decision on the sell-off – which was in fact the aim of his exercise.

Result: success. After closure the collection was not sold off piece-meal, but was moved to ROF Nottingham; which has since closed. The collection is now held at the Royal Armouries Museum, Leeds, as the National Firearms Centre. It remains a unique national resource; thanks in large part to a young civil servant who was overwhelmed by an incredible collection of small arms which he vowed should never just be sold off for a temporary profit but should be preserved for posterity as a national archive.

I understand that later the Mandarin appeared on a national television programme and when interviewed by the presenter expressed the view that Saddam Hussein did not possess weapons of mass destruction; he was sacked the following day.

I recall being told a rather amusing story by the late Herbert Woodend who said he was so disgusted and distraught when Enfield Lock closed that after locking the Pattern Room for the last time he then left the site via the footbridge and threw the keys into the River Lea! If a future archaeologist should find a rusty bunch of keys in the River Lea they will now be able to find out that they once belonged to the world-famous Pattern Room!

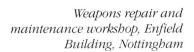

Weapons repair and maintenance workshop, Enfield Building, Nottingham

10. THE CLOSURE OF ENFIELD LOCK

In April 1987 the Government's Royal Ordnance Factories (ROFs), of which the Royal Small Arms Factory at Enfield Lock was one, were sold to the private sector. The Ministry of Defence (MoD), a complex fusion of former government departments, initiated the bidding process for Royal Ordnance plc in October 1986 and received six offers. These were eventually whittled down to just two; Guest, Keen & Nettlefolds (GKN) and British Aerospace, the latter becoming the successful owners of the Ordnance sites with an offer of £188.5 million.

Within months of acquiring the Enfield Lock site British Aerospace announced that the factory would close with the subsequent loss of some twelve hundred jobs. As one might imagine the announcement was met with shock and amazement by the Lockie community. This was a loyal and close-knit workforce with some members claiming that over the past one hundred and seventy years, several successive generations of their families had shared their skills with others, which had contributed to the growth of the factory complex. The announcement of site closure also came as a big economic blow to Enfield Council who, over the latter post-war period, had seen a significant decline in the once vibrant grouping of engineering and manufacturing industries across the borough.

Not unnaturally there was a groundswell of anger locally at the announced closure and in September 1987 the Enfield Gazette reported a large crowd of around five hundred RSAF workers and their families gathered outside Enfield Civic Centre to protest. The gathering was addressed by Jack Dromey of the Transport and General Workers Union, and also Councillor Reg Kendall, the Labour leader.

From the Gazette's report it would appear that a rather acrimonious meeting ensued which continued inside the council chamber with workers shouting abuse from their positions in the packed public gallery. Eventually, after listening to Councillors debating the wording of a resolution regarding

Aerial image of the Great Cambridge Road c1960. Centre image Ferguson and Carter Patterson with Belling in background. Today our industries are missing.

Report of RSAF workforce with their families protesting at the Civic Centre, the Enfield Gazette, September 1987

closure, there was a mass walkout of the meeting by the RSAF workers and their families with their spokesperson claiming "we don't want to hear any more". Apparently the action provoked the warring council members to unanimously agree a compromise resolution that opposed the factory's closure. The following is the full text of the motion:

> The Council notes with deep concern the recently announced intention of British Aerospace to close down the Royal Small Arms Factory.
>
> In view of the fact that the factory is known world wide and is part of Enfield's history and closure will mean the loss of up to 1,200 jobs in the area. The Council opposes the proposals regarding closure but notes that further discussions are being held between unions and management.
>
> In the event of the closure being finally confirmed Enfield Council would wish to see manufacturing opportunities kept alive on the site within any future planning proposals.
>
> The Council authorises officers to continue to take steps to discuss the possibilities with other interested parties in order to retain jobs and skills in the area.

The motion ended with an amendment proposed by Labour Councillor Mark Astirita.

> This Council acknowledges and applauds the Lockies both past and present for their dedicated and often unappreciated contribution to the history and security of Enfield and the British Nation.

It is pretty obvious from the wording of the resolution and amendment that the Council wished to give moral support to the workforce but lacked the power to provide the positive outcome that would have been acceptable to the workforce.

RSAF buildings being taken over by nature after site closure, c1990

The large machine room void of machinery and silent after closure

PART THREE

11. THE EVOLVING RSAF STORY

In September 1988 the Gazette reported that 'the vacant Royal Ordnance factory at Enfield Lock was at the centre of a fresh "asset stripping" storm. It was further reported that in Parliament the Labour Shadow Defence Secretary, Martin O'Neill wanted a full investigation by the Commons Public Accounts and the Trade and Industry Select Committees. The implication being that the Enfield Lock and other Royal Ordnance sites had been sold off too cheaply and taxpayers were shouldering the massive financial loss.

The large machine room in a state of rapid deterioration after closure

In the years that followed several ideas for the Enfield Lock site were put forward; amongst them was one from the National Army Museum who wished to establish an outer London base for some of its larger exhibits. While this particular proposal seemingly gained local popularity at the time, the scheme fell through when the directors of the museum allegedly asked the London Borough of Enfield for a dowry of two million pounds. As various proposals for the site's regeneration came and went the shell of the large machine room began to deteriorate rapidly. Parts of the building were crumbling due to serious water ingress as the structure had not been maintained since the sale to British Aerospace. Furthermore, the overall preservation of the former Royal Small Arms Factory complex, with its surrounding buildings, was not being helped by the fact that a number of local police forces had been allowed to use the site for serious training purposes. I can recall walking through the former factory grounds at the time and they were littered with spent ammunition rounds with a few derelict cars scattered throughout the site's internal roads.

British Aerospace, who had purchased the Enfield Lock site from the government in 1987, made two applications, in the same year, to the London Borough of Enfield to redevelop the land. Later British Aerospace formed a joint venture company with property developer Trafalgar House under the name of Lee Valley Developments (LVD). In 1991 LVD submitted an application to the London Borough of Enfield as they wished to develop the land at Enfield Lock for residential use. However, research carried out by the Enfield historian, the late David Pam, for his book, *The Royal Small Arms Factory Enfield & Its Workers*, states that:

> Local elections in 1994 returned a Labour administration which at once rescinded the plan, demanding more local housing. Deadlock ensued and continued for more than a year. Boundary changes which came into force on 1st April 1995 brought the whole of the site within the jurisdiction of

The new National Army Museum building was opened by the Queen in 2017. The RSAF large machine room at Enfield Lock was once a contender for the museum's secondary collection.

British Aerospace Centre, Farnborough. This company bought the Royal Ordnance Factories from the government when they were put up for offer.

L.B. Enfield [prior to this the land was part of Epping Forest District of Essex]. In April 1996 Trafalgar House sold the site to the local developers Fairview Estates and the Council set up a joint panel under the Chairmanship of Councillor John Jackson to work out a new scheme.

The latest application (September 1996) from Fairview Homes demands even more housing on the site but envisages the re-opening of the canal arm and basin and the conversion of more, although too few, of the mid-nineteenth century buildings.

At this stage in the story it might be worth pausing for a moment as an explanation is required to highlight a number of issues that would have to be dealt with by a potential developer. The regeneration of the former Royal Small Arms Factory (RSAF) site was not just a question of finding a new use for the Grade II listed building; development was further complicated by a range of quite thorny planning issues which had the potential for causing costly delays.

Prior to 1994, the land on which the RSAF site stood had been designated part of the green belt. This would have been the reason why Enfield Council, in 1987, had turned down, on two occasions, the application to redevelop the Enfield Lock site, by the agent Fuller Peiser on behalf of Royal Ordnance plc. Interestingly an application submitted in 1991 on behalf of Royal Ordnance was by a differently named agent, Fairview New Homes plc.

The lifting of the green belt regulations in 1994 and the subsequent boundary changes in 1995 now brought the RSAF site within the jurisdiction of Enfield Council, rather than Epping Forest District of Essex. Between the applications in 1987 to Enfield Council and the later green belt and boundary changes Royal Ordnance had been making a number of other applications to the Authority to redevelop the site. However, all these applications were unsuccessful including at least two appeals, against local planning decisions, that had been lodged with the Secretary of State. To have gained planning approval Royal Ordnance would have had to meet in excess of sixty quite stringent requirements under Section 106 of the Town & Country Planning Act 1990.

Fairview New Homes offices, Lancaster Road, Enfield

Perhaps, after eight years of setbacks, it is possible that Royal Ordnance had become frustrated, which caused them to cut their losses by selling the site, in 1996, to Fairview New Homes plc.

Outsiders watching these long drawn-out negotiations must have wondered whether there was ever going to be a sustainable regeneration plan that would meet all the requirements. And if there was such a plan in the making – was there anyone bold enough and perhaps foolhardy enough to put it forward?

Dark areas depict green belt around London

12. A GLIMMER OF HOPE EMERGES FOR THE ENFIELD LOCK SITE

In 1995, seven years after the government sold off the Royal Small Arms Factory, the Enfield Enterprise Agency (now Enterprise Enfield), a body set up to offer support to start-up businesses and existing small businesses by providing practical help and advice, was approached to discover whether it was possible to develop a sustainable use for the crumbling, unloved large machine room. At the time The Enfield Enterprise Agency was chaired by Ian Ferguson, a director of a successful local company. This is a fine example of successful business people wishing to put something back into their local community.

The Enfield Business Centre, Hertford Road, where the offices of Enterprise Enfield are located

To the surprise of most onlookers three directors of the Enterprise Agency, Michael Polledri, Martin Jewell and Mike Wehrmann came together with Gary Walker, who had joined the Enterprise Agency Board a little later, as these colleagues had come up with an outline for an extremely ambitious plan. Gary was to lead the team of four to see if a sustainable long-term solution could be found for the Grade II RSAF listed large machine room, a building that will be recalled was structurally crumbling after years of neglect.

At the time most thought the four were extremely foolhardy and would fail their impossible mission, probably damaging their reputations and ending up with considerable amounts of egg on their faces. Many thought that as a sustainable use for the machine room had eluded others for the past seven years it was not going to be found now. However, there was a good synergy within the team, who brought together the necessary skills of property development, local authority planning, banking and entrepreneurship.

Best practice suggests that all good business ideas should begin with a feasibility study to test project viability and in 1996 the four businessmen were successful in bringing together British Aerospace and English Heritage to secure funding for an investigation to discover whether the building had a sustainable use.

A specialist company was employed to carry out the work which culminated in a report written by Dr Nicholas Falk of Urban and Economic Development Ltd (URBED). The report recommended that the large machine room be turned into a community village centre to service the everyday needs of a proposed housing development that would be created on the rest of the site. In hindsight these proposals seem blindingly obvious but they had escaped the imagination of all those who had tried previously to find solutions for the large machine room.

13. INTRODUCING THE FOUR FOUNDING FATHERS

At this point in the story it would seem to be a suitable time to introduce the founders of the RSA Trust project. By delving into the backgrounds, skills and personalities of the founders, it is hoped the reader will gain an understanding of their motivation, vision, tenacity and drive that put together a sustainable economic model for a not-for-profit Trust, based on an empty unloved semi-derelict nineteenth-century Grade II listed building that nobody really wanted or cared about. Why did the four take on this mammoth task to the ridicule of their peers? After all, they were successful businessmen who were comfortably off, yet they wished to put something back into their community. They had each recognised that there were many people who had come from similar backgrounds to themselves but for a range of complicated reasons had slipped through the net and had not been given the opportunity to fulfil their individual potential. This was all the motivation the founding fathers needed to drive them forward and to ensure that their vision would succeed and was sustainable.

Gary Walker

Gary Walker, Chairman of RSA Trust

Gary is another one of those remarkable men who, through his business and voluntary work has given so much back to the community. He was brought up in a single parent household by his mother who sacrificed much to get him through The Kings School in Peterborough and then Reading University, where he read Physics. On leaving university he turned down the option to do research and instead entered industry, first joining British Aerospace for a period of four years and then working with IBM for seven years.

In 1981 his entrepreneurial talent finally burst through when he co-founded the Enfield based software development company, Data Connections (now Metaswitch Networks). From a relatively humble start this business has become world renowned. In 1984, the company needed a presence in North America and Gary set up a subsidiary in Washington DC, called Data Connections US, and took his family to live in the States for two years. Remarkably, for a company established for only a little over thirty years, it has been regularly listed in the *Sunday Times* top fifteen "100 Best Companies to work for". This accolade would appear to be no coincidence as the ethos of mutual respect and workforce satisfaction has manifested itself throughout all the interviews carried out for this book and can also be identified in the personalities of directors, staff and clients of those businesses associated with the four founders.

In the years since Gary became a successful businessman he has immersed himself in a phenomenal amount of voluntary and charity work, becoming Chairman of the RSA Trust and Chairman of RSA Island Village Limited and he also remains associated at Board and Trustee level with many worthy youth and children's charities. Therefore, when interviewing Gary the question could not be resisted; "when you became comfortably off what made you devote much of your life to working in the community in pursuit of good causes when you could have opted to put your feet up? The answer came as a bit of a surprise – "when my grandfather, to whom I was very close, died at the age of 65, almost immediately after he had retired as a hardworking painter and decorator, I decided there and then that if I reached my fifties and could afford to step back I would ensure that I did something useful with the rest of my life".

In April 2007 Gary was recognised for his community work when he was made Honorary Freeman of the London Borough of Enfield for his "long and valuable public services".

Gary's passion for doing "something useful with the rest of his life" does not only translate into voluntary and charity work, he loves the challenge of extreme adventure. In 1998 he was one of the crew of the Cable and Wireless Adventurer, which broke the world record for circumnavigating the globe in a power-driven vessel in a time of 74 days, 20 hours and 58 minutes. One of his other extreme achievements was being part of an expedition to Antarctica in 2000 where he provided support and logistics to a party of three adventurers who attempted to walk across South Georgia retracing the footsteps of Sir Ernest Shackleton's epic journey.

These are just two of Gary's maritime and other adventures. How he finds time for his wife, three grown up children and six grandchildren plus his lifelong sporting interests is any one's guess! But clearly the man did not exaggerate when he said that he wanted to do "something exciting with the rest of my life"!

Michael Polledri MBE,
Chairman of Lee Valley Estates Limited

Michael came from a modest family background, growing up in Stepney, East London, where he attended the Coopers Company School. Like many young men when leaving school he had no idea what career path he should take. His grandfather suggested that he should become a barber as he would then be equipped with a skill for life. However his father recognised that young Michael was good with figures and persuaded him to join a firm of accountants and so Michael began working life as an Articled Clerk with KPMG (then known as Peat Marwick Mitchell & Co.).

Michael Polledri MBE

In 1972, after seven years with the firm, Michael qualified as a Chartered Accountant, progressing to a position of Supervising Senior with responsibility for a number of prestigious accounts which included companies like United Artists, Southern TV and G.E.C.

After his spell with KPMG Michael began to think seriously about striking out on his own account and this he did by co-founding the Chartered Accounts and Management Consultants, Mapp & Company. The experience allowed Michael to further increase his business acumen and also gave him the chance to seek out moneymaking business opportunities.

Just as Michael was beginning to develop his long-term business strategy he had to take time to pause as his father's family business had run into financial difficulty. Despite all Michael's efforts to save the business he eventually had to grasp the nettle and put the company into receivership.

The unfortunate distraction of having to wind up his father's business took its toll on Michael's personal finances and he had to find ways of paying the bills. In 1987 Michael saw an opportunity to acquire some property which was ripe for redevelopment on the rundown Argall Avenue industrial estate in Leyton, East London, but he did not have the necessary capital to invest in the enterprise.

Fortunately during his career as a Chartered Account Michael had become acquainted with a number of personable business people, many of whom had become good friends. One of these was the Bank Manager, Denys Downing. Denys was able to secure a loan for Michael to acquire the property which became the first in a long line of real-estate in the property portfolio of what has now become the highly respected Lee Valley Estates, the overarching holding company that was established in 2002.

At the time of writing Michael has set up some fourteen successful companies, which remain as separate entities under the umbrella of Lee Valley Estates. In several instances Michael has chosen the difficult path of taking on a project such as an historic listed building. One such example is the former Leyton Town Hall which he, with his partners, was able to completely refurbish in a sensitive manner and return to its former glory. Should it be possible for all those early artisans who originally worked on the building to view it today they would easily recognise many of the fine features, now restored, that their skills had lovingly created. However, the building now supports a business centre, restaurant, forty-nine homes and a magnificent Great Hall that can be hired for events and functions. All these businesses and homes generate a profit which helps maintain the building in good order and also provides Lee Valley Estates with a revenue stream to invest in further regeneration projects.

Surprisingly Michael finds time to support a range of voluntary and charitable causes. He is a director of RSA Island Village Limited, Trustee of the RSA Trust, Chairman of Waltham Forest Business Board, Trustee of Villa Scalabrini (a multicultural care home in Hertfordshire), Member of CHENEL (College of Haringey, Enfield and North East London), Member of the Canal & Rivers Trust (London), and Founder of The LVE Charitable Foundation.

The LVE Charitable Foundation is Michael's latest creation to help improve the lives of young people; this is something that he is passionate about. Perhaps his zeal can be best summed up in the Foundation's Mission Statement:"To work with young people from North London and the Lee Valley Corridor to help them achieve above and beyond society's expectation of them in terms of work, leisure and their community".

The Foundation aims to identify the individual needs of young people, particularly those who have, for whatever reason slipped through Society's net and to discover what support they need to help them achieve their goals. Support can come in a number of forms such as mentoring, training, financial, work placement etc. and will be tailored to meet individual needs.

To ensure the Foundation has a permanent base Lee Valley Estates has funded the hire of the William Morris Room within the Legacy Business Centre in Ruckholt Road, Leyton. By creating this welcoming space Michael believes that the hidden potential in our young people will be released and they will be helped to become the entrepreneurs, community leaders, innovators, role-models, employers and workforce of the future.

In a world that appears to be growing more concerned with taking rather than giving it is refreshing to have so many examples, within the Lea Valley community, of those who genuinely care and are prepared to demonstrate to us all how to give by creating actual economic models that work.

Martin Jewell, Chairman of RSA Island Village Limited

Martin Jewell

Like many children of his generation Martin's early experience of life was being brought up by his mother while his father served in North Africa with the Devon and Cornwall Light Infantry. Martin was educated at Sefton Park Junior School, Bristol and after passing his eleven plus he attended Cotham Grammar School and then, in 1965, graduated from Southampton University with a degree in geography. Nearing completion of the course he sought advice from the University's recently opened careers office about future job prospects. All they could offer was advice to apply for posts in teaching, something Martin was unwilling to do.

Martin had two ambitions for his working life. The first was to try and leave the world a better place and the second to get a position of influence. He decided that a career in Town Planning was the way forward and in 1965 answered a newspaper advertisement for the post of Junior Assistant in the Planning Department in the London Borough of Lewisham and, after interview, his first application was successful. He then took a three-year postgraduate course in Town Planning at the Regent Street Polytechnic, now Westminster University, attending three nights a week after a normal working day.

As Martin admitted, the career ambitions that he had set himself motivated him to become a Chief Planning Officer and he achieved this through sheer determination as he worked his way up the promotion ladder by moving to different Local Authorities; from Lewisham to Westminster, to Croydon then back to Lewisham and finally, in 1973, to the London Borough of Enfield where he initially took up the post of Group Leader in charge of the Borough Development Plan team. Martin remained in that post for the next eleven years while overseeing the first Development Plan which shaped the future development of the Borough. In 1984 Martin was appointed Deputy Borough Planning Officer. Then in 1987, 22 years after setting his goal, Martin finally achieved his lifelong ambition when he was appointed Borough Planning Officer, a position he held until his first retirement in 1997.

Towards the mid 1980s job opportunities within the Borough of Enfield were becoming scarce, mainly because of cheap imports and the failure of British industry to modernise after the Second World War. Household names in the manufacturing sector like Belling, Belling & Lee, Sangamo Weston, the Thorn group of companies and subsequently the Royal Small Arms Factory at Enfield Lock eventually succumbed to external pressures. Fortunately Enfield Council saw that the lack of jobs would quickly lead to wide-scale social deprivation and Martin was charged with writing a report, which was circulated to the appropriate Council Committees, on what measures the Council could take to assist local business.

In the report Martin suggested that Councillors might like to consider setting up an Enterprise Agency to support small businesses and perhaps more importantly help unemployed people to set up in business on their own account. The Councillors agreed with Martin's proposal and to help take the idea forward the Mayor invited business leaders to a reception to discuss the plan. This resulted in the setting up of a working party of business leaders and Council members, of which Martin was one, and in 1985 Enfield Enterprise Agency was born. The Agency is now more familiarly known as Enterprise Enfield.

Martin's part in and his connections with the development of the large machine room at the Royal Small Arms Factory site highlights an important lesson for many aspiring business leaders; to ensure that a strict focus is kept on the business objective and not to over commit resources by taking on extra projects.

The Enfield Enterprise Agency had recently taken over a redundant building in Queensway, Ponders End and had it converted it into 53 small business units with the idea of encouraging new business start-ups. The reader will probably recognise that this particular project may have planted, in Martin's mind, the germ of an idea about finding a possible use for the rapidly deteriorating RSAF large machine room.

Perhaps more pertinent to the story within this book, Martin in his role as Borough Planning Officer, was only too aware that despite all the efforts, no commercial organisation was prepared to take on the challenge of the Grade II listed large machine room at Enfield Lock. However, Martin seems to have been harbouring other thoughts!

Once the Queensway project was underway and attracting clients there was the opportunity for the Enfield Enterprise Agency to take on another regeneration project. Could the "Queensway model" somehow provide the blueprint that would unlock the long-standing problem of the large machine room? Interestingly clause 4.6 in the Deed pursuant to S.106 of the Town & Country Planning Act 1990 relating to the Royal Small Arms Factory Site Enfield, dated 28th June 1996 (see Bibliography) requires "the owner to submit to the Council its proposal for a marketing campaign which is to seek to find an alternative use/user or uses for the listed machine shop...". And according to Martin "this was part of the catalyst, as well as the initiative of Enfield Enterprise Agency, to promote seeking a future for the building".

With the Queensway project and the earlier planning requirement in mind Martin took the opportunity to introduce the ideas at an Enfield Enterprise Agency meeting. It would appear that others at the Agency saw the vision and it was agreed to take on the challenge of turning the large machine room into a commercially viable business. Fortunately the four Agency directors, Gary Walker, Michael Polledri, Mike Wehrmann and Martin Jewell had the good business sense to form a separate company, RSA Island Village Limited, to deliver the project. This was done to prevent sinking the Enfield Enterprise Agency should the initiative fail. Of course we now know the project, with its not-for-profit ethic, became a runaway success, creating jobs, new businesses and, at the time of writing, over £4 million generated for good causes.

After his first retirement in 1997 Martin was subsequently appointed Planning Director of Fairview Estates (Housing) Ltd, a post he held until 2003 when he left to set up his own Planning Consultancy. In 2005, with three friends, Martin became a founding Director of Chase Green Developments Ltd (now Chase Green Homes Ltd), a position he held until his final retirement. Since then he devoted much of his time to the activities of Enterprise Enfield until resigning from the Board in 2015 after thirty years of service. While Martin has taken two retirements in his life, escaping the increasing demands and pressures of business, he has now taken on extra responsibilities by becoming Chairman of Enfield Island Village Limited and a Trustee of the RSA Trust. However, he has actually managed to relax a little by finding time to play golf twice a week!

Martin's wife Doreen Willis also shares his passion for community good causes as she is a Trustee of the Enfield Youth and Community Trust and also a Trustee of Children's International Voices Enfield. Doreen and Martin have five children and five grandchildren between them which have probably added to Martin's retirement relaxation!

Mike Wehrmann, former Banking Executive with Barclays Bank

Mike Wehrmann

Mike is another example of how to succeed in life even after his education suffered a disastrous start as his parents moved house thirteen times to seek new job opportunities. Despite this early setback he discovered that he was one of those young men with practical skills excelling in woodwork, metalwork and vehicle restoration. He also possessed a good understanding of Physics and Maths which allowed him to receive a grant to read Physics at London University. To help support himself he got a Saturday job at the Charing Cross Branch of Barclays Bank suggesting that he had knowledge of computers, although he confided to the author that at the time he had never used one! Fortunately for Mike the Branch did not have any computer equipment and he no doubt breathed a huge sigh of relief.

After a year at University Mike realised that to progress to a reasonable career in Physics he would need to acquire a First Class Honours Degree, which he did not feel he could achieve, so in November 1968 he returned his grant and went to work for Barclays Bank full time. Mike's work with the Bank took him to various places around London and he recalled that on one occasion when working as Office Manager at the Covent Garden Branch he had to oversee the relocation of two Branches into temporary premises while being involved with the restoration of an historic building. This is when Mike's hands-on skills became extremely useful as he attended meetings with the architects and oversaw operations on site wearing a hard hat. Unbeknown to Mike at the time the hard hat experience would stand him in good stead when he became involved with the large machine room regeneration project at Enfield Lock.

Mike had joined Barclays at a time when businesses were beginning to install computer systems and it would be fair to say that not many people knew too much about them and in some quarters there was resistance rather than acceptance as people thought their jobs would be put at risk. As Mike freely admitted his computer skills are completely self-taught. However, he must have acquired a good grounding as he was able to look after the programme for the new Small Firms Loan Guarantee Scheme for the whole of Barclays Bank. Apparently there was nobody else in the Business Development Department that could operate the recently acquired "not so portable" IBM computer.

In the late 1980s Mike was given clearance by the Bank to take up a Non Executive Director position at the Enfield Enterprise Agency (later named Enterprise Enfield). Mike's banking and business credentials immediately made him the obvious candidate to take on the role of bidding for the recently released European grant funding scheme that had been launched to support new business start ups in economically and socially deprived areas; parts of Enfield had already met the criteria. Not surprisingly Mike's first bid was successful and this helped fund the Agency's various training programmes to re-skill the Borough's unemployed.

During Mike's time as Corporate Manager of the Bank's Enfield Business Centre he had made it a priority to visit his customers regularly as he believed that this was essential good business practice. In getting to know his clients he hoped to gain their respect and trust but perhaps more importantly he would get to swiftly understand problems and take the necessary remedial action. This approach, in Mike's view, would be beneficial to both Bank and clients in the long term.

When Mike finally left the Bank in 1995 his customer-centric approach to business banking was deemed old fashioned by the new young blood that was then beginning to populate the banking sector. Interestingly, when working for the Enfield Company Thorn EMI Ferguson I experienced a similar situation shortly after the death of my old boss, Sir Jules Thorn, in 1980. This man, an Austrian Jew, came to Britain in the 1920s selling gas mantles for his homeland manufacturer. When his employer went bust he was stranded in a foreign country but through sheer hard work and determination he was able to acquire a small light bulb manufacturing business in Enfield and from there he founded a worldwide empire that employed over eighty thousand people. When the new brigade of managers came in after his death, Sir Jules, a very hands-on businessman, was referred to as nothing more than a shopkeeper!

Perhaps if those in the worldwide banking industry had remained customer-centric and applied some of Mike's "old fashioned" methods we may have avoided the serious financial meltdown of recent years.

Back row left to right: Gary Walker, Mike Whermann, Martin Jewell, Michael Polledri MBE, photographed with community police officers

14. MAKING THE VISION REALITY

By 1997 the URBED recommendations had been accepted and the four directors appear to have been left alone to take the Enfield Lock project, now known as the Enfield Island Village, to the next phase. This would mean creating a business plan and also seeking and securing the necessary regeneration funding to complete the construction work. By now a credible visionary plan had emerged for the village centre which would act as a hub for the local community, supporting a proposal for 1,300 new homes, of which 25 per cent would be social housing. This part of the plan would be completed by the local developer, Fairview New Homes, the company who had recently bought the Enfield Lock site from British Aerospace.

Large machine room with head pond filled in, c1990

The large machine room had been added to in the fifties and sixties, so there was 200,000 square feet to play with. The RSA IV directors developed plans to turn it into retail space for local shops and units for small businesses (a community hall, a health centre and youth centre would come later). Fairview released the freehold of the large machine room to RSA IV to deliver the project. The transfer of the building was arranged for a peppercorn fee and a dowry of £0.5 million completed the deal.

While initially things were looking good for the embryonic RSA IV there was still a long way to go before the four directors could achieve their target of £4.0 million, the amount that they estimated was needed to secure their vision of a bustling community hub.

The area next to Benedict House where the extensions to the large machine once stood

In the period following the Cold War, which had ended with the dissolution of the Soviet Union in December 1991, many defence industries across Europe had closed or had drastically run down their operations after seeing a rapid decline in armament orders. The industries' demise had resulted in great hardship amongst many skilled workforces as countries right across Europe struggled to create new jobs or training opportunities for their unemployed. This situation was quickly recognised by members of the European Union and in 1993 a special programme was approved, under the one of the Europe's "Cohesion and Structural Funds" which was given the acronym KONVER. The initiative was to make funding available for "the redevelopment of former military bases and barracks, the creation of leisure areas, the repair or creation of infrastructure networks and the renovation or conversion of former military buildings to other uses".

The directors of the RSA IV made an application to the KONVER fund and were successful in securing funding of almost £2.0 million.

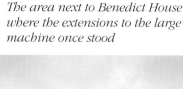

However, there was still a shortfall of £1.5 million to reach the target needed to start the regeneration of the Grade II listed building that, over the past few years, had seen further weather damage to its shell. The target figure was finally achieved through a successful application for £0.5 million from English Partnerships (now incorporated into the Homes and Communities Agency) which gave the directors the financial stability to secure a commercial loan of £1.0 million from the Anglo Irish Bank plc.

15. A PROGRESS HICCOUGH OCCURS

Just as everyone thought that things were beginning to move along nicely with the regeneration of the redundant brown-field site, delays to Fairview's building programme and to the development of the large machine room into Enfield Island Village occurred. In the 1990s concerns had been raised by the Enfield Lock Action Group and Friends of the Earth regarding possible site contamination. The group believed that over the years, when the factory was active, random dumping of toxic materials had occurred and they expressed their concerns in a 154 page report entitled *Unsafe as Houses*. The issues were also aired in a BBC Panorama programme.

To investigate the claims the Royal Small Arms Review Panel was set up by the London Borough of Enfield. The Panel took evidence from witnesses, looked at site environmental reports that had been produced over the previous ten years and also took evidence from the Head of Land Quality at the Environmental Agency. After the investigation the Review Panel came to the conclusion that the site was safe for housing development. The findings of the Review Panel were endorsed by the European Union.

In is only in recent years that developers have turned their attentions towards brown-field sites, because suitable land for building purposes has become scarce. The post-war brown-field technique of treating mildly contaminated sites was used at Enfield Lock to facilitate the building of the housing estate by Fairview New Homes. The method of treatment is achieved by first removing the top soil and before replacing the earth sealing the site with a one-metre thick clay cap. Initially, after the work was completed, test samples were taken from the site every six months but now checks take place just once a year.

Interestingly the large machine room, which has now become the RSA Island Centre, has a solid concrete base and did not raise the same concerns as the land designated for the housing estate although, as a precaution, the site was subject to monitoring.

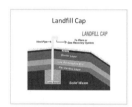

A diagram showing a typical system of capping a brownfield site

16. REGENERATION COMMENCES

In 1998, after a tendering process, the construction company Mansell Group was chosen to begin the major task of turning the large machine room into attractive shops and workspace units. During the 1960s and 1970s the large machine room had had extra buildings added, increasing the overall footprint from 180,000 square feet to 200,000 square feet. As the extra 20,000 square feet did not form part of the 1856 Grade II listed building, English Heritage agreed with the decision to demolish these rather ugly appendages. The decision was helped by the fact that only the first twelve bays of the machine room, with their distinctive "north light" roofline, were listed and the later additions were not deemed important to retain although they had been originally included in the listings curtilage. This was a sensible and crucial decision as it had the advantage of enabling the improvement of access by creating a roadway through the listed building to the new shops and business units that were about to be built. The demolition work also freed-up building space on the east side of the site that would in future provide an ideal area for the construction of Benedict House, the headquarters of Christian Action (Enfield) Housing Association Limited, a provider of much needed accommodation that complimented the ethos of the four founders.

The large machine room prior to change of use into the Enfield Island Village community hub

Below: *Inside the large machine during the first construction phase*

Below right: *The large machine room construction, phase two*

Now that work was underway the four businessmen took tight commercial control of proceedings and monthly meetings were introduced to drive the project forward and to ensure that budgets and timescales were being met.

While all the construction was taking place the hard task of getting tenants for the shops and business units was begun so that rents could start flowing in once the project was completed. However, Gary Walker seems to have had time on his hands! Not only was he involved with his own business interests and the task of driving the Enfield Island Village Centre regeneration forward but he was also itching to start a second project that would celebrate the heritage of Enfield Lock (more about this in the following chapter).

A red sandstone grinding wheel from the RSAF grinding shop. The building once stood south of the head pond

17. CELEBRATING ENFIELD LOCK'S HERITAGE

Acutely aware that the history of the Royal Small Arms Factory and the successive generations of its highly skilled workforce should be acknowledged and celebrated, Gary Walker instigated the creation of an Interpretation Centre and also the restoration of the ancient clock, whose giant bell, Albert, once reminded the workforce that time was a necessary discipline.

Of course the second project required extra funding and a successful application for £50,000 was made to the Heritage Lottery Fund which was matched by contributions from company sponsors. These were mainly businesses that had an association with the project and included Data Connections Ltd, Charterhouse Mercantile Properties Ltd, Enfield Enterprise Agency, Capita Property Services, Mansell plc, London Development Agency, London Borough of Enfield and RSA IV. Individual private sponsors were also invited to contribute. These included Martin Jewell, Michael Polledri, Gary Walker, Mike Wehrmann and members of the RSAF Apprentices Association.

Civix, a specialist heritage contractor, were appointed project managers. This company had previously worked on several high profile projects including Lego Land, Windsor and the Royal Gunpowder Mills at Waltham Abbey. Civix were tasked with the design of an Interpretation Centre in space allocated directly beneath the iconic clock tower with the aim of showcasing the history of the site through a series of information panels and a selection of relevant artefacts. The contractor worked with Ray Tuthill, President of the RSAF Apprentices Association and a local historian to complete a series of site interpretation boards and panels that would allow interested residents and visitors to understand the former significance of the place in keeping Britain safe during times of conflict.

A plaque on the former RSAF pattern room. A number of these plaques are placed on buildings around the site, providing historical information

The regeneration programme, by virtue of its nature, had caused changes of use to important buildings that surround Enfield Island Village Centre and these were given small information panels to explain their former use.

The Enfield Pattern Room

The history of this world-famous building has been covered earlier in the book. Through Fairview's site development the Pattern Room has now seen a change of use which has allowed the building to sensitively retain its external Victorian characteristics. Internally its weapon associations have vanished and the building's interior has been supplanted by much needed living accommodation. No doubt the late curator Herbert Woodend MBE would be happy to see that his beloved building still remains, although it is now providing a different service for the community. A plaque on the outside of the building, unveiled by his daughters and sister, commemorates his stewardship.

From left to right at plaque unveiling: the late Herbert Woodend's two daughters, Sarah Lever, Arleen Vince, and his sister, Helen Montgomery

The former RSAF pattern room, now part of Enfield Island Village housing stock

The pattern room at Enfield Lock before the collection was transferred to Nottingham after closure

The rescued factory church font

A church was built in 1857 within the grounds of the Royal Small Arms Factory to serve the Lockie congregation. After the church was demolished by government order in 1921, on reasons of economy, the font was removed and eventually found its way to a place within the grounds of St Peter & St Paul Church that had been built in Ordnance Road in 1928 (a later church now stands on this site). There it remained unloved and exposed to the elements yet fortunately surviving when the church suffered bomb damage during the Second World War.

The font that once stood in the RSAF on-site church, now restored and in a protective glass case

The RSAF church, built c1850, was demolished in 1928.

These railings once stood inside the large machine room and were used to section off the gun stocking shop area

With the help of the RSA Trust the font was rescued and restored and can now be seen placed in a purpose-built glass pyramid that stands within the courtyard adjacent to the RSA Trust and RSA IV offices within the precincts of Enfield Island Village Centre.

On 27th October 2001, Fr. John Vaughn, parish priest of St Peter and Paul, held a special ceremony to dedicate the font.

Railings from the large machine room stocking shop

As the name implies the stocking shop was the part of the factory that manufactured the wooden gun stocks that formed an important part of the small arm. The railings were originally placed within the large machine room to divide the stocking shop from other areas of manufacture. At some time in the railings' life they were removed and placed outside on the west side of the site and were often used by various senior factory personnel to tie up their horses. When regeneration of the factory took place in the 1990s the railings were removed by contractors and stored for safe keeping. After restoration they were reinstated in their former position on the west side of the site.

Cast iron machine room columns and guttering saved

Perhaps people might wonder why the decision was taken by RSA IV directors to save and restore surplus columns and guttering that were removed during the regeneration of the large machine room rather that sell them to the scrap-man for a little cash. If this latter option had been taken the opportunity would have been lost to expose a great piece of Victorian ingenuity.

The guttering, which is probably better described as a cast iron trough, caught and channelled rainwater from the north light roof sections to the various columns that had hollow centres that acted as drain pipes. Also the columns served as roof supports and provided places on which brackets were positioned to hold the overhead line shafting that drove leather belts that powered the factory's machine tools. The columns held a further set of brackets which supported the steam pipes that warmed the building.

Visitors to the site will note that cast iron columns stand to the west of the Christian Action Housing building. Should visitors wish to venture northward through the housing estate towards the edge of the island a rather attractive domed artwork has been created out of other surplus columns.

When admiring the various flower containers that populate the Enfield Island Village Centre, take a closer look and some Victorian cast iron guttering might be observed!

RSA Trust business units in the background, with flower containers in the foreground made from sections of Victorian guttering

An artwork made from Victorian iron columns removed during the redevelopment of the large machine room

Note. The north light roof, sometimes referred to as saw-tooth, due to its distinctive shape, was designed to supplement the poor lighting in Victorian factories by allowing in natural light and due to its north-facing position shield the workforce from direct sunlight. Several examples of these mono-pitched roofs can be seen across the country and the preserved roof-line of the large machine room is a particularly good example.

The narrow boat and head pond

Although not strictly part of the RSAF history the narrow boat has been placed on the opened-up area of the original head pond and barge turning basin that once served the RSAF's barrel grinding mills with power. Now re-named Harold Turpin the boat commemorates the work of an Enfield Lock weapon designer who, with his colleague Reginald V. Shepherd, invented and developed the Sten light machine gun. The narrow boat acts as a vivid reminder that water transport once formed an important part of the working of the factory by moving goods and material to and from the site.

The space created around the head pond has been designed to form a pleasant area where people can sit and relax and has the added bonus of allowing the visitor to observe the insect and bird life that has now been attracted to the area.

The water tower

When approaching Enfield Island Village Centre across the new road bridge that crosses the River Lea and Lee Navigation it is impossible to miss the restored water tower on the roundabout directly in front. This building, with its large water tank, once acted as part of a distribution system to quench factory fires and not, as commonly thought, to provide drinking water to the

This water tower provided water to extinguish factory fires which was not suitable to drink

Albert, the bell that hangs in the clock tower, above the Interpretation Centre, was cast at the Royal Arsenal Brass Foundry, Woolwich

site buildings. Water was pumped from the River Lea to fill the tank and a story which has now become part of a Lockie legend was that small fish used to get sucked up too. Apparently, over time, these captured fish grew to be quite large specimens but it is not known if they ended up on dinner plates or were returned to the river!

Visitors to the site with an interest in its history can obtain walking trail maps from the RSA Trust office.

Restoration of the ancient clock

The Royal Small Arms Factory clock was built by the clockmakers Thwaites & Reed, a firm of famous horologists established in 1740. For thirty years Thwaites & Reed looked after the clocks in the Palace of Westminster, including the Great Clock, incorrectly called Big Ben by many. It is the large bell which chimes the hourly strike which is called Big Ben.

Built c1783 the RSAF clock, which is installed in the iconic Italianate style tower, pre-dates the large machine room by over seventy years and is believed to have been taken from another building. As we have seen the large machine room was built in 1856 to house the machine tools purchased from America which allowed the production of the Enfield 1853 rifle by a system of mass production. Incidentally, 1856 was the same year that Albert, the clock's chiming bell, was cast at Woolwich Arsenal.

Since closure of the Royal Small Arms Factory the clock had remained neglected and unloved. When engineers from the makers were engaged to inspect the clock, prior to renovation, it was discovered that the moving parts had rusted so badly that they no longer moved. What is more, not wishing to miss this static opportunity and no doubt thinking of a room with a view, the local pigeon community decided to take up nesting rights in the stationary mechanism which further added to the ancient clock's woes.

Thwaites & Reed finally removed the clock's mechanism and many long hours were spent removing years of neglect and also damage that had been caused by the pigeons. Each individual part had to be removed and restored to high conservation standards. During this conservation work it was noted that the clock mechanism bore five different dates (frame plate 1783, setting dial 1808, clockmaker's mark 1857 and barrel 1856 & 1883). It was thought by the writer that these various dates might suggest that, over the years, parts

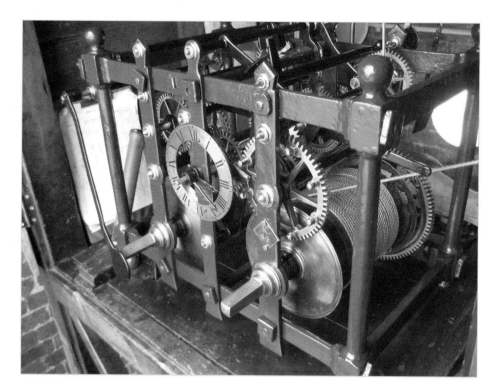

from different clocks had been used to replace failed originals. However, when speaking with Melvyn Lee the Managing Director of Thwaites and Reed it was explained that it was not unusual for clocks of this age to be assembled from parts of different dates (stamped into the metal) that the clockmaker would have held in stock. I find it difficult to accept this theory because; if the clock was built in c1783, the eighteenth century, how could the clockmaker have parts stamped with nineteenth-century dates in his stock?

As the clock had been installed after the building had been completed in 1856, probably in 1857, one date, 1883, post-dates this period. Therefore, it was presumed that this particular date might have been scratched rather than stamped, like marks left by jewellers today to indicate when a clock or watch was repaired. This theory was put to voluntary clock winder Ray Tuthill who said that he would check next time he visited. When Ray tried to check the date in question he discovered that it was inconveniently obscured by other clock parts.

Never a man to be beaten by such trivialities, Ray equipped himself with a mirror and returned. Once more climbing the vertical maintenance ladder then painfully contorting his body around the clock frame he was able to just make out some letters stamped onto the metal which he thought could be the latter half of the makers name Thwaites. Ray also remarked that he could see "something else which was unclear; I am not convinced that it either is or includes a date, but that is possible", he said. Defeat is not a part of Ray's character as he confidently remarked "I shall try to have another look when I next visit on Tuesday". When this further attempt was announced serious concerns began invading thoughts regarding Ray's aching body parts as he stoically volunteered for yet another clock dating mission impossible. By now there was an overpowering wish that the question of the 1883 date had never been raised in the first place.

At the time of his next visit Ray had equipped himself with a powerful inspection lamp to accompany his mirror and then once again made the tenuous vertical climb to have a further look at the clock's innermost parts.

After the inspection the author received a full A4 email from Ray. For brevity the author will not reproduce it here, but he is "now certain as he can be that the date is 1837" and not 1883. In qualifying this Ray was absolutely certain that he had correctly identified the first three digits of the date and then remarked that "there could be a slight dispute over the last one"!

It is now my view that Ray's dogged observations have enabled me to confidently conclude that the puzzle has been solved and all the dates, so far discovered, are prior to the clock tower being built. However, it has now been learned that Ray is looking for a suitable magnifying glass so that he can **definitely confirm** the last digit of the 1837 date. Ray; if you think that this chapter is going to be re-edited for the fourth time you are very much mistaken!

The fully restored clock was re-installed in its original tower setting and now sports four beautiful solid slate dials set into cast iron bezels. The hands, made from copper, have been sensitively restored and ribbed for strength. With consideration for the sleep of the local community the clock has had a clever little mechanism fitted to silence Albert's chimes during the hours of night.

Volunteers manually wind the clock once a week and if necessary it is possible to regulate the time by adjusting a rating nut at the end of the pendulum.

Patrick Gray, the RSA Trust Heritage Manager, outside the Trust's office at Enfield Island Village

The RSA Interpretation Centre

Students from Birkbeck and Goldsmiths Colleges in the RSAF Interpretation Centre, February 2018

Ray Tuthill, President of the RSAF Apprentices' Association, who, out of the goodness of his heart appears to have become the clock's winder in chief, told an amusing story about Albert's timing. The "clever little mechanism", referred to above to silence the bell consists of a highly technical arrangement. This is an off-the-shelf AM/PM central heating timer wired to a solenoid that is connected to a mechanism which holds off the hammer to prevent the bell from striking. The arrangement was installed when the refurbished clock was returned to the tower. When everything was nicely working Thwaites & Reed sent their Dutch technician to set the off time of the clock but it would seem that he became confused by the unfamiliar AM/PM timer terminology. However, his thought processes persevered and eventually he had a "light bulb" moment; of course, AM must mean, **after midday**! Complaints came rolling in from bleary-eyed villagers!

Note. Ray; determined to the end, did eventually acquire a suitable magnifying glass and can now confirm **100 per cent** that the elusive clock date is 1837! Therefore, as this number has been stamped into the clock, rather than scratched, it can probably be concluded that at some time in the past a recording error had been made when copying this date to paper.

18. THE BIG DAY ARRIVES

Finally on 27th October 2001, before a crowd of local people invited to witness history in the making, the Deputy Mayor of London, Nicky Gavron, accompanied by Gary Walker, Chairman of RSA IV and RSA Trust, cut a red ribbon suspended across the doorway of the Interpretation Centre and declared the RSA Island Centre officially open. The ceremony was also attended by local MP Joan Ryan and the Deputy Mayor of Enfield, Councillor Ivor Wigget.

Guests were taken on tours around the site by knowledgeable volunteers and were shown the new history boards and panels which had been placed on those buildings that were of particular importance to the unique history of the site. Children were treated to face painting, while a circus skills workshop provided further entertainment. Rhino, from the popular television show Gladiators greeted his fans and expressed the view that the RSA Island Centre captured the spirit of the urban village and was an excellent model for future developments throughout London. A jazz band had been hired to play while guests mingled and talked on a beautiful autumn day which added a party atmosphere to the occasion. In the large newly constructed community room an illustrated presentation was given by a local historian to a full audience, followed by a buffet.

It would be fair to conclude that, by the expressions on the faces of guests departing the event, they were leaving with warm contented feelings. Directors of the RSA Trust and RSA IV must have also felt great satisfaction as their dreams had been partially realised.

Following the celebrations the directors received a letter from the attending MP Joan Ryan. The observations that she made (reproduced below) capture the atmosphere of the day and the importance of the regeneration project to Enfield and the local community.

The opening of the RSA Island Centre at the Enfield Island Village was certainly one of the nicest events an MP can attend. The sun shone, the band played and the people laughed and chatted. This was a real community event. Of course, what we were all doing was celebrating the opening of what was the 'heart' of the Enfield Island Village community. One major concern when new developments are built is the fact that infrastructure such as schools, community centres, shops and doctors surgery do not have to be included in the plans. A community can in theory come into being with none of the facilities it needs to ensure its well-being. This is fortunately not the case at Enfield Island Village.

The old machine shops of the original Royal Small Arms Factory have been completely transformed and the residents now have some very welcome shops, café, community centre and heritage centre. The new primary school on Innova Park for the children of Enfield Island Village is under construction and just a few weeks ago I opened the doctor's surgery and dental access centre.

Some of these facilities had to be campaigned and argued for, but they have been achieved and Enfield Island Village will have the facilities that a new community needs. The RSA Island Centre is the heart of the development, provides a focal point for the residents and this will help to support the development and the transition from residents to 'community'. Well done everybody and seasons greetings.

Joan Ryan MP

However, with all the praise and nice words there could be no taking eyes off the ball because the model that the directors had created had now to be managed and constantly and carefully monitored.

The grand opening of Enfield Island Village

19. LONG-TERM SITE MANAGEMENT BEGINS

As already alluded to, completing the regeneration of the large Grade II machine room and having an enjoyable opening ceremony did not mean that it was time for resting on laurels, as this was the completion of just one, although an important, phase in the overall plan. Now the real work of delivering the four directors' vision of having a long-term sustainable business model to invigorate the local community would begin in earnest. If the directors got this particular part of the project wrong then all those earlier criticisms of foolhardiness from the negative soothsayers would come home to roost and this would no doubt seriously dent respected business judgements and damage personal reputations.

One of the directors' first actions was to decide that RSA IV was to be the overall management company for the RSA Island Centre with a focus on maintenance and the cleanliness of the surrounding area to ensure that the site was welcoming to new and prospective clients. Dr Mike Taylor, formerly with Bush Boake Allen, was appointed Estate Manager and was given the important task of managing the commercial arm of the business. This would include the collection of rents from the various businesses that were now being installed in and around the large machine room. The profits generated from the rent revenue stream would be donated to the RSA Trust that was planned to be set up within the coming months. As might be imagined Mike had to get up to speed quickly with his new challenge and was provided with an Administrative Assistant, Michelle Kyprianou who took control of organising the office and also the day-to-day liaison with the incoming clients.

Mike's task of managing the estate and servicing the new business clients as they moved in was one thing, but the RSA IV directors quickly realised that the RSA Island Centre that they had created to act as a shopping and community hub for the whole of the residential development did not perform in the same way as a typical village centre or high street model. To rectify the situation the directors agreed to engage the services of Annette Mitchell who had considerable experience in the field of marketing and event management. Annette was given a two-year contract and set the extreme challenge of marketing and populating the newly constructed units with the right mix of businesses to a level of 80 per cent within the first year of the RSA Island Centre opening. Remarkably this seemingly impossible task was achieved.

Once the smooth running of the site had been established, which had been achieved by tight commercial management from a fully staffed office located within the Grade II listed building, the continuing role of managing the estate was contracted out to Lee Valley Estates, a local property company with a strong community ethic and a sound track record, for a short period until the management function was brought back in house. Since the opening of the RSA Island Centre the annual unit occupancy has consistently reached on or near 100 per cent which has generated rent revenues in excess of £0.5 million per annum and climbing.

The success of the four directors' sustainable business model can be judged by the diversity of the businesses that have been attracted to the site which are crucial to maintaining and supporting the needs of the local community; businesses like Enfield Island Medical Centre, a pharmacy, Island Village Library, Island Fitness, Splash Day Nursery Crèche, Tesco Express, Enfield Christian Action Housing and the Youth Centre.

As will have been observed earlier, these and other businesses based in the thoughtfully and carefully restored former large machine room, sit within a pleasant setting of a mains water channel feeding into a wildlife supporting pond with a themed narrow boat gently bobbing on the surface. There are also ample parking spaces for visitors and residents. The area has been specifically designed to serve and act as the heart for the local community which now consists of over four thousand people. It is also hoped that this particular space will promote a safe and friendly environment for years to come.

When government first decided to build the armoury at Enfield Lock in the early nineteenth century to compete with the poorly organised private gun trade, they could not have foreseen that two hundred years later their project would have turned into a "from swords into ploughshares" ending.

20. CONCLUSIONS

It would appear that Britain, after 200 years, is in a similar position to when it had to rely on overseas manufacturers for arms to fight Napoleon

Looking back at the history of the Royal Small Arms Factory from the twenty-first century the reader will probably conclude that successive governments have changed little when it comes to arranging and managing contracts, particularly in areas of defence. Here we seem to have learned nothing from past mistakes and now find ourselves in a similar position as we were in the late eighteenth century when we relied on small arms purchases from manufacturers abroad to fight the armies of Napoleon.

Today, the great majority of our military small arms are manufactured abroad as are much of our heavy armaments including aircraft, naval vessels and their various weapon systems. It would appear that the best that British manufacturers can hope to achieve is to receive the odd contract for making a part for some off-shore produced military equipment. In time of war, such reliance on others leaves Britain extremely vulnerable.

Regularly we read articles in the press or see programmes on television about serious product delays and gross overspending. Also we hear about costly modifications having to be made to military equipment as compatibility issues come to light. Public rage and frustrations surface as we learn from the media that the taxpayer will have to bail out, yet again, another government contractual or purchasing blunder in the area of defence. Not to mention other issues that regularly get reported in the media regarding the National Health Service, public utilities and transport infrastructure projects.

Not having sufficient experienced and knowledgeable personnel overseeing our military procurement, particularly as the technology has become more sophisticated, has left our country, as we have already mentioned, exceedingly vulnerable. Now increasingly we rely on overseas sources for weapons and homeland security. This type of unsatisfactory situation leaves us exposed to external financial pressures, without the necessary controls that we could have with more in-house manufacturers and contractors. In the long term, in-house manufacture could prove more cost-effective as it would give government greater and closer control of the contract system.

The post 1987 period, after closure of the RSAF site, turns into a really good news story for the local community. This is due to the vision of the directors of the not-for-profit charity, the RSA Trust and the model they created to regenerate an unloved Grade II listed building and its surroundings into a thriving community hub to support Enfield Island Village, generating to date, £5 million for good causes. Future governments might like to look closely at this particular model with a view to encouraging entrepreneurs within local communities to become involved in similar not-for-profit projects that can stimulate jobs and enhance well-being. **The challenge has been set; who will pick up the baton?**

21. APPENDIX

The following are just a few examples of those community organisations that have benefited from start-up funding from the RSA Trust. As already mentioned the funding for good causes has already reached £5 million and will no doubt grow and help create more community start-ups. The funding has also been set up to support established worthwhile projects.

Gladys Anoquah. Natgab Services Limited

Gladys, a former senior nurse and care team manager who had worked within several leading NHS hospitals explained that in later years her job had become too bureaucratic with "80% of her time being taken up with report writing". This had caused her much anguish as she felt the increasing amounts of paperwork were preventing her from providing the caring services that she had been trained to perform. Gladys said that the everyday pressures which she had encountered became so great and stressful that it was felt there was no alternative but regrettably to quit the service. After a period of redundancy and recuperation when Gladys struggled to plan her future career, she saw an Enterprise Enfield advertisement for the RSA Trust *Inspiring Women* programme which is designed to give women the necessary skills to get back into work or start their own businesses. Successful candidates are invited to join the six-month, completely free, programme where they first attend a residential weekend followed by weekly six to nine hours of intensive training seminars and also one to one support sessions with expert advisers. During the course candidates are introduced to all the various aspects of business and also have the opportunity to develop their own particular business ideas. At the end of these courses it has been found that most of the candidates have gained the confidence and self esteem to enter employment or to pursue their own dreams of starting a business.

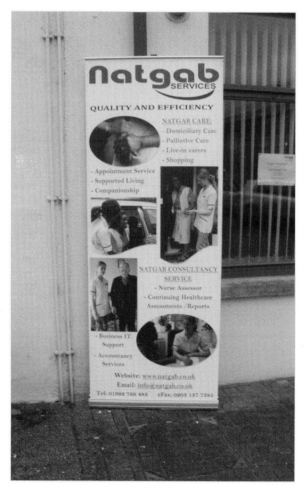

Natgab Services Limited offices at the Enfield Island Village Centre

Gladys applied to join the programme and was accepted, then introduced to a range of subjects like financial management and analysis, raising finance, book keeping, business planning and Information Technology, all areas that she fully admitted "were completely alien to her". Nevertheless, she persevered and readily devoured all the coursework and by the end of the course, with the help of her advisors, was able to develop her ideas into a credible business plan. Gladys, through her former NHS experience, had identified a gap in the care market which in 2013 allowed her to form Natgab Services Limited, a company that is a Care Quality Commission (CQC) registered community domiciliary service provider.

Anyone who has experienced the problems of finding the right kind of care support package for a loved one will know how stressful, for all parties, this can be. Researching what is available from diminishing and limited local authority and private sector services can also be a harrowing experience. Until meeting Gladys I had absolutely no idea what care services could be offered and speaking to friends and relatives afterwards they were also amazed at the range of services that her company could provide.

Natgab provide domiciliary care for the physically frail, those in our community with mental health issues and people with disabilities and also those who have different levels of learning difficulties. Gladys has assembled a team of around forty experienced carers and support workers that can provide a comprehensive range of services that cater for just about every care need that you can think of. After each client's needs are initially assessed an individual bespoke care plan will be arranged and if care is required 24/7 this can be provided.

Areas such as domestic cleaning, laundry, shopping, cooking meals (even special dietary needs are catered for and the ingredients sourced), arranging client outings, administering medication, and continence needs are serviced. Also a service is provided when a carer will sit with a client who is facing the end of life. Currently Gladys offers care services to clients in Enfield, Haringey, Camden and Islington and currently works from an office located within Enfield Island Centre. However, Gladys has ambitions to grow the business nationally and if this should happen her care services are sure to be welcomed by many frail and vulnerable people.

When speaking with Gladys it was impossible not to notice her passion and enthusiasm for care with dignity within our community. What a loss might have occurred if she had missed seeing the advertisement for the RSA Trust's *Inspiring Women* programme administered by Enterprise Enfield!

Dr Kostakis Evangelou. Edmonton Eagles Amateur Boxing Club

It must be confessed that this particular interview was approached with a little apprehension as it did not seem logical that a club, which put two young people together into a ring to beat each other to a pulp, could have beneficial outcomes. As this interview would eventually prove, this rather impulsive thought by the writer, was completely unjustified as it was shown that the club could provide facilities which would fulfil, rather than damage, young lives. Therefore, it just goes to show how we can often seize the wrong end of a stick if we have not taken the trouble beforehand to engage with those who run activities with which we are not completely familiar.

The Edmonton Eagles Amateur Boxing Club was established in 2004 in an area of North London that is recognised as one of the most socially and economically deprived in the country. Founding members of the club had recognised at an early stage that something had to be done to steer our young people away from street violence, gang culture and knife crime. In establishing the club, the founders invited young people to sign up to a range of fitness based activities that were designed to allow them a real opportunity to put their energies towards developing self esteem, personal worth and other skills.

Kostakis, who is a fully qualified head coach, runs the club which is based in Montague Road, Edmonton with the help of volunteers, many of whom are licensed professionally and are Amateur Boxing Association (ABA) qualified (CRB checked) boxing coaches. As might be imagined the club has strict rules governing injury and personal safety and has trained medical staff and experienced clinicians on hand. Young people under the age of eleven are not allowed into the ring to take part in contact training. Later when they do enter the ring protective headgear is always provided.

As the club progressed, the number of volunteer helpers grew (at the time of writing seventeen) and partnerships with other organisations were formed which allowed the facilities on offer to be considerably expanded. For example, a partnership with the Access Sport Ignite Programme has meant that the club can now offer an inclusive range of boxing activities to young people with learning difficulties and also those with physical disabilities. Another activity offered by the club is a programme called Boxercise. This is a series of fitness classes which have been designed to deliver a full body work out for men and women. The training is modelled on a typical boxing keep fit programme.

As word of the club's success spread they were contacted by the Gang Co-ordinator for Enfield Police and asked to set up dedicated mentoring and boxing sessions for young people who needed to be shown that there were better things in life than the influence of the gang. Also Enfield Local Authority and London Sport were so impressed with the levels of crime reduction and the noticeable improvements in the health and fitness of young people that Edmonton Eagles Amateur Boxing Club were achieving that the club was invited to set up a satellite at an Enfield school modelled around the facilities offered at Montague Road.

Article in the Enfield Independent *featuring the Edmonton Eagles Boxing Club*

Currently the club boasts a weekly attendance of around two hundred and fifty users and the free after school sessions, funded by the RSA Trust, have become very popular. Speaking with Kostakis he explained that if the club did not receive this funding support it could not offer these free sessions and "many families would be unable to send their children to enjoy the benefits".

From a relatively meagre beginning the club has gone from strength to strength winning, in 2015, the prestigious Queen's Award for services to volunteering. However, it is probably fair to say that the best award that Kostakis and his team have achieved so far is that of giving our young people a new direction in life and a positive vision for the future.

Joan Kearns. Nightingale Cancer Support

Joan Kearns is Director of Services and Development at the Nightingale Cancer Support Centre. The charity was set up in 2002 in Enfield by a group of concerned people who had witnessed many cancer suffers slipping through the net of the various local care services. The founders had identified a particular set of needs and were determined to develop a comprehensive package that gave the necessary support to those affected by cancer and they were also resolved to ensure that links were maintained or established with the traditional cancer service providers. The primary aims and objectives of the founders were to work with cancer professionals and others to fill the gaps in this sector of the community rather than to establish a separate stand alone body.

Fourteen years on Nightingale Cancer Support has developed into a highly respected body within the Enfield local community and is supported and receives referrals from the local authority and also NHS clinicians. Often, when people are diagnosed with cancer they feel frightened and alone and there is an urgent need for both emotional and psychological support. The slogan that is often used by Joan and her colleagues is, "remember, you are not on your own".

Nightingale Cancer Support offers a full range of services not just to people living with cancer but to their carers, family and friends. Complementary therapies are also on offer which include acupuncture, massage, reflexology, chiropody and Indian head massage. These treatments are dispensed in private rooms and can be accessed throughout the week via the regular drop-in sessions. A Lymphoedema Clinic is also available to ease the painful side effects of cancer treatment. Many people have found the one-to-one counselling sessions, which are arranged by appointment, extremely helpful. The sessions, normally one per week for a period of six weeks, are confidential and are held in private. Initially they are offered to give people the space to discuss their fears and concerns and go on to explore ways of coping and adjusting to their particular condition.

In 2014, after identifying an increasing need, the Nightingale Cancer Support Centre, in collaboration with Macmillan Cancer Support and the University of Coventry, launched the six-week Hope Course (Helping Overcome Problems Effectively). The course is run by a Clinical Nurse Specialist and also someone who has been affected by cancer. Courses are open to all people over the age of eighteen who have survived cancer and may be struggling with health problems caused by their treatment. Also the course will help those who are having difficulty coping with the thought of their disease returning. These particular issues are of major concern for many and often have long-term side effects like anxiety, distress and depression. The course is designed to teach people how to cope emotionally, psychologically and practically.

The Nightingale Cancer Support Centre receives no statutory financial backing and relies solely on fund raising events by volunteers, donations from businesses and a regular annual grant from the RSA Trust. As demand for Nightingale's other services like home sitting and transport for hospital appointments and to and from drop-in centres have increased, other methods of sustainable funding had to be found. With support from the RSA Trust a trading company was founded which has grown to three charity shops run by fully paid managers and several volunteers. The shops collect and sell recycled household goods and the venture helps to fund many of the free services provided by the Nightingale Cancer Support Centre.

In a world of seemingly bad news stories, it is a privilege to be able to write yet another good news story about a wonderful charity that is doing much needed work in our community.

The Nightingale Cancer Support Centre, Baker Street, Enfield

Enfield Island Youth and Community Trust – How the RSA Trust model works to support youth provision at Enfield Island Village

As families began populating the residential development it soon became clear that there was a need to provide recreational and other facilities for the growing numbers of young people who were living within Enfield Island Village complex. Originally the location for the Royal Small Arms Factory had been chosen for its isolated position on the River Lea flood plain some distance from the area now known as Enfield Highway. Now that the site had changed use from manufacturing to a housing development it had also isolated its young residents from the places of entertainment and interest within the borough. The lack of local youth facilities became particularly noticeable during the evenings when young people found themselves with absolutely nothing to do and this began generating concerns among the local residents.

Fortunately the problem was recognised at an early stage and after discussions between RSA IV and local residents it was agreed to set up a facility to address the problem and the Enfield Island Youth and Community Trust (EIYCT) was born. Gary Walker was the driving force in creating a board of Trustees to manage the youth activities. The board consisted of Gary Walker, Chair of RSA IV and the RSA Trust, a Local Ward Councillor, a nominee from the Residents Association and two representatives, Sue Gatrell and Steve Yanni, from RSL London & Quadrant (a not-for-profit housing association and the largest social housing provider on the Enfield Island Village complex). At the beginning a part time administrator was employed funded by the RSA Trust and the London Borough of Enfield provided two part time youth workers.

The Youth Club was set up in the on-site Community Hall and catered for young people aged from eleven to nineteen. Initially programmes were run for the younger group during the school holidays and the seniors were catered for two evenings per week.

As the Club grew, its popularity increased and it quickly became apparent that a full time youth worker with administrative support was needed. It was also identified that a separate home for the Youth Club was needed so that its activities did not clash with the various functions that the Residents Association had planned to be held in the Community Hall. Luckily a suitable unit became available within the Grade II building and after modest modification the Youth Club moved in. Naturally the premises commanded a full commercial rent and the problem of paying this was solved by the RSA Trust which provided an annual grant to the Youth Club equivalent to the rent payable to RSA IV.

The move had been specifically designed to extend the Youth Club's recreational and educational facilities and to do so it was necessary to address the urgent need for further support, as the provision of the two part time youth workers from the London Borough of Enfield had become insufficient. The EIYCT came up with the idea of approaching the recently built OASIS Academy Enfield, conveniently located on the nearby Innova Park. It was believed that there could be mutual benefits from collaboration between the academy and RSA IV. Gary Walker met with the founder of the Oasis Academies, Steve Chalke and the initiative to establish a collaborative undertaking, which has now developed into a long-term partnership, proved successful.

The Enfield Oasis Academy was the first in a group of academies started by Steve Chalke, and is a coeducational secondary school and sixth form with academy status that offers GCSEs and BTECs as study programmes. In the sixth form students can choose from a range of A Levels and additional BTECs.

The collaborative arrangement, between Oasis and EIYCT, allows the youth worker to be employed by Oasis while EIYCT is involved in the recruitment process and is responsible for servicing youth provision. In the first three years the youth worker was jointly funded by the RSA Trust and the Jack Petchey Foundation, a body set up in 1999 by an East End rags to riches entrepreneur that has already given millions of pounds towards supporting youth projects. As the EIYCT grew the RSA Trust continued to provide core funding. However, as the rate of expansion quickened it became necessary to seek other funding streams and these came primarily from the London Borough of Enfield and the Big Lottery with contributions from a range of other partners. It is now part of the EIYCT youth worker's role to seek and secure ongoing funding.

By 2010 the Youth Club was proving to be a runaway success and a further need had been identified to cater for young people between the ages of seven to eleven. It was therefore decided to establish a pilot scheme called KIDZ Club as part of the EIYCT. Another youth worker was employed using the same joint arrangement with the Oasis Academy and the collaboration was able to attract a number of volunteers to the project. Since September 2010 the KIDZ Club has been formally established and the London Borough of Enfield has also been able to provide youth workers.

Enfield Island Youth and Community Trust, a welcome addition to the Enfield Island Village Centre

As the appeal of the EIYCT increased the youth provision also had to expand and to accommodate this, the EIYCT hired the community centre from the Residents Association at the prevailing hiring charge.

With the youth club's growing popularity, and the increasing age range of the young people living in the Island Village it was inevitable that further provision would soon be required. This came in the shape of a "transition club" for the age group eleven to thirteen. To serve this emerging cohort a new youth group has now been established under the umbrella of the EIYCT and named Club 6-8. Core funding was provided by the RSA Trust and the London Borough of Enfield although significant additional funds have also been acquired from a variety of other sources. No doubt the good working relationship built between the RSA Trust and the Oasis Academy has given the funding bodies the added confidence to support the Enfield Lock youth projects.

With such a large and diverse youth provision in operation at Enfield Lock it was crucial to apply the sort of business disciplines that had allowed the RSA Trust model to perform so successfully. Additional representatives have been added to the founding member structure of the EIYCT and include a delegate from the London Borough of Enfield and also the youth workers from the Youth Club and KIDZ Club attend the regular Trust meetings. This has had a marked effect on improving understanding and communication between the various disciplines at the monthly Trust meetings which have rapidly learned to keep a business-like grip on the management of accounts and also a close eye on the current funding status.

The Trustees have developed a policy which encourages them to regularly meet with the young club members who have their own steering group which identifies current and future needs. Another brilliant initiative developed by the RSA Trust over the past few years was to fund three university students doing youth work degree courses and this really paid dividends. In September 2013 two of the graduates from the scheme joined the EIYCT team on a full time basis.

However, the youth projects are not in any way static and are constantly developing and evolving. This makes it almost impossible, at the time of writing, to capture and record all the events that are currently occurring or are projected for the future. These various initiatives clearly demonstrate how the RSA Trust model, with its good management and financial disciplines, can "spin out" to create community cohesion, improved youth provision and create jobs.

Note. 1. In December 2015 EIYCT put out the following statement:

> *For the avoidance of doubt, Enfield Island Village Trust (EIVT) is not to be confused with Enfield Island Youth Community Trust (EIYCT) also known as ENACT which is a different entity.*

> *Enfield Island Youth and Community Trust (EIYCT) was set up in 2003 to support young people who live on the newly developed Enfield Island Village. In 2009 the work expanded to include children aged 7 - 11 as there was no other provision for them. Quickly we created a transition group for 10 - 13's so they could move between the groups. Then we started a club 4 - 7's as well as a Community Garden, Family Events and trips. Over the last year we have seen many young people and parents volunteering to help run the clubs.*

> *We realise that EIYCT no longer describes what we are or what the community can engage in. That's why we are calling ourselves 'enact'. This is a single name that runs across the whole provision - that describes the ambition that can be supported through what can be participated in.*

> *More information and ways to engage coming soon. In the meantime, sign up for updates at **info@enact.community***

Note. 2. The brief of the RSA Trust is to invite applications for funding from local people with start-up business ideas and to accept applications from others who champion local good causes. The Trust part funds, and works closely with, Enterprise Enfield and financially supports training and other business initiatives, in particular, ones designed to get women back into work. All applications received by the Trust are professionally scrutinised to assess their business plans for future viability. In this way it is hoped to build sustainable community businesses that will boost the local economy and create jobs.